ENDORSEMENTS

I and the entire Arken Congregation would like to congratulate you from the bottom of our hearts on your book *The Miracle Code,* because this book is more important than ever. We previously published your book *The Healing Creed* into Swedish through our publishing house, and it has been very well received. It provided a good foundation in the Word regarding healing, a secure foundation of certainty and conviction. Healing truly belongs to us. We have a long history of collaboration with you in Guatemala and Life Tender Mercy Home. It is so wonderful to see in your life how the healing ministry connects with love for abandoned and suffering children.

Becky, you are not a theorist; what I love about you is that you practice everything you teach.

Your heart is present in every chapter of the book, and one can clearly feel how Jesus speaks through all the wonderful examples in the Bible. When I meet speakers and evangelists who have been in ministry for many years, my questions are often: "How did you get through the trials, illness, and difficult circumstances? Could you hear Jesus' voice? What words did He give you in your time of need? What did the Holy Spirit's guidance look like, and what fruits grew out of the trial? What steps of faith did He ask you to take?"

The Miracle Code book is more important than ever. The world is not waiting for a gospel based on human wisdom but on the power of God. The book comes at the right time. God wants to equip His people in the miracle ministry but also teach them how to approach Jesus and receive healing for themselves. In every story that describes a miracle and all the encouraging stories in the Bible, there is a key, a revelation from Heaven. Every story breathes God's goodness and care. In different ways, He approaches people, sees their needs, and meets their needs. What is so important in Becky's book is the clear Bible teaching with a strong and clear focus on Jesus.

My desire is that you read the book thoughtfully and in prayer. Jesus longs to meet you, and miracles are even more important in the end times. Sickness and need will increase, but so will God's power, which will make everyone understand that Jesus has truly risen from the dead and that all names and powers are under His feet. He is our Teacher and Mentor. He will introduce us step by step into His miraculous ministry. This book will be a great blessing to the body of Christ.

Linda Bergling
Arken Church, Sweden
Doctor in Pastoral Counseling, Bible Teacher, Author

Becky Dvorak has written another wonderful book! *The Miracle Code* is about the one subject that I as a minister have desired to explore for years—an in-depth study of the miracles of Jesus! In this book, Becky opens to the reader the glorious revelation of what each of Jesus' amazing miracles means in our lives on a distinctly personal level. *The Miracle Code* will inspire your faith to believe God when faced with impossible situations, and it will embolden you to embrace life's challenges with renewed confidence and expectation! Through Scripture and her life experiences, Becky's book is certain to propel you, as it has me, into new levels of faith for the supernatural for the purpose of fulfilling one goal—to prove that Jesus is alive! Get ready for a life-changing book!

Pastor Joan Boethel
Joan Boethel Ministries

The Miracle Code is not just a book. It's a divine tool for transformation. Becky Dvorak writes with piercing clarity about the importance of following Jesus' example to allow the supernatural to become the normal part of our life as it was for the disciples. Becky describes all of the 37 recorded miracles of Jesus and reveals a miracle code for each, and then gives us a faith assignment to pursue God's calling on our lives to be like Jesus. This new book will help you get a grip on the supernatural life and walk in God's promises at a brand-new level.

Dr. Douglas Bailes
Family Physician
Codirector, Healing Hearts Healing Rooms
Glendale, Arizona

So blessed by this Scripture-based, Jesus-focused account that builds faith in the miracle power of Christ. This book is a model for teachers seeking to know how to build vibrant faith for miracles without sacrificing consistent biblical mooring. *The Miracle Code* encouraged my faith by exalting God's Word.

Pastor Chad Budlong
Availing Truth Bible Church
Goodyear, Arizona

We have the distinct honor of knowing and pastoring Becky Dvorak and her wonderful family, who have personally encountered the miraculous healing power of God. In *The Miracle Code,* Becky not only highlights the miracles of Jesus, but also takes readers behind the scenes to reveal the cultural context, Greek language insights, and deeper spiritual meanings that uncover the very heart of God. This book offers a powerful revelation of the love and power of Jesus working in and through us today. With personal application and activation prayers at the end of each chapter, *The Miracle Code* is a must-read for anyone desiring to experience the fullness of their salvation—including signs, wonders, and miracles. Curt and I love the book. We're doing it as a devotional with the questions at the end of each chapter.

Pastors Curt and Rhonda Edwards
Founders and Senior Leaders
New Promise Church and Phoenix House of Prayer

In this amazing book, Becky has so simply and clearly broken down what we need to do as God's people to not only receive healing, but to walk in divine health. You may ask, why do we need a code? Because people on their own sometimes get overwhelmed and life becomes hard, and that is not what Jesus wants for us. It is a simple gospel when broken down in this manner. We all need hope. Sometimes we get hopeless, the battle rages, and we need a word; and this book is a beautiful guide through Scripture to show you the heart of our Lord and Savior Jesus Christ and what the Father can and will do in our lives.

Apostle Don & Pastor Shari Gray

The Miracle Code reveals the miracles of Jesus. It is an insightful deep-dive into 37 of Jesus' recorded miracles. Becky provides well-researched, historical context to each of these biblical stories, yet presents them in a way that is not only easy to understand, but to also apply throughout everyday living. We are in a time when God is igniting His Church to walk boldly in the authority of the Holy Spirit, and *The Miracle Code* is an instruction manual that gives guidance on where to begin. Jesus said, *"Very truly I tell you, whoever believes in me will do the works I have been doing, and they will do even greater things than these, because I am going to the Father."* Through Becky's personal experiences, thought-provoking questions, and depth of knowledge, she shows her readers that these words are very possible to live out.

Jordan Oliver
His Glory / Creative Production

Discover *The Miracle Code* and step into the heart of God's unfolding power on earth. In this groundbreaking release, Becky Dvorak has done a masterful job blending prophetic insight with the wisdom of apostolic grace, painting a vivid portrait of what happens when the Church fully aligns with God's heart and prophetic principles. As you explore each New Testament miracle through her eyes, you'll see how Jesus moved then—and learn how to partner with the Holy Spirit now to propel Kingdom agendas forward. Within these pages, you'll embark on a deep dive into every miracle Jesus brought forth, each chapter unlocking a prophetic code that activates the supernatural power of God in and through your life. Enjoy richly crafted word studies that open doors to deeper intimacy with the Father and reveal practical pathways for bringing signs and wonders into our day. Becky's combination of Scripture, revelation, and application will challenge you to shift from simply partaking in the Word—to boldly demonstrating its power.

The Miracle Code will inspire you to step into a new dimension of His glory, releasing miracles, signs, and wonders that leave no doubt about the reality of God's Kingdom. You'll discover how the visible world can be over-come by supernatural manifestations of His Spirit, flowing through you for His glory and the transformation of lives all around you. The book you hold in your hands has the power to change not only your story but the stories of everyone you encounter. We are crossing into a fresh move of God—one where the Kingdom of Heaven is more tangibly demonstrated than ever before. *The Miracle Code* will equip you to move with the wind of His Spirit, partner in every miracle, and ignite a revival of Heaven's power on earth.

Apostle Cara Nordeen
Senior Leader, High Tower Ministries, International Apostolic Network
Founder and President, Word Up Daily, Inc., Christian Media Network
Author, Unlocking Glory

Becky Dvorak has given us a treasure that will touch your heart deeply! As a seasoned healing evangelist and missionary who has witnessed countless miracles—including raising her own son from the dead—Becky brings both biblical wisdom and tender, real-world experience to *The Miracle Code.* This beautiful book perfectly aligns with walking in God's fullness by showing you how to encounter His supernatural love and power for breakthrough in health, relationships, and purpose. With such warmth and hard-won wisdom, Becky breaks down each of Jesus' 37 miracles into practical, life-changing principles that will transform how you approach challenges and step into your God-given potential. Every page invites you into a deeper encounter with the heart of God. If you're ready to move beyond limitations and truly walk in the abundant life He has for you, this book will ignite your spirit and equip you with divine tools for breakthrough!

Liz Wright
Host, Live Your Best Life Podcast
Founder and CEO, International Mentoring Community

Becky Dvorak has given us a masterful blueprint for walking in supernatural power. In *The Miracle Code,* she systematically unlocks the spiritual principles within Christ's 37 recorded miracles, transforming familiar stories into practical keys for breakthrough. What makes this book exceptional is Becky's ability to combine rigorous biblical scholarship with real ministry experience. Her Greek word studies uncover truth most miss, but this isn't academic theory—it's revelation from someone who has witnessed genuine miracles.

The faith assignments don't just inform—they activate. This book will revolutionize how you read Scripture and transform your expectation of God's power.

Dr. Faisal Malick
www.faisalmalick.com

THE MIRACLE CODE

DESTINY IMAGE BOOKS BY BECKY DVORAK

The Miracle Code

Decrees That Heal

The Waves of Healing Glory

Conquering the Spirit of Death

The Prophetic & Healing Power of Your Words

The Healing Creed

Greater Than Magic

Dare to Believe

THE MIRACLE CODE

A BREAKTHROUGH BLUEPRINT FOR RECEIVING YOUR HEALING AND DELIVERANCE

BECKY DVORAK

DESTINY IMAGE® PUBLISHERS, INC.

P.O. Box 310, Shippensburg, PA 17257-0310

"Publishing cutting-edge prophetic resources to supernaturally empower the body of Christ"

This book and all other Destiny Image and Destiny Image Fiction books are available at Christian bookstores and distributors worldwide.

For more information on foreign distributors, call 717-532-3040. Reach us on the Internet: www.destinyimage.com.

ISBN 13 TP: 979-8-8815-0610-0

ISBN 13 eBook: 979-8-8815-0611-7

For Worldwide Distribution, Printed in the U.S.A.

1 2 3 4 5 6 7 8 / 30 29 28 27 26

DEDICATION

I dedicate this work, *The Miracle Code*, to Sid Roth, host of *It's Supernatural!* I so appreciate your faithfulness to stand with me as a prophetess, healing evangelist, and as a woman in ministry. Your invitations to share about my supernatural experiences with our Messiah with your audience mean a great deal to me. And the opportunity you entrusted me with to host my own teaching program, *Empowered for Healing and Miracles* on your network is honoring. Sid, you're the best!

Shalom, Shalom!

ACKNOWLEDGMENTS

I thank Destiny Image Publishers for their amazing job and professional touch to put this work, *The Miracle Code,* together for readers. Special thanks to Larry Sparks (publisher). It is a privilege to work with you.

CONTENTS

FOREWORD xix
PREFACE xxiii
INTRODUCTION xxv

PART ONE
MIRACLES 1-10

Miracle 1 3
Whatever He Says to You, Do It!
Miracle 2 13
Believe by Faith, Not by Sight
Miracle 3 20
Delivered from an Unclean Spirit
Miracle 4 29
See Through the Father's Eyes
Miracle 5 34
Healed Spiritually and Physically
Miracle 6 43
Take the Limits off God!
Miracle 7 50
He Is Willing to Heal
Miracle 8 57
Great Faith
Miracle 9 63
Forgiven and Healed
Miracle 10 69
Defy the Religious Spirit and Heal

PART TWO
MIRACLES 11-20

Miracle 11 77
Life Overpowers Death
Miracle 12 83
Where Is Your Faith?
Miracle 13 90
Delivered and Clothed in His Right Mind
Miracle 14 99
A Special Touch
Miracle 15 106
Guard the Atmosphere

Miracle 16 113
Have Mercy on Us
Miracle 17 119
Irresistible Force
Miracle 18 125
Do You Want to Be Made Well?
Miracle 19 132
Spiritual Multiplication
Miracle 20 138
Rescued from the Storms of Life

PART THREE
MIRACLES 21-30

Miracle 21 147
Healing in His Wings
Miracle 22 152
Unrelenting Faith
Miracle 23 158
Spittle and a Command of Faith
Miracle 24 165
The Empowerment of Compassion
Miracle 25 171
Restored and Clearly Sees
Miracle 26 179
Recreated Eyes and Something More
Miracle 27 187
Come Down from That Mountaintop Experience
Miracle 28 193
Miracle Money to Pay the Temple Tax
Miracle 29 201
Questions, Rumors, and the Big Lie
Miracle 30 208
Loosed from Your Bondage

PART FOUR
MIRACLES 31-37

Miracle 31 217
Hypocrisy Versus Grace
Miracle 32 223
One Out of Ten Returns to Give Thanks
Miracle 33 231
That You May Believe
Miracle 34 240
What Do You Want Jesus to Do for You?

Miracle 35 246
Curse a Spirit of Lack in Your Life
Miracle 36 254
Ears to Hear
Miracle 37 260
Faith Revives

Answer Key 267

Notes 285
About Becky Dvorak 289

FOREWORD

by Patricia King

It is with great joy and expectation that I commend to you this powerful work by Becky Dvorak, *The Miracle Code: A Breakthrough Blueprint for Receiving Your Healing and Deliverance.*

We are living in a time when it is crucial for the people of God to walk in the fullness of the Gospel—a Gospel of power, healing, deliverance, and wholeness. Too often, believers have been content to know Christ theologically, but have not stepped into the full reality of who He is and what He came to do. This book is a bold and needed invitation to recover that reality.

Becky Dvorak has long walked as a prophetic healing evangelist with a deep passion to see the body of Christ rise in faith and authority. In *The Miracle Code*, she takes readers on a remarkable journey through 37 miracles of Jesus, unpacking the spiritual keys hidden within each one. These are not merely stories from history, they are living codes of breakthrough—divine patterns that unlock healing, freedom, provision, and restoration today.

The miraculous has never been a theory for me—it has been a reality. From the earliest days of my walk with God, I was blessed to be taught not only the truth of Scripture but also given the invitation it holds to live a supernatural life. My teachers didn't just preach miracles—they stepped out in childlike faith and watched God move—and I was right there to witness it! It was life-transforming to see the love of God at work through the miraculous.

Because of their example, I was able to follow in faith to see Jesus touch the lives of those I was led to minister to: the deaf heard; the lame walked; terminal diagnoses were overturned; captives were set free from demonic oppression; and yes—on occasion—even the dead were raised. Just like in the Bible.

The working of miracles isn't a message reserved for the spiritual elite. It's the inheritance of every believer. Neither is the miraculous reserved for those with titles or platforms. The Lord needs everyone on board to represent Him with the truth of the Gospel and His supernatural power—mothers, fathers, teenagers, even young children. Every believer can minister healing, deliverance, and miracles in the power of Jesus' name. All it takes is courageous faith. Not a mountain of it. Just a mustard seed's worth, firmly planted in the soil of trust in a *very big Jesus*.

That is why I'm so excited about *The Miracle Code*. Becky Dvorak has written a powerful and practical guide that doesn't just inspire—it equips and mentors. When I started reading the book, I was amazed at the depth of revelation and insight Becky extracted from each miracle. There is so much to meditate on and ponder. You will be stirred in your heart to follow Christ into the activation of the miracle realm.

In these pages, you will not only discover biblical accounts of miracles, but you will be introduced to the heart of the miracle worker Himself. You will discover His invitation and blueprint to access healing and deliverance, not as a rare exception but as a regular expression of your walk with God.

From Jesus' first miracle at Cana to His resurrection of Lazarus, to the miraculous provision of temple tax money in a fish's mouth—each account reveals a blueprint for faith. Becky teaches with clarity and prophetic insight, leading the reader to see how obedience, belief, compassion, faith, and spiritual authority open doors to the miraculous. This is not just theory—it's truth designed to activate you.

I further believe that this book is much more than a study of miracles—it is a manifesto of Kingdom living. It calls believers to rise above religious limitations, to defy the spirit of unbelief, and to embrace the ministry of Jesus in all its fullness. Healing, deliverance, and miracles are not optional side notes of the Gospel—they are part of our inheritance in Christ.

The Miracle Code is filled with biblical insights, real-life testimonies, and

Spirit-led activations that will stir your hunger, draw your heart to the Source of miracles Himself, and strengthen your confidence in what is possible with God. This book is a valuable mentoring tool created for you!

The miracle-working Jesus still lives—in you and through you. As you absorb and apply the truths revealed in *The Miracle Code,* your faith will arise, your spirit will be stirred, and your body and soul will experience the miracle-working power of God.

Whether you're contending for your own breakthrough or longing to minister healing and miracles for others, let this book inspire you and expand your training ground in the Spirit. Read it with expectation. Take it to prayer. And most of all, act on what you learn. The miraculous life is not only possible —it's *normal* for those who believe...for you!

Get ready. The miracle code is not locked. It is open. And it's yours.

Patricia King
Minister, Author, Media Host

PREFACE

We live in very troubling times with wars and rumors of wars, deadly earthquakes, famines, pandemics, hatred, and lawlessness to depths we were not able to imagine before. This has upset the souls of many. And yet, Jesus gently reminds us to be strong and courageous, not to be afraid or discouraged, because He is with us to the very end. He desires more than survival for His people and creates us for victory. In order to fulfill the plans and purposes He has for us, we must encourage our spirits in His Word and allow His Spirit to equip us to win the world for His glory, by the power of His might.

> *Yet through it all, the good news of heaven's kingdom will be proclaimed all over the world, providing every nation with a demonstration of the reality of God. And after that the end of this age will arrive* (Matthew 24:14 TPT).

INTRODUCTION

In this exciting work, *The Miracle Code,* we will go beyond the oohs and the aahs of the supernatural and journey back into time and witness the amazing miracles of Jesus. We accept His personal invitation to observe, listen, and even question the who, what, when, where, why, and how of each event. We will go beyond mere goose bumps and dig for the hidden secrets of each recorded miracle of Jesus. And enter His realm of deliverance, healing, miracles, signs and wonders, and discover the miracle code.

God's Word makes it plain in John 21:25, *"And there are also many other things that Jesus did, which if they were written one by one, I suppose that even the world itself could not contain the books that would be written. Amen."* This Scripture calls out to my spirit and begs me to ask, "What is so unique about these 37 recorded miracles that stops all of Heaven to say, 'Hey, Holy Spirit, make sure to record this one for the benefit of our people, for generations to come'?"

Let's decode the good news of the operations of Heaven's Kingdom on earth with these miracles and celebrate healing for all people from all sickness and all disease, and release those who all their life were in bondage to satan's wicked works by the power of the blood of Jesus to deliver and make them whole again.

PART ONE
MIRACLES 1-10

Dear Holy Spirit, as we purpose to seek revelation with these first ten recorded miracles of Jesus, we ask, Holy Spirit, lead and guide us into spiritual truths that will help us to be healed and delivered. In the name of Jesus we pray, amen.

With the help of Holy Spirit, let's begin with who was at this wedding in Cana by checking out the wedding guest list.

MIRACLE 1

WHATEVER HE SAYS TO YOU, DO IT!

Jesus Turns Water Into Wine

> *On the third day there was a wedding at Cana of Galilee, and the mother of Jesus was there. Jesus also was invited with His disciples to the wedding. And when the wine was all gone, the mother of Jesus said to Him, They have no more wine! Jesus said to her, [Dear] woman, what is that to you and to Me? [What do we have in common? Leave it to Me.] My time (hour to act) has not yet come. His mother said to the servants, Whatever He says to you, do it* (John 2:1-5 AMPC).

How appropriate it is for us to open this work, *The Miracle Code,* with this portion of Scripture that begins by saying, *"On the third day."* Why? The number three has significant meaning throughout the Bible. For one, it represents the Trinity—Father, Son, and Holy Spirit. To embark into the supernatural realm of healing, miracles, signs, and wonders we must have all three beings of God operating in our life:

- Father God, the Creator (Genesis 1:1).
- Jesus, the Creative Word made visible (John 1:1 TPT). Let's delve into this a bit. *Word* in the Greek language is *logos*, but *logos* is more than mere words on a page, it is *self-revealing* or a *message*.

Plainly put, Jesus Christ is the eternal Message, the Creative Word, and the Living Expression of God made visible.[1]

- And then we have Holy Spirit, the third Person of the Trinity, who is coequal, coeternal with the Father and the Son. He is the *Dunamis* (Greek: power, ability, strength), explosive power of God, and it is He who empowers us (Acts 1:8.). With every miraculous encounter, we need the Creator, the Creative Word made visible, and the empowerment of Holy Spirit to work a miracle. And yes, we will work via the Trinity a miracle.

In John 14:12-14, Jesus assures us with His promise, *"Most assuredly, I say to you, he who believes in Me, the works that I do he will do also; and greater works than these he will do, because I go to My Father. And whatever you ask in My name, that I will do, that the Father may be glorified in the Son. If you ask anything in My name, I will do it."*

Let's walk on over to the wedding in Cana and witness Jesus' first recorded public miracle, where He turns water into wine. This miracle is packed with prophetic insight about how we receive our manifested miracles today.

THE WEDDING GUEST LIST

Along with the bride and the bridegroom and their families, there is the master of ceremonies of the banquet, the servants, and all the invited guests. And even though they do not realize it at the time, included on this guest list are a few very world-renowned invites such as Jesus, Mary, the mother of Jesus, and the disciples who were traveling with Jesus. Let's talk about this wedding guest list and how Jesus fulfills the type and shadow of everyone on the list.

Jesus, being the most important guest, can relate to each person in attendance—for the couple to be wed He is the eternal Bridegroom for all the people, the Church, the bride of Christ who accepts His invitation to be eternally united to Himself.

Revelation 19:7-9 says, *"'Let us be glad and rejoice and give Him glory, for the marriage of the Lamb has come, and His wife has made herself ready.' And to her it was granted to be arrayed in fine linen, clean and bright, for the fine linen is the righteous acts of the saints. Then he said to me, 'Write:*

"Blessed are those who are called to the marriage supper of the Lamb!"' And he said to me, 'These are the true sayings of God.'"

Mary, Jesus' mother, is the one who surrenders to God's will and physically carries and births the gift of salvation—Jesus within her. In the Hebrew language the name of Jesus is Yeshua, and it means "Yahweh is salvation." Jesus is our Savior, and He came to deliver and rescue us. Luke 1:30-31 reveals to us who Mary will carry in her womb, *"Then the angel said to her, 'Do not be afraid, Mary, for you have found favor with God. And behold, you will conceive in your womb and bring forth a Son, and shall call His name Jesus.'"*

And just as Mary is obedient to the Father, Jesus is willing and obedient to carry this eternal gift of salvation on His own physical body so we can be spiritually birthed anew.

Philippians 2:8 (AMPC) shows us to what point Jesus obeys the will of the Father for us, *"And after He had appeared in human form, He abased and humbled Himself [still further] and carried His obedience to the extreme of death, even the death of the cross!"*

And like the master of ceremonies is responsible for the wedding plans, so too is Jesus. The ultimate wedding of all weddings, the plan of salvation is the plan of Elohim (Father, Son, Holy Spirit)—not only do they plan the event, but Yeshua (Jesus) is responsible to carry out this amazing plan.

John 3:16 (AMPC) shares this good news, *"For God so greatly loved and dearly prized the world that He [even] gave up His only begotten (unique) Son, so that whoever believes in (trusts in, clings to, relies on) Him shall not perish (come to destruction, be lost) but have eternal (everlasting) life."*

The duty of the servants is to attend to the needs of the guests, and Jesus is the Master who serves and attends to the needs of all the people.

Philippians 2:6-7 (AMPC) tells us, *"Who, although being essentially one with God and in the form of God [possessing the fullness of the attributes which make God God], did not think this equality with God was a thing to be eagerly grasped or retained, but stripped Himself [of all privileges and rightful dignity], so as to assume the guise of a servant (slave), in that He became like men and was born a human being."*

And then we have the wine; as the natural wine runs dry, Jesus cares for all who receive a supernatural supply of new wine by performing His first recorded public miracle. It demonstrates Jesus' authority over the natural realm and over the power of lack. It shows another side of Him. He's not just the miracle worker who turns the water into wine, He also takes upon Himself the shame of the master of ceremonies and supplies the natural needs necessary for a weeklong wedding feast.

Philippians 4:19 assures us that, *"My God shall supply all your need according to His riches in glory by Christ Jesus."*

And I should like to add to this stunning list of fulfillments the fact that in one powerful moment in His life, Jesus fulfilled the requirements of "The Blood Covenant" by filling that precious Communion cup with the power of His own blood. Luke 22:41-42 (NIV) describes this very agonizing moment in His life, *"He withdrew about a stone's throw beyond them, knelt down and prayed, 'Father, if you are willing, take this cup from me; yet not my will, but yours be done.'"*

And last, there's the disciples traveling with Jesus, He set the bar high for future evangelism, removes natural limitations, steps into the supernatural, and begins to share the good news with miracles, signs, and wonders, just as we should too.

In Mark 16:15-18, we read just how high Jesus raises the bar of evangelism for all of His disciples, including us, when He says,

> *Go into all the world and preach the gospel to every creature. He who believes and is baptized will be saved; but he who does not believe will be condemned. And these signs will follow those who believe: In My name they will cast out demons; they will speak with new tongues; they will take up serpents; and if they drink anything deadly, it will by no means hurt them; they will lay hands on the sick, and they will recover.*

So, by checking out the wedding guest list, we can get a pretty good glimpse of the big picture and see how Jesus not only meets the needs of everyone on the wedding guest list, but He spiritually fulfills their roles too.

And here we thought it was just going to be an ordinary wedding. Well, let's raise the bar of our own expectations and know that every event with Jesus will not be common or mundane, but instead miraculous and stunning in every way.

"JESUS, WE HAVE A PROBLEM."

Mary says to Jesus, *"They have no more wine!"* At first Jesus responds with a question, then interjects a reassuring response, and then adds a puzzling comment. He responds, *"[Dear] woman, what is that to you and to Me? [What do we have in common? Leave it to Me.] My time (hour to act) has not yet come."* At first glance, we might think Jesus is being rude, but rudeness involves a sinful attitude, and Jesus is without sin, so rude He is not, frank He is. In the natural He is not the bridegroom; but spiritually speaking, a prophetic conversation is taking place. And as briefly shared earlier, Jesus is an invited guest, and therefore, the supply of wine would not be His responsibility. But He then fulfills the role of the eternal Bridegroom by supplying the wine for the invited guests.

And I for one, believe Jesus' life on earth, while short, was a constant fulfillment of prophecy spoken by the prophets of old, and His daily encounters were a continual reminder to Him about what He was preparing to do for us at Calvary and then for eternity. And if not spiritually minded, what He says would utterly confound the mind of the listener. But His mother, Mary, knew Him—which is a main code buster to walk in the divine. Because of her close relationship with Jesus, she understood Him. This is also why she immediately commands the others, *"Whatever He says to you, do it."*

SIX WATERPOTS OF STONE

> *Now there were six waterpots of stone standing there, as the Jewish custom of purification (ceremonial washing) demanded, holding twenty to thirty gallons apiece. Jesus said to them, Fill the waterpots with water. So they filled them up to the brim. Then He said to them, Draw some out now and take it to the manager of the feast [to the one presiding, the superintendent of the banquet]. So they took him some* (John 2:6-8 AMPC).

This portion of Scripture tells us that there are six waterpots of stone standing there. The number six in the Bible symbolizes people and all our frailty. God created people in His image on the sixth day of creation (Genesis 1:26-28). When God created the first humans, Adam and Eve, they were without fault, but then came the fall, when they chose to disobey God's command (Genesis

3). And this is when corruption, including lack for our daily needs and all other forms of the curse, came into this world and into the human body as well. With this information let's return to this special wedding being held in Cana.

SPIRITUAL CLEANSING

This Jewish custom of purification (ceremonial washing) is also part of this prophetic act taking place at the wedding. I see these six water pots of stone as symbolizing people who are spiritually dirty and lost, needing a spiritual bath in the redemptive blood of Jesus. But because it is not yet His hour to shed His blood for us at Calvary, this is a foreshadow of things to come.

Without Christ, the Anointed One, we are nothing more than empty clay vessels that are spiritually contaminated inside, in need of a spiritual cleansing. And the only thing that can cleanse us is the spiritual wine, the blood of Jesus that takes away the sin of the world, so that our spiritual vessels can be filled with His eternal living water.

> *But whoever takes a drink of the water that I will give him shall never, no never, be thirsty any more. But the water that I will give him shall become a spring of water welling up (flowing, bubbling) [continually] within him unto (into, for) eternal life* (John 4:14 AMPC).

THE SERVANTS' RESPONSE

The servants' response to Jesus' command is beautiful. Without question they respond immediately and fill the water pots with water, and they fill them to the brim. May we all be as quick to respond to His commands as these servants are.

MARY TREASURES AND PONDERS

Mary's ability to give such profound advice, *"Whatever He says to you, do it,"* to these servants came from living a lifestyle of service to her Lord. She heard that the wine had run out, and even though this was a major problem for the hosts of this big event, she knew there was someone present in the house who could easily take care of the problem. So, she turns to Jesus to help them in their time of need. She receives a strange response from Jesus, *"[Dear] woman, what is that to you and to Me? [What do we have in common? Leave it to Me.] My time (hour to act) has not yet come."*

We can agree that this woman of faith has witnessed amazing and unexplainable events in her personal life. She receives a bewildering message from the angel Gabriel that she was going to supernaturally conceive, carry in her womb, and give birth to the long-awaited Messiah, Jesus Christ. Her response to such shocking news is, *"Behold the maidservant of the Lord! Let it be to me according to your word"* (Luke 1:38). The entire conception and birth of Jesus is filled and confirmed with supernatural events and messages. And it says in Luke 2:19 (NIV), *"But Mary treasured up all these things and pondered them in her heart."*

I love how Mary treasures, preserves and keeps these memories safe in her heart as she ponders upon them. The King James Dictionary tells us *to ponder* means to consider carefully or to meditate.[2]

Joshua 1:8 instructs us, *"This Book of the Law shall not depart from your mouth, but you shall meditate in it day and night, that you may observe to do according to all that is written in it. For then you will make your way prosperous, and then you will have good success."*

We, like Mary, are to do the same, treasure and ponder upon these supernatural interventions of Jesus that take place in our lives. And as we contemplate, we encourage our faith by what He has done for us and share testimonies of God's goodness and grace with one another.

THE IMPORTANCE OF FAITH AND OBEDIENCE

John 2:5-8 demonstrates the importance of faith and obedience when the servants heed Mary's instructions, *"Do whatever He tells you"* and do what Jesus asks of them, *"Fill the waterpots with water."*

In the Gospel of John, chapter 1, verses 1-18 we read a beautiful declaration of the divine nature of Jesus, how He and the Father are one (John 10:1) and whatever His Father God says and does so He does (John 5:19). He loves the Father and walks in obedience to Him and expects us to obey Him too.

What does Jesus tell us to do in Matthew 22:37-39: *"'You shall love the Lord your God with all your heart, with all your soul, and with all your mind.' This is the first and great commandment. And the second is like it: 'You shall love your neighbor as yourself.'"*

SEVEN THINGS JESUS ASKS OF US

There are many commands in the Bible for us to obey that will enrich our lives in every way. The following is a list of seven to begin with:

1. Be born again (John 3:5-7).
2. Believe (James 1:6).
3. Repent (Acts 3:19).
4. Forgive (Matthew 16:14-15).
5. Love (Matthew 5:44).
6. Pray (Philippians 4:6).
7. Seek (Matthew 6:33).

Examine your heart, ask yourself if there is anything on this list that you have not done yet, but need to. Activating this list will open your spirit to freely receive the manifestation of that miracle.

THE MANIFESTED MIRACLE

> *And when the manager tasted the water just now turned into wine, not knowing where it came from—though the servants who had drawn the water knew—he called the bridegroom. And said to him, Everyone else serves his best wine first, and when people have drunk freely, then he serves that which is not so good; but you have kept back the good wine until now! This, the first of His signs (miracles, wonderworks), Jesus performed in Cana of Galilee, and manifested His glory [by it He displayed His greatness and His power openly], and His disciples believed in Him [adhered to, trusted in, and relied on Him]* (John 2:9-11 AMPC).

John sets down in writing the first recorded miracle of many more miracles to come, so many in fact that he states in John 21:25, *"And there are also many other things that Jesus did, which if they were written one by one, I suppose that even the world itself could not contain the books that would be written. Amen."* And in our text from John 2:11, He emphasizes the reason for miracles, signs, and wonders, which is to manifest His glory.

Manifest in this occasion means to become known, to be plainly recognized, thoroughly understood for who and what someone is, and comes from the Greek word *phaneroō.*[3] Let's add this to Who is being manifested, made known for Who and What He truly is by doing a quick study of the word *glory*. Defined according to Strong's Concordance #G1391: "In reference to Jesus, the Messiah it means, splendor, brightness, magnificence, excellence, preeminence, dignity, grace, majesty. And comes from the Greek word, *doxa.*" Take a few moments and cherish this gemstone of revelation.

THE RICHES OF JESUS ON DISPLAY

As we seek to discover the riches of Jesus on display in this recorded miracle, we see that these are actual clues to breaking into the miracle code:

- He activates divine authority and power over creation.
- Lack does not restrain Him.
- He is willing to help others in need.
- For our benefit, He requires faith and acts of faith from us to His commands.
- Our everyday matters matter to Him.
- Preserving the honor of others is important.

CRACK THE MIRACLE CODE

The power of true faith in His deity overrides a spirit of lack.

When you read Miracle 2, you will learn what it means to believe by faith, not by sight.

A PRAYER OF FAITH

Dear Lord Jesus, I desire to fulfill Your will for my life. Yet, there are times I struggle with the smallest of requests. Remind me, Holy Spirit, that obedience to the seemingly unimportant daily tasks leads to greater opportunities of service. And perhaps, what You are really asking of me is to take part in a much bigger miracle that will affect many lives around me, by doing the little things first. Whatever You ask of me, I choose to do it. Speak Lord, for Your humble servant listens. Amen.

FAITH ASSIGNMENT

Jesus' mother said to the servants, "Whatever He says to you, do it." What is Jesus asking of you to do now in your life? List 1 - 3 assignments.

1. ____

2. ____

3. ____

Questions for Miracle 1: Whatever He Says to You, Do It!

1. Who do you need in every miracle?
2. What role does Jesus fulfill when He supplies the wine at the wedding of Cana?
3. What is a main code buster that allowed Mary to walk in the divine?
4. What does the number 6 symbolize in the Bible?
5. Mary's ability to give such profound advice, "Whatever He says to you, do it," to these servants came from what?
6. What does Mary do when she treasures, preserves, and keeps these memories safe in her heart?
7. What is the Greek word for *manifest?* And what does it mean?
8. What is the Greek word for *glory?* And what does it mean?

MIRACLE 2
BELIEVE BY FAITH, NOT BY SIGHT

Jesus Heals the Official's Son at Capernaum

In this next portion of Scripture, we read how Jesus heals the son of a royal official who is near death. During the study of His second recorded miracle, we will carefully consider how Jesus responds to this nobleman, clear up confusion concerning this passage, His revelation about why people believe, and then make it personal and see how we should believe.

> *So Jesus came again to Cana of Galilee where He had made the water wine. And there was a certain nobleman whose son was sick at Capernaum. When he heard that Jesus had come out of Judea into Galilee, he went to Him and implored Him to come down and heal his son, for he was at the point of death. Then Jesus said to him, "Unless you people see signs and wonders, you will by no means believe"* (John 4:46-48).

My initial thought to Jesus' response to this man is, *"Whoa!"* But then I ask myself, *Why would Jesus rebuke this man?* And then clarity comes. As we reread this Scripture, Jesus doesn't say, "You," He says, "You people." And this is the correct interpretation, as this is the plural form of *you*. What a relief this little revelation brings to my heart. He did not rebuke this individual who traveled almost 20 miles to invite Jesus to come and heal his son who was sick and on his deathbed. Jesus was rebuking the crowd of people who were constantly following Him, only to see signs and wonders.

RIGHTFULLY, DIVIDE THE WORD OF GOD

There is quite a bit of confusion concerning this portion of Scripture, but if we slow down, reread and study the passage it becomes clear.

The apostle Paul writes under the inspiration of Holy Spirit, *"Study and be eager and do your utmost to present yourself to God approved (tested by trial), a workman who has no cause to be ashamed, correctly analyzing and accurately dividing [rightly handling and skillfully teaching] the Word of Truth"* (2 Timothy 2:15 AMPC).

I teach my students enrolled in my online healing school the following:

1. If you don't understand something in the Bible, pray and ask Holy Spirit to teach you, and then reread the portion of Scripture carefully.
2. If possible, read this portion of Scripture from three different versions of the Bible.
3. Do a little study of words and pay attention to what you think are unimportant words.
4. And ask yourself these basic questions: who, what, when, where, why, and how about the portion of Scripture.

In time you will cut through the confusion in your mind and answer the questions you have.

Now, let's return to this second recorded miracle of Jesus.

WHY JESUS PASSES THROUGH SAMARIA

> *He left Judea and departed again to Galilee. But He needed to go through Samaria* (John 4:3-4).

This heart-revealing miracle begins as Jesus journeys to Galilee from Judea through Samaria. It says that Jesus needs to pass through Samaria.

Although the road through Samaria was the shortest route from Jerusalem to Galilee, pious Jews often avoided it. They did so because there was a deep distrust and dislike between many of the Jewish people and the Samaritans.[1]

The Samaritans were looked down upon by the Jews. But despite this pride and prejudice, Jesus, who is also a Jew, chooses the shorter route through Samaria not because he was in a hurry and needed to save time, but because He needed to save the Samaritans. "*Jesus wants all people to be saved and to come to the knowledge of the truth*" (1 Timothy 2:4 NIV). This was their hour to hear and believe the Gospel of Jesus Christ. Jesus wills for all people to come to know Him as Savior and Lord. And I tell you the truth, miracles, signs, and wonders are the bait He uses to reel them in. They point to Jesus.

The word *miracle* in biblical terms refers to an event that defies the laws of nature, often attributed to divine action.[2]

In the Bible, *signs* refer to indicators or symbols that signify something greater than themselves, often pointing to God's authority and purpose. The biblical meaning of *signs* encompasses both miraculous occurrences and everyday events that carry spiritual significance.[3]

And the term *wonders* in the Bible often refers to extraordinary events or acts that invoke awe and amazement. The Hebrew word for wonders is *mofet,* while in Greek, it is *teras.* Both terms encapsulate the essence of miraculous phenomena that transcend ordinary experiences. These wonders are portrayed as manifestations of God's power and sovereignty, serving as signs to affirm faith and reveal divine truth.[4]

THE SAMARITANS HEAR AND BELIEVE

For numerous reasons there is great animosity between the Jews and the Samaritans, so this is their opportunity to be introduced to our glorious Lord. It is truly His choice to pass through Samaria, and He spends two days there to share Himself, the Creative Word made Visible, with them. This is where He ministers to the woman at the well, teaches the Word, and makes more disciples, while His disciples traveling with Him baptize the new believers. (See John 4:39-45.)

Jesus makes His way to Galilee from Judea through Samaria. And it is here in Samaria where He ministers the Word among a different group of people—a people who believe what He has to say. In John 4:39-42, we read how their faith matures.

And many of the Samaritans of that city believed in Him because of the word of the woman who testified, "He told me all that I ever did." So when the Samaritans had come to Him, they urged Him to stay with them; and He stayed there two days. And many more believed because of His own word. Then they said to the woman, "Now we believe, not because of what you said, for we ourselves have heard Him and we know that this is indeed the Christ, the Savior of the world." (John 4:39-42).

You see in this portion of Scripture that the Samaritans have spiritual ears that are wide open, and the message Yeshua preaches witnesses to their hearts, and they believe Jesus is the Savior without having to see signs and wonders—they believe His words as truth.

A WORD OF FAITH

The Samaritans believe Jesus at His Word. The Jews will not believe unless they see signs and wonders. Jesus is testing, not tempting this man's faith. He is testing this man's heart. He is causing him to make an inward decision, to believe by faith and not by sight. Which is real faith. As I see it, this nobleman was going to receive this healing for his son by a word of faith, or he wasn't going to receive at all. Did he believe the words of Jesus or not?

First, what do I mean when I write, "a word of faith"? A word of faith is a biblical promise declared over someone or a given situation that is backed with trust in the redemptive work of Christ to keep His promise found in the Holy Bible. Like I declared over my son, Marcos, whom I raised from the dead. *"You will not die, but live and fulfill your destiny in Jesus' name."* Now with this clarification of what a word of faith is, let's find out if this royal official believes the word of faith Jesus speaks over his son.

And this is a strong message for the Church today—we receive by faith, because we believe His healing promise to be truth. And it comes from a deep-seeded conviction that Jehovah Rapha is the God who heals us (Exodus 15:26), and our faith in Him is the only evidence (Hebrews 11:1) we need for our healing. As written in John 20:29, *"...blessed are those who have not seen and yet have believed."*

CRISIS-DRIVEN VERSUS VICTORY-BELIEVING FAITH

The nobleman said to Him, "Sir, come down before my child dies!" (John 4:49)

We often reach out to Jesus when we are in deep trouble, when what He really desires from us is to move from crisis-driven faith to victory-believing faith.

Why did Jesus not go with the man to Capernaum to heal his son? This is a good question, with a logical answer that leads to a spiritual challenge. This man is facing a real crisis, his son is on his deathbed. He has heard of Jesus and His power to heal. So he gives the invitation, but it involves a 17-mile hike.[5] Jesus is aware that time is of the essence but also knows that there is no distance in the spirit realm, so He issues a word of faith, *"Your son lives,"* and tells the man to go home. The challenge is placed upon the man—will he change gears from crisis-driven to victory-believing faith?

Jesus said to him, "Go your way; your son lives." So the man believed the word that Jesus spoke to him, and he went his way. And as he was now going down, his servants met him and told him, saying, "Your son lives!" (John 4:50-51).

Praise Jesus! His glory manifests once again. This nobleman starts out in the crisis-driven mode, but makes that important heart decision that we all must make, he believed Jesus at His word and received the power that drives victory-believing faith.

Then he inquired of them the hour when he got better. And they said to him, "Yesterday at the seventh hour the fever left him." So the father knew that it was at the same hour in which Jesus said to him, "Your son lives." And he himself believed, and his whole household. This again is the second sign Jesus did when He had come out of Judea into Galilee (John 4:52-54).

Jesus desires us to believe Him at His Word. To believe Him is to trust Him, and to trust Him we must get to know Him.

He does not desire us to seek after signs and wonders but to chase Him down, get to know Him for who He really is. And it is from this type of relationship that supernatural happenings just happen.

A DANGEROUS ZONE

When signs and wonders become our foundation to believe, we've entered a dangerous zone of weak faith. We might not like hearing this, but we need to mature in the faith to the point where our faith in Jesus and in His promise to heal is the only evidence we need to know that we are healed. Now that's real faith. Let's be mature believers. And be ready to share the benefits of our victory-believing faith with others as well.

THE RICHES OF JESUS ON DISPLAY

There are actual clues that we can discover as we observe the riches of Jesus on display to help us break into the miracle code.

- Jesus is not moved by the pressure of others.
- Circumstances do not control Him.
- He activates authority over time and distance.
- Jesus operates by faith.
- He uses wisdom and activates the most effective form of healing.
- He takes the time to win the Lost.

CRACK THE MIRACLE CODE

Jesus wants us to mature in our faith and believe because He says it's true—not because we insist on seeing a sign or a wonder.

As you read Miracle 3, you will learn the difference between demon-possession and oppression, and how to be free from an unclean spirit.

A PRAYER OF FAITH

Dear Holy Spirit, help me to step out of this dangerous zone of having to see to believe. I desire to believe because Your Word tells me so. And to mature in my faith from being crisis-driven to victory-believing faith.

Remind me to put my trust in Your promises, and not in the circumstances around me. I thank You for Your leadership in my life. Amen.

FAITH ASSIGNMENT

Examine your life, are you being crisis-driven in any area? If so, pray the prayer of faith, ask Holy Spirit for His help, and allow Him to lead you to the point where you live in victory-believing faith in this area of your life.

Questions for Miracle 2: Believe by Faith, Not by Sight

1. Who does Jesus rebuke with these words, "Unless you *people* see signs and wonders, you will by no means believe"?
2. Why does Jesus pass through Samaria?
3. What is the biblical definition of the word *miracle?*
4. What is the biblical definition of the word *signs?*
5. What is the biblical definition of the word *wonders?*
6. To what different people group does Jesus minister the Word of God?
7. What is Jesus doing to the nobleman if He is not tempting his faith?
8. According to Hebrews 11:1, what is the only evidence we need for our healing?
9. Jesus desires for us to move from crisis-driven faith to what type of faith?
10. Why does Jesus not go with the nobleman to heal his son?
11. What do we enter when signs and wonders become our foundation to believe?

MIRACLE 3
DELIVERED FROM AN UNCLEAN SPIRIT

Jesus Drives Out an Evil Spirit

We are going to discuss a rather difficult subject matter, demon-possession and oppression. To my dismay I have found that this is an unwelcome topic in most religious establishments worldwide, but we are the Church, and we will not be defeated. And as tough as this topic may be, I find everywhere I go the people of God are crying out for help—and I am here to do just that, help you to heal in Jesus' name.

> *Then He went down to Capernaum, a city of Galilee, and was teaching them on the Sabbaths. And they were astonished at His teaching, for His word was with authority. Now in the synagogue there was a man who had a spirit of an unclean demon. And he cried out with a loud voice, saying, "Let us alone! What have we to do with You, Jesus of Nazareth? Did You come to destroy us? I know who You are—the Holy One of God!" But Jesus rebuked him, saying, "Be quiet, and come out of him!" And when the demon had thrown him in their midst, it came out of him and did not hurt him. Then they were all amazed and spoke among themselves, saying, "What a word this is! For with authority and power He commands the unclean spirits, and they come out"* (Luke 4:31-36).

Verse 31 says, *"Then He went down to Capernaum, a city of Galilee, and was teaching them on the Sabbaths."* This unpretentious verse is one that many quickly skim over, but I tell you it is chock-full of prophetic insight for the man who is suffering and about to be delivered from an unclean spirit.

We will begin with the first word in the opening statement of this portion of Scripture, *"Then,"* and see all that had just transpired with this unassuming word recorded in God's Holy Word. Let's look at some verses in Luke 4:14-30. Verse 16 says, *"So He came to Nazareth, where He had been brought up. And as His custom was, He went into the synagogue on the Sabbath day, and stood up to read."* And He continues with verses 18-19 telling us, *"The Spirit of the Lord is upon Me, because He anointed Me to preach the gospel to the poor; He has sent Me to proclaim release to the captives and recovery of sight to the blind, to set at liberty those who are oppressed; to proclaim the acceptable year of the Lord."*

Jesus closed the book and began to speak from the heart with frankness. He boldly declares in verse 21, *"Today this Scripture is fulfilled in your hearing."* But as He continues to speak, they take offense because He is a member of their hometown of Nazareth. And Scripture is clear in verse 24, *"Assuredly, I say to you, no prophet is welcome in his own country."* The religious community became enraged and drove Him to the edge of town to throw him off the cliff. But by the supernatural grace of Abba Father, Jesus passes through their midst, and continues along His way.

PROPHETIC INSIGHT IN THE MEANING OF THE NAMES

Now, let's take a day's walk (about 90 miles) with Jesus from His hometown, Nazareth, down to what will become His base of operations, Capernaum, accurately located in the "Village of Comfort,"[1] a city of Galilee, "a circuit,"[2] a place where the miracles and teachings of Jesus Christ are manifested[3] and where Jesus is teaching the people on the Sabbath(s). The Hebrew word for *Sabbath* is *Shabbat,* and it means to rest.[4]

What I shared with you here are not just interesting facts, but a prophetic insight to what Jesus came to do in the life of this man and others enslaved to an unclean spirit. Jesus left His hometown of Nazareth, to set up His base of operations in the Village of Comfort, to circuit the area with the message of Himself, the Creative Word made visible to give rest to those bound by an unclean spirit.

DEMON-POSSESSED WITHIN THE SYNAGOGUE

Notice where this demon-possessed man is, in the synagogue. This should put us all on high alert that people within our religious and Christian establishments can have issues with demons and need spiritual help—deliverance.

> *Now in the synagogue there was a man who had a spirit of an unclean demon...* (Luke 4:33).

AN UNCLEAN SPIRIT

First, let us tackle *the basics* of this pertinent miracle for today. In the Bible a demon is named after what they do. For example, a spirit of divination is someone entrapped by witchcraft. Another example is an epileptic spirit, who is someone suffering from epileptic seizures.

And now we will confront an unclean spirit. We will begin with a mini study about this type of spirit, an unclean spirit that Jesus casts out of a man in the synagogue.

According to the Strong's Concordance G169, *akathartos* is the Greek word for *unclean spirit.* And in a moral sense it is unclean in thought and life. It's impure (ceremonially, morally (lewd) or specially, (demonic)—foul, unclean.

Prime examples of unclean spirits in today's world are pornography, drug addiction, alcoholism, child abusers and groomers, drag queens, transgenders, and the LGBTQ+ community in general. These people have lost their moral compass, have no respect for sexual norms or the boundaries of others.

I have had many honest conversations and prayer sessions with people who are struggling with these very sinful issues and want out or have been abused by people possessed by these unclean spirits, or with concerned family members and friends witnessing the lives of their loved ones being destroyed by this lifestyle.

This problem is real and is extremely prevalent today. It is deeply rooted in the demonic realm, the Church has been infested, and it's time for the true lovers and worshippers of Jesus to rise and take a stand against this satanic attack—to do what our Lord expects us to do by setting the captives free. (See Luke 4:18-19.)

The following are a few questions from my readers about this sensitive topic, and my answers.

1. How do we break off a homosexual spirit from someone who does not recognize this is a sinful lifestyle?

- Pray and fast for this individual's salvation.
- Pray the demonic strongholds in their life would be broken.
- Command soul-ties of the people they are having relationships with to be cut off.
- Pray that they would find the courage to forgive those who have hurt and/or abused them in any way.
- Pray that they would encounter the true love of God in a supernatural way.
- Also pray that they hear about others who had struggled with the same sin, but have truly been delivered and set free from this unclean lifestyle.

2. A sister in Jesus asks, "Am I possessed by a demon from my husband's porn addiction? And what should I do about it?"

- No, you are not possessed, but probably oppressed by the weight of his sin.
- Pray and fast for him.
- Break off from him the demonic soul-ties of these emotional fantasies, and their connection now with you.
- Pray for God's strength to forgive him. There is a difference between freely forgiving someone and being able to trust that person again; a new foundation is a must to heal a broken relationship.
- Pray that he sees into the spirit realm the actual demons behind the porn, and that it scares these hellish ways out of him.
- Plead the power of the blood of Jesus over your mind and emotions.
- Fill yourself with the Word of God concerning Jesus' love for you, and your identity in Christ.

As we continue in this real story, we read the response of the demons to Jesus. "*Let us alone! What have we to do with You, Jesus of Nazareth? Did You come to destroy us? I know who You are—the Holy One of God!*" (Luke 4:34).

Believe me when I tell you that demons want to be left alone. They certainly do not want a follower of Yeshua exercising their God-given authority against them. They want to remain and fulfill their mission which is to steal, kill, and destroy people. (See John 10:10.)

3. "Can I effectively remove demons from someone who does not want me to pray for them?"

This is a great question, and the answer is, "Yes, you can." First, I would figure out who does not want you to pray—the demon or the person being oppressed or possessed by a demon. A demon will never want you to evict them out of their host. But nevertheless, Jesus gave you His authority over satan and over all his wicked works.

> *Behold! I have given you authority and power to trample upon serpents and scorpions, and [physical and mental strength and ability] over all the power that the enemy [possesses]; and nothing shall in any way harm you* (Luke 10:19 AMPC).

And demon possession is certainly a wicked work of the devil.

Second, someone struggling with demons, or demonic strongholds, is probably blinded to this issue, but it doesn't mean that you cannot pray for them. Even if the person is not right there with you, you can pray in faith for them. Pray away! Your prayers of faith will weaken the power of the demon. Pray like this:

> *In the mighty name of Jesus, I renounce the power of this demonic stronghold over (name of person). By the authority of Jesus living in me, I command you to release this person and leave. I will not tolerate you and your torment over my loved one. I bind you, unclean spirit to defeat and ineffectiveness in (name of person's) life. I plead the power of the blood of Jesus over this individual's mind, emotions, dreams, visions, physical body, and over all daily activities. I call down a garrison of God's angelic forces to war against you on (name of*

person's) behalf. In the mighty name of Jesus, I declare (name of person) is set free. Amen.

Also, you need to be willing to fast on behalf of this person. Jesus tells us in Scripture, *"[But this kind of demon does not go out except by prayer and fasting.]"* (Matthew 17:21 AMP).

- You pray and fast.
- Build yourself up in the Holy Scriptures concerning your identity in Christ.
- And when you have the release of the Lord, put your faith into action. Go to the person and cast out the demon(s), in the name of Jesus.

As always, it is up to the individual to remain free and clear of future demon possession. The individual may ask, how is this accomplished? Answer: by filling your mind and emotions with God's Word.

- Read the Word of God.
- Listen to biblical teachings.
- Play worship music constantly.
- Pray in your heavenly language—tongues.
- Declare the Word of the Lord over yourself, *"I am free in Jesus' name!"*
- And as a word of wisdom, someone who just experienced deliverance should not be left alone for a time. They need to be protected.

4. What if the person struggling with an unclean spirit is you?

If you are the one in bondage to an unclean spirit, you must defeat the darkness within yourself. The only pathway to victorious living is by cleansing yourself from an unclean spirit, which is by repentance. And let's make sure we are all singing from the same hymnal, so to speak, only the blood of Jesus can deliver you from your own destruction, and His Word will purify your mind and emotions. I strongly believe that most people will be delivered from demonic strongholds by living daily life in the Word. But you must be willing to be free and seek the Lord and His ways to do so.

- Ask Jesus to forgive you of your sins.
- Join a local church or Bible study.
- Read and study God's Word.
- Pray in your supernatural language—tongues.
- Confess God's promises over yourself, aloud.
- Play worship music 24/7.
- Do not hang around old friends who struggle with these same demonic strongholds.
- Rid yourself of the internet or install parental locks on your own personal devices.
- Find support.

Why Did Jesus Rebuke This Demon?

> *...And he cried out with a loud voice, saying, "Let us alone! What have we to do with You, Jesus of Nazareth? Did You come to destroy us? I know who You are—the Holy One of God!" But Jesus rebuked him, saying, "Be quiet, and come out of him!..."* (Luke 4:33-35).

People are often confused as to why Jesus rebukes this demon when it says, *"I know who You are—the Holy One of God!"* Why did He rebuke this demon when it began to reveal His true identity as the Holy One of God? It has to with timing and the vessel that was announcing who He was. It was not for demons, especially unclean spirits to declare the deity of Christ to the world. And so, He was not going to permit them to get ahead of God's timing. Also, crowds were growing larger and larger, making it difficult to minister to the needy individuals. So, Jesus rebuked, sharply charged this demon into silence, and then cast it out.

THE RICHES OF JESUS ON DISPLAY

- Jesus stays true to His calling.
- He does not bow down to control of the religious spirit.
- He takes total command over demons.
- He does not allow demons to get ahead of God's timing.
- He does not allow an unclean spirit to declare to the world His deity.
- He takes time to minister to the individual in need.

CRACK THE MIRACLE CODE

There are people even within our religious and Christian establishments who need deliverance from unclean spirits.

When reading Miracle 4, you will discover how Jesus demonstrates the reality of His caring compassion for the sick.

FAITH ASSIGNMENT

Look at your life, are you or a loved one enslaved to an unclean spirit? If so, take the steps necessary to get yourself free, or help another be delivered from an unclean spirit.

PRAYER OF FAITH

Father God, You created me in Your mirror image (Genesis 1:26-28), but instead of mirroring Your image, I have become enslaved to an unclean spirit, and in bondage to sinful ways. Holy Spirit, I need Your empowerment to work this personal deliverance in my soul. Lead me and guide me into the manifestation of my freedom. In Your name, Jesus, I pray, amen.

Questions for Miracle 3: Delivered from an Unclean Spirit

1. What did the enraged religious people try to do to Jesus in Luke 4:28-29?
2. Where was Jesus' base of operations located?
3. His base of operations in Capernaum was accurately located where?
4. The city of Galilee means what?
5. Galilee is a place where what happens?
6. The Hebrew word for *Sabbath* is what? And what does it mean?
7. In a moral sense, what is an unclean spirit?
8. In Luke 4:18-19, what is one thing the Lord expects us to do?
9. In Matthew 17:21 some demons will not leave unless we do what?

MIRACLE 4

SEE THROUGH THE FATHER'S EYES

Jesus Heals a Fever-Sick Mother-in-Law

> *Now when Jesus had come into Peter's house, He saw his wife's mother lying sick with a fever. So He touched her hand, and the fever left her. And she arose and served them* (Matthew 8:14-15).

The Bible says in Matthew 8:14 that Jesus *saw.* The phrase *to see* in Greek is the word *eidō* and means to perceive, notice, discern, discover.[1] I believe as followers and lovers of Jesus we need to have our spiritual eyes wide open, and see people as Jesus sees, through the eyes of Abba Father. And we need to be ready in season and out of season to minister to the needs of those we encounter. Jesus sees Peter's mother-in-law, a woman sick and suffering with a fever. We don't know the cause of the fever, but we do know that her immune system is fighting off some type of infection or illness. What does He do? Jesus reaches out and touches her hand, and the fever lifts off her.

A HEALING TOUCH FROM JESUS

Jesus would often reach out and touch the infirmed and they would heal. This healing touch is a demonstration of the reality of His caring compassion. As His healing power cleanses their every cell, tissue, organ, and system from sickness and disease, I also believe it cures them of doubt and unbelief about His divine nature.

DOES JESUS WORRY ABOUT GETTING SICK?

Did you notice that Jesus is not worried about getting sick? He isn't using a face mask, gloves, or grabbing for the hand sanitizer. First John 4:18 tells us that, *"There is no fear in love; but perfect love casts out fear, because fear involves torment. But he who fears has not been made perfect in love."* His compassion, which is His love in action, reaches out to this infirmed woman, just as He would with someone suffering with leprosy, and without fear releases a healing touch.

Let's dissect this verse, the Greek word for this fear is *phobos.*[2] It's not a common fear, but that of exceeding fear, dread, or terror. And it has no place in *agapē* love, which possesses no earthly perversion. *Agapē* love is benevolent brotherly love and affection from God.[3] And this form of love is perfect, *teleios,* and lacks nothing necessary for completeness.[4] In fact, *agapē* love is so complete that it violently casts, [or in Greek, *ballō*, to throw or let go of a thing], in this case fear without caring where it falls.[5] This Scripture tells us that this fear involves *torment*, correction, punishment, penalty, and it comes from the Greek word, *kolasis.*[6]

When we understand the true nature of our Lord Jesus and how great He suffered to rescue, deliver, and redeem us from satan and all his wicked works including tormenting fear, we can accept His perfect love that lacks nothing and begin to move in His glory realm where life, health, and healing abound.

JESUS IS WILLING AND ABLE TO HEAL

Jesus' fame continues to increase, so much so that the multitudes follow Him everywhere He goes. But even still, He remains humble and takes notice of the individual in need, like Peter's mother-in-law, and takes the time to minister to her. His mission is to undo the work of the devil, and when someone is on a mission, that call is taken very seriously. A vital part of work on earth is to heal the sick spiritually, emotionally, mentally, and physically too.

AN INWARD POWER CALLED GRATITUDE

We read in this short-written testimony that she rises from her bed and serves them. This is an example of faith in action, which is something Jesus requires from those He ministers to, but in this situation, He does not have to require an action of faith, because she offers this of her own accord. Why? Why does she just naturally rise off the sick bed and serve Him? I believe it has to do with an inward power called gratitude. And I believe this is another reason Holy Spirit took note of her acts of faith and includes her testimony for the ages to read and learn from. Lovers and followers of Jesus, there is power in gratitude. A thankful heart goes a long way with the Lord, and He records it within the pages of His heart. In Psalm 7:17 (AMPC), David writes, "*I will give to the Lord the thanks due to His rightness and justice, and I will sing praise to the name of the Lord Most High.*"

HEALING CHANGES LIVES AND PRODUCES GRATEFULNESS

I personally see time and time again how this healing touch changes lives. A couple of years ago, one of our employees at our children's home in Guatemala was suffering with severe neck pain. She had injured her neck. And like most, she went through the buffet of earthly medical cures, without healing. She suffered with daily pain and sometimes missed work because of it. I was visiting the home, and it was one of those times she could not come to work because the physical pain was too much for her to bear. She knew I was in the country and requested that we come to her home to pray for her healing. So we went to her home that afternoon. I briefly encouraged her with a word of faith for healing and reached out and touched the back of her neck. She was instantly healed.

This woman reminds me of Peter's mother-in-law. I see her several times a year, and every time she shares her grateful heart for her healing. She gives me thoughtful gifts beautifully wrapped, but what blesses my heart more is her willingness to express her thankfulness.

Like many, she grew up with a whole lot of religion, but not a lot of faith, especially not for supernatural healing. And I am sure you know quite a few people just like her. If so, hold true to your confession of faith about a wonderful Savior who is alive and well, and abounds with caring compassion for all people. I believe that eventually opportunity will present itself and you will be the one reaching out in the name of Jesus with His healing touch and another is healed physically, emotionally, mentally, and the doubt and unbelief about our Jesus is spiritually cured.

THE RICHES OF JESUS ON DISPLAY

- Jesus is perfect love.
- There is no fear in Him.
- He is observant and sees what others do not see.
- He often heals the contagious and untouchable with a gentle healing touch.

CRACK THE MIRACLE CODE

A touch of Jesus' healing power demonstrates the reality of His caring compassion for the sick.

When reading Miracle 5, you will learn the difference between demon possession and demon oppression and how to minister to both.

FAITH ASSIGNMENT

While at the store, step out of your comfort zone, and ask someone you do not know if you can pray for them. If the person says yes, ask if there is a specific need. And then pray for the person.

PRAYER OF FAITH

Father God, this healing testimony of Peter's mother-in-law, and the healing testimony of the woman in Guatemala calls out to my heart. I desire to see what You see, to be spiritually in tune with Your Spirit and take notice and discern the pain and the hurt in others around me. Forgive me for all the time I am consumed with myself and my own needs that I forget to be a real, live demonstration of Your caring compassion to others in my arena of influence. Open my eyes to see people as You see them. This I sincerely pray in Your name, dear Jesus, amen.

Questions for Miracle 4: See Through the Father's Eyes

1. In Matthew 8:14, what did Jesus do?
2. The phrase *to see* in the Greek is what?
3. What does the Greek word *eidō* mean?
4. What would Jesus often do with the infirmed?
5. In 1 John 4:18, what is the Greek word for *fear*?
6. What does *phobos* mean?
7. What type of love is expressed in this verse?
8. Describe this type of love.
9. What is the definition of *teleios?*
10. What is the Greek word for *casts?*
11. What is the Greek word for *torment?*

MIRACLE 5
HEALED SPIRITUALLY AND PHYSICALLY

Jesus Heals Many Sick and Oppressed After Sunset

> *When evening came, they brought to Him many who were under the power of demons, and He drove out the spirits with a word and restored to health* ***all*** *who were sick. And thus He fulfilled what was spoken by the prophet Isaiah, He Himself took [in order to carry away] our weaknesses and infirmities and bore away our diseases* (Matthew 8:16-17 AMPC).

UNDER THE POWER OF DEMONS

Now, more than ever before, God's people are under attack. Why? The devil is on a mission to steal, to kill, and to destroy us (John 10:10), and he uses his dirty agents, demons (the fallen angels), to deliver his nasty blows.

As we see in this portion of Scripture, *"When evening came, they brought to Him many who were under the power of demons."* Demons are comfortable with darkness; they are afraid of the light. They want to remain hidden and not be exposed. But I have every intention to expose them. For too long they have wreaked havoc on unsuspecting people, and it is time for God's people to shed the light on all this darkness so the people can be free.

According to Scriptures, these people were under the power of demons. In other words, they were either possessed or oppressed; and from my own personal experience of ministering to groups of people, I would say they were both, and some worse off than others. But regardless of the severity of demon hostility in their lives, these demons were no match for Jesus. They came possessed and oppressed by the devil, but then we have Jesus, the Creative Word made visible. And that devil and his demons do not stand a chance with Him.

WHAT IS DEMON POSSESSION?

Demon possession is a serious offense against God's greatest creation, people. When demons have possession of an individual, it means that a demon (or demons) has taken ownership of this person. Somewhere, somehow a spiritual entrance has been opened for the demonic spirit to enter in and take partial or total control of a human being.

When someone is demon possessed, they lose control of their mind and emotions, and their actions too. I have witnessed many bizarre behaviors from demon-possessed individuals, such as animal-like behaviors including growling, howling, walking on all fours, eating and using the bathroom like an animal would, grabbing frozen meat out of a freezer and eating it frozen and raw. I have witnessed the typical behaviors of foaming at the mouth, rolling, thrashing, and slithering around on the ground. I have seen the unusual and humanly impossible such as ears literally flapping.

I have walked into homes of Christians where someone in that home is totally possessed and have physically felt the unseen touching me and licking my ears. I have heard the voices of these tormenting demons, seen photographs of their family members change back and forth before my eyes from the tormented to what I believe to be their tormentors. I have witnessed spirits of death in the form of skeleton masks appear on the faces of the demon possessed.

But what stands out to me more than anything about these possessed individuals is the sheer terror in their voices, and the utter loneliness in their cries. And with the discernment of Holy Spirit, I readily see the look of demons in their eyes. And I kid you not, so many people, particularly within the United States right now, have demons who need to be delivered and set free. And we lovers and followers of Jesus possess the power and the authority to set them free in the name of our Lord, Jesus Christ.

WHAT IS DEMON OPPRESSION?

With *demon oppression,* the demon does not have actual possession or ownership, but a stronghold, an evil influence to lead him or her into sinful behavior. Oppression in this sense of the word is an overwhelming pressing force working against you to submit to do wrong.

So when it comes to demon oppression, does the devil force you to do something? No, but with tremendous pressure he does tempt you. The Bible makes it clear in James 1:14 (AMPC), *"But every person is tempted when he is drawn away, enticed and baited by his own evil desire (lust, passions)."* This action word *tempted* in the Greek language is *peirazō* (Strong's G3985), and it means to try, make trial of, test: for the purpose of ascertaining his quality, or what he thinks, or how he will behave himself. The phrase *drawn away* is *exelkō* in the Greek language, and it means to *entice* (Strong's G1828). And it's perfectly clear here that we are enticed and baited by our own evil desire. This little word, *own*, in Greek is *idios,* and it forces us to take responsibility of our own shortcomings. It plainly states that *own* means belonging to one's self. So, yes, we are responsible for our own sin issues. And no, the devil as evil as he is, cannot force you to do anything you do not want to do. So use caution!

Our flesh, when under the control of selfishness, has great power to do evil. This is why we need the Savior. Jesus purchased our freedom from the oppression of the devil with the redemptive power of His blood. And His precious blood holds the power to save, to heal, and to give us forgiveness for sins and eternal life if we will believe in its redemptive power. As Christians, we have been gifted with other spiritual weapons to overcome every attack of the enemy.

The following are four more spiritual weapons:

1. We have been given the privilege to call upon the name that is above every other name, Jesus (Romans 10:13).
2. All lovers and followers of Jesus have been given the opportunity to be endued with power by the baptism of Holy Spirit (Luke 24:49).
3. We have been given a spiritual map, the Holy Bible that guides us through this life (Psalm 119:105).

4. We have been given a direct line of communication with our Lord through the power of prayer (Psalm 4:3).

FREEDOM FOUND ONLY IN JESUS

Whether someone is possessed or oppressed by demons, both need deliverance. And freedom from both, possession or oppression, is found *only* in Jesus. Acts 4:12 (AMPC) reads like this, *"And there is salvation in and through* ***no one else****, for there is* ***no other name*** *under heaven given among men by and in which we must be saved."*

PROPER INTERCESSION COVERING

One of my students asked while discussing exercising authority over demons, "I have been told that it is dangerous to approach anyone without proper intercession covering. Do you agree?"

Yes, I do agree with this advice, but not if it is being used as an excuse not to reach out and offer true help to people who need deliverance. And here is why I believe this. Jesus empowers us to set the captives free in numerous ways. In Luke 10:19, He gives to us His authority over satan and over all his wicked works. And He does not expect us to do this in our own strength but by the power of His Spirit (Zechariah 4:6).

We are advised to always be ready in season and out of season (2 Timothy 4:2), to pray without ceasing (1 Thessalonians 5:17), to edify ourselves (1 Corinthians 14:4), to be about our heavenly Father's business (Luke 2:49), and we are commissioned to go into all the world (Mark 16:15-18), and one specific assignment in the Great Commission is to drive out demons in His name, (Mark 16:17).

CLEANSING PRAYER

After ministering over these hurting people, it is very important to pray a prayer of spiritual cleansing over yourself. Pray like this:

> *In the name of Jesus, I declare the power of the blood of Christ over me, and no evil will befall me, and any curse or assignment formed*

against me will not prosper. No transferring of evil spirits will enter or follow me. I am protected in Jesus' name, amen.

IS IT OKAY TO WATCH A GOOD HORROR MOVIE?

One of my students asked, "I know horror movies can be dangerous. But I still love to watch a good horror movie. However, if I get scared or it feels odd, I immediately turn it off. I'm very careful. If I feel or have any hesitation and/or it feels like more than entertainment I don't watch. Is that okay? If not why, Since I am vigilant about not watching if gets too scary."

No, it's not okay to date the devil, or for God's people to flirt with a spirit of fear. First Peter 5:8 gives us this warning concerning the devil: *"Be sober, be vigilant; because your adversary the devil walks about like a roaring lion, seeking whom he may devour."* Let's take this verse apart to see the seriousness of God's warning.

- **Be sober:** *nēphō,* discreet, be sober, and watch Strong's G3525
- **Be vigilant**: *grēgoreō,* give strict attention to, be cautious, we are to be awake and watchful Strong's G1127
- **Our adversary**: *antidikos,* our enemy Strong's G476
- **The devil**: *diabolos,* is a false accuser, a slanderer Strong's G1228
- **He walks about**: *peripateō,* makes due use of opportunities Strong's G4043
- **As (KJV), Like (NKJV)**: *hōs,* as, like, even as, etc. Strong's G5613
- **Roaring**: *ōryomai,* to roar, to howl (of a lion, wolf, dog, and other beasts) Strong's G5612
- **Lion**: a brave and mighty hero Strong's G3023
- **He seeks**: *zēteō,* he plots against us Strong's G2212
- **To devour**: *katapinō,* to swallow up, and destroy us Strong's G2666

We are to be sober and vigilant, awake and watchful. Because our enemy, the devil, is the accuser and the slanderer, and makes use of every opportunity to do us harm. With a roar, he pretends to be like Jesus, strong, courageous, and a brave and mighty hero, but it's all a lie. Really, he plots against us, to devour, swallow up and destroy us.

THE LIONS ARE ROARING

Lions in the Bible symbolize the authority, courage, power, and strength of Jesus. But both our Lord, Jesus and our enemy, satan (the devil), are depicted as lions in Scripture. It can be confusing at first, but as we take a closer look at God's wording, it becomes clear. The devil is described as *like* a *"roaring lion"* in 1 Peter 5:8 while Jesus Christ is *"**the** Lion of the tribe of Judah"* (Revelation 5:5). We can sum up these two verses like this: the devil pretends to represent our authority, courage, power, and strength, but remember he's pretending while Jesus really is who He says He is. The little foxes can spoil the vine, so be watchful of the grammar being used such as prepositional words and phrases as well as the articles too.

OPEN DOORS TO DEMONIC ACTIVITY

What exactly are the open doors to demonic possession? In the many cases that have presented themselves to me over the years, the tormented individual has been severely physically, mentally, emotionally, and sexually abused.

Sexually speaking, the two become one in a marriage covenant. And so also is the case of sexual abuse, but not in a loving way as within the contents of marriage but violently forced upon the victim. And this sexual tie between the victim and the perpetrator(s) becomes an unwanted and ungodly soul tie that must be broken.

PRAYER OF FAITH TO BREAK SOUL TIES

In the name of Jesus, I renounce this ungodly soul tie with (say the person's name), or between (say the names of the people). Father, I plead the power of the blood of Jesus heavily over the mind and the emotions of (say the victim's name). I command this unclean spirit of violence to come out of (name of person) and all unhealthy emotional attachments to be broken. I release the healing balm of Gilead into (name of person's) mind and emotions. And by the grace of God, the power of the redemptive blood of Jesus be delivered, be healed, and be made whole for the glory of our Lord and Savior, Jesus Christ, amen.

DEMONIC POSSESSION ON PUBLIC DISPLAY

I was seated at the movie theater in the United States to see a family-approved movie with my family, but the announcements before the show were so graphically demonic—an open display of demon possession. Right from my seat with a loud voice I renounce this spirit of death and demonic possession and boldly tell the demons that they cannot and will not enter anyone in this place, and especially not my family in Jesus' name. I am not about to sit still and allow a spirit of fear or any other demon have access into my family. And what surprises me, no one in that theater tells me to be quiet.

Another instance happens over Easter in a movie theater in Guatemala, when we take the children from our children's home to go watch an animated movie of the life, death, and resurrection of Jesus, "King of Kings." Here we are working to get all the little children settled in their seats with their bags of popcorn and sodas when the announcements begin with an advertisement for a very demonic movie, again an open display of demonic possession. Of course, I loudly exercise my God-given authority for protection over the children against the power of demons right then and there. And then I march right out of that theater into the lobby and make a strongly worded complaint to those in charge and rebuke them for having no discretion for a theater full of children. Just as we cannot remain silent when demons enter our domain, we cannot tolerate their wicked public displays either.

HE DROVE OUT THE SPIRITS WITH A WORD

In our text for this miracle in Matthew 8:16 (AMPC) it says that *"He drove out the spirits out with a word...."* The spoken word is one way Jesus heals people. Words possess power, they have life and death within them (Proverbs 18:21). Also, Jesus is releasing a command, not a wish or a plea, but a demand with no other option, but to leave these individuals. And when we believe in the power and authority that has been given to us by Jesus Himself in Luke 10:19, our commands of faith are empowered by the Spirit of the Living God. And when we truly believe those demons have no other option but to leave, just as they did in this night of miracles.

RESTORED HEALTH TO ALL WHO WERE SICK

In the same line of Scriptures, with a word Jesus restores health to all who were sick. Again, it is the principle of the spoken word of faith released into the atmosphere, and the wicked works of satan become null and void of power, and the people are healed and made whole for the glory of our Lord.

THE RICHES OF JESUS ON DISPLAY

- Jesus is the Deliverer.
- Jesus is the Healer.
- Jesus drives demons out with a word of authority.
- The demons obey Jesus' authority over them.
- Jesus didn't leave anyone behind; He delivered and healed them all.
- Fulfilling the Scriptures is important to Jesus.

CRACK THE MIRACLE CODE

We have the power to drive out demons with a word of faith.

When you read Miracle 6, you will learn how to catch unlimited miracles.

FAITH ASSIGNMENT

Examine your heart. Is there any place in your life where the enemy is pressuring you to fall into sin? If so, pray to God for help. Ask for forgiveness. If needed, reach out to someone for accountability.

PRAYER OF FAITH

Father God, this chapter is a strong message that speaks to my heart. Forgive me for the times I walk past troubled people without even thinking to stop and pray for them. Help me to understand and believe that You gave me the same authority over demons. And along with the rest of the body of Christ, I have a great work to do in these latter days —set the captives free in Jesus' name, amen.

Questions for Miracle 5: Healed Spiritually and Physically

1. How did Jesus drive out the evil spirits?
2. What did Jesus do for *all* the sick who came to Him that evening?
3. What does it mean when demons have possession of an individual?
4. With *oppression of demons* the demon does not have actual possession or ownership, but what?
5. Our flesh, when under the control of selfishness, has great power to do what?
6. Freedom is found only in whom?
7. What must happen with a sexual tie between the victim and the perpetrator(s)?

MIRACLE 6
TAKE THE LIMITS OFF GOD!

First Miraculous Catch of Fish

Our whopper of a fish story begins on the shores of Lake Gennesaret, the garden of riches. This is where Simon hears the call of his Master, Jesus, to become a fisher of men for Him; and later Simon becomes the rock, a strong leader of the Church. Here Jesus also gives the same call to the sons of Zebedee, a gift from God, and James, the one who follows, and John, the gift of God. These men leave all and follow Him. This story and more is recorded in Luke 5:1-4.

> *So it was, as* ***the multitude pressed about Him*** *to hear the word of God, that He stood by the Lake of Gennesaret, and saw two boats standing by the lake; but the fishermen had gone from them and were washing their nets. Then He got into one of the boats, which was Simon's, and asked him to put out a little from the land. And He sat down and taught the multitudes from the boat. When He had stopped speaking, He said to Simon, "Launch out into the deep and let down your nets for a catch."*

When I describe this miracle as a "whopper," I don't mean to imply that it's an overly exaggerated fish tale. There's no need for embellishment here, it's already an amazing fish story; but it's not about the one that gets away, but the ones that keep on coming, both physically and spiritually.

It all begins as Jesus was near the Lake of Gennesaret, which means "a garden of riches"[1] where Jesus met the fishermen including Simon Peter.[2] The name *Simon* means "he has heard," and "Peter" is derived from the Greek *Petros,* meaning "rock." James in Hebrew is *Yaakov,* meaning "supplanter" or "one who follows."[3] John means "God is gracious."[4] James and John were the sons of Zebedee, Zebedee means the "gift of God."[5] Jesus was teaching the Word of God to the multitude who followed Him.

THEY CROWDED AROUND HIM TO HEAR THE WORD

I love this detail added to the story, *"the people were* ***crowding around him*** *and listening to the word of God"* (Luke 5:1 NIV). This hunger for the Word has been buried by the cares and the problems of this world today. And yet, it is what we need to transform our hearts and minds to believe in the miraculous. In this situation, there is a problem with a lack of provision, a lack of products (fish) to sell to the people to provide for their families and fill their bellies.

You might be in this situation right now, and not sure how to make ends meet, let alone get ahead and walk in the realm of prosperity. God's Word gives us the solution to this dilemma:

> *But seek (aim at and strive after) first of all His kingdom and His righteousness (His way of doing and being right), and then all these things taken together will be given you besides* (Matthew 6:33 AMPC).

It's the pressing, crowding, seeking, and the hunger for God and His ways that releases profound miracles such as boatloads of fish into our lives.

DISCOURAGEMENT WILL STOP YOUR MIRACLE

Discouragement is a thief; it steals courage right from our hearts. If Peter had allowed this negative force to control his actions, he would never have received this tremendous supply of fish.

We, along with Peter, James, John, and the multitude, are about to witness a miracle of sizable proportion:

Simon answered and said to Him, "Master, we have toiled all night and caught nothing; nevertheless at Your word I will let down the net." And when they had done this, they caught a great number of fish, and their net was breaking. So they signaled to their partners in the other boat to come and help them. And they came and filled both the boats, so that they began to sink (Luke 5:5-7).

Peter's act of sheer obedience to Jesus' command not only broke the nets due to the overload of fish given to him, but it broke off the chains of discouragement too.

Look at how quickly circumstances can change if we just trust and obey the Word of our Lord.

MIRACLE, SIGN, OR WONDER?

In the second miracle of this work, we learn about the biblical meanings of miracles, signs, and wonders. A *miracle* defies the laws of nature; *signs* are symbols that point to something greater than themselves; and *wonders* invoke the awe of amazement. Even though I refer to this supernatural large catch of fish as a miracle because it defies the law of nature, I also believe that it is a sign as it directly points to the deity of Jesus—so much so that Luke 5:8 tells us, *"When Simon Peter saw it, he fell down at Jesus' knees, saying, 'Depart from me, for I am a sinful man, O Lord!'"*

And this supernatural catch also invokes the awe of amazement within us about the wonder of our God:

For he and all who were with him were astonished at the catch of fish which they had taken; and so also were James and John, the sons of Zebedee, who were partners with Simon. And Jesus said to Simon, "Do not be afraid. From now on you will catch men" (Luke 5:9-10).

DON'T BE AFRAID

The Lord may be asking you to trust Him and to do something entirely different from how you have been doing it. And yes, that can be a scary thought to consider, but you know in your heart that something must change. You cannot keep going in the same direction. I'm telling you, times are different. Either you trust Him, or you don't. And if you won't do what He is leading you to do because you fear failure, then you have already lost the battle. And this type of negative thinking does not line up with the message from Isaiah 41:10 (AMPC) that encourages us with these words,

> *Fear not [there is nothing to fear], for I am with you; do not look around you in terror and be dismayed, for I am your God. I will strengthen and harden you to difficulties, yes, I will help you; yes, I will hold you up and retain you with My [victorious] right hand of rightness and justice.*

What are you going to do?

WHAT DO THE FISH REPRESENT?

This profound catch of fish represents the great number of people who will be harvested and brought into the Kingdom of God when we do what He has asked of us. James, John, and Peter were His earlier followers and started this work of the Father to win the Lost.

THEY LEFT ALL AND FOLLOWED HIM

As a missionary, the next and last verse of this story has great meaning to me, *"So they pulled their boats up on the shore, left everything and followed him"* (Luke 5:11 NIV). It's a giant leap of faith to leave everything and follow Him. But throughout all the years, and the struggles, my faith has grown in leaps and bounds, and I can honestly say, I haven't lost, only gained. Yes, I lived through years of hardship, going without many materialistic things that most take for granted, but I have lived what many only dream about living. I have learned to be content in whatever state I am (Philippians 4:11). I have overcome hurt and betrayal in life in the ministry and life in general, and I tell you the truth, *"He will never leave you nor forsake you"* (Deuteronomy 31:6 NIV). And know that *"your God will be with you wherever you go"* (Joshua 1:9 NIV).

In the good times and in the bad times, Jesus has always been faithful and true (Revelation 19:11). And I am honored to say Jesus and I are friends (James 2:23). Time and time again, He has rescued me from the darkness

(Colossians 1:13) and even death, for I stand on the fact that *"No weapon formed against me shall prosper"* (Isaiah 54:17). I have been blessed to obey the Great Commission (Mark 16:15-18), I have witnessed the blind see, the deaf hear, the mute speak, the paralytics walk, cancerous tumors disappear, the possessed set free, and so much more. I know and I hear His voice call me by my name (John 10:27). And I am confident that He hears me when I call to Him (Psalm 4:3). I am loved (Jeremiah 31:3), forgiven (Mark 11:26), and taken care of by Him (Psalm 23:1-4). Hallelujah!

AN INVITATION

He gives each one of us an invitation to launch out into the deep and let down our nets to bring in this great harvest of fish for Him. Do you hear Him calling? And will you answer this call? Romans 10:14-15 (AMPC) beautifully explains it like this:

> *But how are people to call upon Him Whom they have not believed [in Whom they have no faith, on Whom they have no reliance]? And how are they to believe in Him [adhere to, trust in, and rely upon Him] of Whom they have never heard? And how are they to hear without a preacher? And how can men [be expected to] preach unless they are sent? As it is written, How beautiful are the feet of those who bring glad tidings! [How welcome is the coming of those who preach the good news of His good things!]*

If you would make this your life's goal, more people would hear the Gospel of Jesus Christ. You would be going about your heavenly Father's business and begin to win people to Jesus. It's really that simple.

THE RICHES OF JESUS ON DISPLAY

- Jesus prioritizes the teaching of the Word.
- Jesus knows what we need.
- He is willing to provide for our needs.
- Jesus is aware of the power of miracles, signs, and wonders and makes the most of every situation to use that power to win the Lost, and to meet our needs.

- He is willing to journey with us to answer our prayers.
- Jesus has authority over nature, in this case the fish.

CRACK THE MIRACLE CODE

Press, crowd around, seek, and hunger for God and His ways, and you will catch unlimited miracles.

As you read Miracle 7, you will be encouraged by the Lord's ability and willingness to heal the sick.

PRAYER OF FAITH

Father God, I am being challenged to let go of my discouragement and fear of failure. I confess that my mind and emotions have been in turmoil as I have been unwilling to trust and change the course of my destiny. Forgive me for doubting that You really do care about me and have my best interests in mind. Help me to launch out into the deep knowing that You will never leave me, nor forsake me. In Your precious name dear Jesus, I pray, amen.

FAITH ASSIGNMENT

Take out a sheet of paper and write down 1-3 things you fear the most. Ask God for a plan to overcome those fears.

1. ______________________________

2. ______________________________

3. ______________________________

Questions for Miracle 6: Take the Limits Off God!

1. What did the multitude do to hear the Word of God?
2. What does discouragement steal from our hearts?
3. What two things were destroyed by Peter's sheer act of obedience to the command of Jesus?
4. What does a miracle defy?
5. Signs are symbols that point to what?
6. What do wonders invoke?
7. What does the profound catch of fish represent?

MIRACLE 7
HE IS WILLING TO HEAL

Jesus Cleanses a Man with Leprosy

Many people lack the confidence that Jesus wants to heal them. We will read about one such man from Luke 5:12-16:

> *And it happened when He was in a certain city, that behold, a man who was full of leprosy saw Jesus; and he fell on his face and implored Him, saying, "Lord, if You are willing, You can make me clean." Then He put out His hand and touched him, saying, "I am willing; be cleansed." Immediately the leprosy left him. And He charged him to tell no one, "But go and show yourself to the priest, and make an offering for your cleansing, as a testimony to them, just as Moses commanded." However, the report went around concerning Him all the more; and great multitudes came together to hear, and to be healed by Him of their infirmities. So He Himself often withdrew into the wilderness and prayed.*

WHAT IS LEPROSY?

First things first, what is leprosy? Leprosy, also known as Hansen's disease, is a chronic infectious disease caused mainly by a type of bacteria called

Mycobacterium leprae. The disease affects the skin, the peripheral nerves, the mucosa of the upper respiratory tract and the eyes. Apart from the physical deformity, persons affected by leprosy also face stigmatization and discrimination.[1]

A LEPER'S LIFE IN BIBLE TIMES

Life for a leper in Bible times was very harsh. A leper was considered physically unclean, highly contagious, and spiritually unclean. Someone suffering from leprosy was so feared, that an accidental touch or breathing the same air with a leper would make someone unclean. They were utterly shunned by society. They were not allowed in public places; this meant everyday life they had once known was over. They were forced to live in leper colonies or caves.

Imagine being shunned from worshipping God because of something you were not responsible for. What great hopelessness these individuals suffered. But then we have Jesus, the Healer not only of our physical bodies, but also the spiritual Healer of our souls, our minds and emotions.

FULL OF LEPROSY AND SHAME

This man in Luke 5 was full of leprosy; he didn't just have a suspicious spot—his body was consumed with this deadly and highly contagious disease. And leprosy was not the only thing he was full of, we could also add shame. Back in the day when someone had leprosy, they would have to warn a passerby and throw a rock at them and call out to that person about themselves that they were *"unclean."* What utter shame and rejection this man and others like him must have felt. And the result of being full of leprosy, shame, and rejection led to another obstacle, doubt. He wasn't sure if Jesus would heal him.

Perhaps you are in a similar situation as this leprous man, and you have been labeled with a deadly and/or contagious disease, and you find yourself struggling with the same issues as he does. You really are unsure if Jesus is willing to cleanse you from this disease, and all the inner wounds that are eating away at your mind and emotions such as shame and rejection. You know He has the power to heal, but on the inside, there is this nagging doubt, "Will You heal me?"

INSECURITY IN GOD'S PROMISE TO HEAL

I want to address this issue of insecurity in God's promise to heal us. Isaiah 53:5 declares that *"by His stripes we are healed."* This word *healed* comes from the Hebrew word *rapha'*, which means healer, to cure, heal, repair, and make whole (Strong's H7495). Throughout Messiah's teachings we read the healing Scriptures and His promises to heal us too. And yet, we often hear slanderous preaching against His will to heal His people from today's pulpits. It's not biblical to say that Jesus withholds healing. But when we make our negative experiences the foundation of our beliefs, we will be insecure in His promise to heal us.

For a deeper understanding of Isaiah 53:4-5, *"By His stripes we are healed,"* read my book, *The Healing Creed,* Chapter 2, pages 33-42.

WHERE INSECURITY STEMS FROM

So often I find that people are insecure in God's promise to heal because they lack the confidence of His love for them. This misunderstanding happens when we wrongfully judge God's love for human love. God's love is unconditional. It's not based on our behavior, good or bad. In fact, He loves us even if we do not love Him. Romans 5:8 (AMPC) describes His unconditional love like so, *"But God shows and clearly proves His [own] love for us by the fact that while we were still sinners, Christ (the Messiah, the Anointed One) died for us."*

JESUS' RESPONSE

The Messiah could have spoken a word of faith and sent the man on his way, but He didn't. Scriptures accurately tell us, *"Then He put out His hand and touched him, saying, 'I am willing; be cleansed.' Immediately the leprosy left him."* Jesus is very intentional in what He says and does, and this is no exception. He was defying a spirit of fear by demonstrating that He has authority over contagious and deadly disease. And He began to remove this man's shame by doing the unthinkable, He reached out, touched him, and healed him instantly from leprosy. He delivered the man from the dirty label of being "unclean," and cleansed him from shame and rejection.

This reminds me of a filthy elderly man who lived on the streets in a village in Tanzania. He obviously had suffered from leprosy in the past, and was shunned by the people, even by the elders of the church. He was not all together mentally and emotionally stable, and this type of cruelty does great damage to a person's spirit. I was the minister in the pulpit during a conference, and I did something that upset the head apples in the cart. I stopped when I saw this man on the street corner, held out my hand to him and invited him to the church meeting as my guest of honor. Yes, while we were dressed in our Sunday best and he in his torn rags, he sat right next to me throughout the entire meeting. This man was overwhelmed with joy; someone reached out and touched him in the name of the Lord and invited him into the house of the Lord—and years of shame and rejection were being healed that day.

GO TO THE PRIEST

Why did Jesus send this man to the priest after he was healed, and not to a physician? It's a great question, and we misunderstand a major part of this man's testimony when we don't dig into the Word to find out. Back in biblical times it was the priest who diagnosed someone with leprosy, not a doctor. And if there were symptoms, the person was declared "unclean" with leprosy. Why? The religious beliefs were strong that this disease was a direct result of sin. And the letter of the Law was very strict.

THE RESULT OF AN INQUIRING HEART

Out of all the lepers during this time, what was different about this man? Why did his testimony make it into The Book? This man possessed an inquiring heart. He did not falsely accuse God by placing the blame on Him for his misfortune, as was and still is today a major problem within the religious community. Let's contemplate upon this man's inquiring heart.

Out of all my years of study and living out this healing message I find this to be truth. All the whining, begging, and tears do not move God. Those are all emotional pleas, and God does not operate by emotions, but by faith. So even though I write that this man is plagued with doubt as to whether it is God's will to heal him, he is strong in the faith of one thing, that Jesus *can* heal. He just has an honest question, *"Are You willing to heal me?"* And we see to the glory of God, He is willing, and the man is cleansed and healed from leprosy, and His testimony is recorded in the Holy Scriptures for people throughout the ages to learn from and to be encouraged.

WHY DID JESUS HEAL THIS MAN?

Like me, as you read through this miraculous testimony, your imagination is probably recreating this scene in your mind and thinking about why He healed this man. Luke 19:10 (NIV) gives us a clear answer to this question: *"For the Son of Man came to seek and save the lost."* Again, this man was full of leprosy, shame, and rejection. *Sōzō* is the Greek word for *save*, and it means "to save a suffering one (from perishing), i.e. one suffering from disease, to make well, heal, restore to health" (Strong's G4982). This man was not only in need of physical healing, but also a spiritual cleansing. And the most life-changing miracle anyone of us can receive is spiritual cleansing from sin and the consequences of sin—death and hell. As I consider the depth of Messiah's love and care for the Lost, my heart fills with awe. And may each of us purpose within our hearts to follow in His footsteps.

Deep healings such as this one bring to my heart one of my faithful students, Jennifer. This beautiful woman has suffered a lot of injustices in life. And over the past few years I have witnessed a powerful transformation by the power of the Spirit and the Word of God. She is free from the bondage of past abuse from Free Masonry, healed from the suffering of Lyme's disease, and she continues to shine brighter and brighter with Jesus.

WHEN DID THIS MIRACLE TAKE PLACE?

According to the Gospel of Matthew, when Jesus came down from the mountain after teaching the Sermon on the Mount, large crowds followed Him. And this leprous man *"fell on his face and implored Him, saying, 'Lord, if You are willing, You can* make me clean.'" We can figure that this leprous man followed Jesus like the rest, but because of this disease, from a cautious distance.

It says that *"he fell on his face,"* this word *fell* in the Greek language is *piptō* and it means "to prostrate" (Strong's G4098). I love how this man humbled himself and lay face down before Jesus, and it says he *inquired* of Him. In other words, with a humble heart he seeks truth and finds it. These words of Jesus are recorded in John 8:31-32 (AMPC), *"If you abide in My word [hold fast to My teachings and live in accordance with them], you are truly My disciples. And you will know the Truth, and the Truth will set you free."*

THE RICHES OF JESUS ON DISPLAY

- Neither the religious leaders nor society control Jesus.
- Jesus came to undo the letter of the Law by fulfilling it.
- He is not given to fear contagious or deadly disease.
- Jesus' compassion for hurting and rejected people is outstanding.

CRACK THE MIRACLE CODE

Have no fear about the strength or spreadability of any disease, because Jesus is able and willing to heal it.

As you read Miracle 8, you will discover how Jesus honors faith and how it transcends physical distance.

PRAYER OF FAITH

Dear Jesus, this miracle about how You cleansed this man of leprosy brings up negative emotions that I struggle with such as doubt, unbelief, shame, and even rejection. I too desire to be free from the bondage of these things, along with the disease itself. Help me to rid myself of this nagging doubt, "Will You heal me?" I know You can, and now I ask for forgiveness for any doubt that You will heal me. I see one of the first steps to the manifestation of my healing is to ask You to cleanse me from the chains of doubt and unbelief that You are willing to heal me, too. In Your precious name I pray, amen.

FAITH ASSIGNMENT

On a sheet of paper write down your doubts and fears. Then turn to His Word and search out His response to these doubts and fears and write them down. And then take His promises with you in prayer.

Questions for Miracle 7: He Is Willing to Heal

1. What is one thing that many people lack concerning His will to heal them?
2. What was someone with leprosy considered to be?
3. What does the Hebrew word *rapha'* mean?
4. Why are people insecure about God's promise to heal them?
5. What was the unthinkable thing that Jesus did with the leprous man?
6. Why did Jesus send this man to the priest after he was healed, and not to a physician?
7. This man has an honest question for Jesus, what is it?
8. What does the Greek word *piptō* mean?

MIRACLE 8
GREAT FAITH

Jesus Heals the Centurion's Servant

We are about to read the story about a controversial man of power and authority, a centurion, a member of the Roman army, and oppressor of the Jews whose faith caught the attention of our Lord Jesus and receives an honorable mention in the Holy Scriptures. Let's start at the beginning with this amazing read from Luke 7:1-10:

> *Now when He concluded all His sayings in the hearing of the people, He entered Capernaum. And a certain centurion's servant, who was dear to him, was sick and ready to die. So when he heard about Jesus, he sent elders of the Jews to Him, pleading with Him to come and heal his servant. And when they came to Jesus, they begged Him earnestly, saying that the one for whom He should do this was deserving, "for he loves our nation, and has built us a synagogue." Then Jesus went with them. And when He was already not far from the house, the centurion sent friends to Him, saying to Him, "Lord, do not trouble Yourself, for I am not worthy that You should enter under my roof. Therefore I did not even think myself worthy to come to You. But say the word, and my servant will be healed. For I also am a man placed under authority, having soldiers under me. And I say to one, 'Go,' and he goes; and to*

another, 'Come,' and he comes; and to my servant, 'Do this,' and he does it." When Jesus heard these things, He marveled at him, and turned around and said to the crowd that followed Him, "I say to you, I have not found such great faith, not even in Israel!" And those who were sent, returning to the house, found the servant well who had been sick.

Let's begin this interesting study by examining the individuals and groups of people involved in this recorded miracle of Jesus. First, we have the centurion introduced in the first paragraph of this chapter. Who, despite working for the enemy of the people, heard about Jesus and His authority over sickness and disease. The centurion curiously sent the Jewish elders to plead in his stead for his servant who was on his deathbed.

When did this miracle take place? According to Luke 6:17-19, *"And He came down with them and stood on a level place with a crowd of His disciples and a great multitude of people from all Judea and Jerusalem, and from the seacoast of Tyre and Sidon, who came to hear Him and be healed of their diseases, as well as those who were tormented with unclean spirits. And they were healed. And the whole multitude sought to touch Him, for power went out from Him and healed them all."*

And then He continues to teach them about the Beatitudes.

CAN GOOD WORKS PURCHASE HEALING?

Let's take a quick look into this question, "Can good works purchase healing?" You might think this to be an odd question, but how often do we hear people inquire about someone who is ill, "They are a such good person, so why are they sick?" In Luke 7:3-5, the Jewish elders were pleading with Jesus to come and heal this man's servant, and touting the good deeds of this servant, *"for he loves our nation, and has built us a synagogue."* Obviously, he was a good man, but do our good works purchase blessings from God? And by this response to Jesus concerning this man, it's apparent that both the centurion and the Jewish elders seem to think so. And many people today believe so too. But this is not the case, it's a myth.

MYTH BREAKER

Considering what you just read, "Can good works purchase healing?" I think it's important to address this issue that you must be a good person or a person of good works in order to be healed or to receive blessings from God.

Certainly, the biblical teaching is truth when it says that we reap what we sow (Galatians 6:7). But Jesus makes it clear in John 16:33, *"These things I have spoken to you, that in Me you may have peace. In the world you will have tribulation; but be of good cheer, I have overcome the world."* The Greek word for *tribulation* is *thlipsis*, and it means "trouble" (Strong's G2347). So just because someone is facing troubling times, it does not mean they are up to something bad. Let's not be so rigid, but instead be balanced in our beliefs, I believe sickness and disease are a direct result of the fall of man back in Genesis 3. (For a deeper understanding about this, read my book *DARE to Believe,* Chapter 1, "Redeemed from the Curse.")

WORTHY TO BE HEALED

Allow me to make it perfectly clear—it is our good works or our righteous acts that buy us salvation or any other blessing from God, such as supernatural healing. That's a "works mentality." Isaiah 64:6 tells us that our righteousness is as filthy rags. Our generous acts of kindness do not make us worthy. Romans 3:10-12 tells us that no one is worthy. It's all about what Jesus did for us at Calvary. The foundational truth for healing is this: *"by His stripes we are healed"* (Isaiah 53:4-5). And He only asks one thing from us, to believe. Jesus tells us clearly, *"All things are possible for the one who believes and trusts [in Me]!"* (Mark 9:23 AMP).

UNDERSTANDS AUTHORITY

This centurion, a Gentile man, has experiential knowledge about authority; not only is he under authority, but he also exercises authority over others too. He explains why he understands this authority in Luke 7:8, *"For I also am a man placed under authority, having soldiers under me. And I say to one, 'Go,' and he goes; and to another, 'Come,' and he comes; and to my servant, 'Do this,' and he does it."* The revelation of authority goes hand in hand with great faith. You cannot have great faith without this revelation about how authority operates. Very few had, and I would add have, this type of understanding about faith: "If Jesus says it, that settles it." As far as the centurion is concerned, "It's a done deal!" And we should all have this type of faith.

JESUS MARVELS

The centurion's understanding of authority causes Jesus to marvel in Luke 7:9.

> *When Jesus heard these things, He marveled at him, and turned around and said to the crowd that followed Him, "I say to you, I have not found such great faith, not even in Israel!"*

The Greek word for *marvel* is *thaumazō*, and it means "to wonder" (Strong's G2296). And there is only one other recorded place in Scripture (Mark 6:6) where it says that Jesus marvels, and it wasn't at someone's faith, but at their lack of faith in Nazareth.

Not only does Jesus publicly credit this man with great faith, but his faith marvels Him. Let us pray, *"Lord Jesus, may our faith marvel and honor Your authority."*

Throughout the recorded miracles of Jesus, there is another who receives an honorable mention concerning great faith—another Gentile, a Canaanite woman (Matthew 15:21-28). We will study about her later in this work.

THE RESULT OF GREAT FAITH

The result of great faith is clear in Luke 7:10, in the life of this centurion, *"And those who were sent, returning to the house, found the servant well who had been sick."* And this is true for anyone who takes Jesus at His word, *"The blind receive their sight, and the lame walk, the lepers are cleansed, and the deaf hear, the dead are raised up, and the poor have the gospel preached to them"* (Matthew 11:5 KJV). Does the faith of this unlikely man, the centurion, cause a disturbance within your spirit. I pray it does. I want you to crave great faith, and cause Jesus to marvel about your faith.

SPIRITUAL DISTANCE

Did Jesus go to where this sick man was? Did He lay healing hands upon this sick man? Did He send a cloth anointed with oil? Did we hear Jesus pray a prayer of healing for the man? The answer to all these questions is "No." This divine healing proves to us that in the realm of faith, there is no distance. Faith transcends all physical barriers such as distance.

Hey, I raised my son, Marcos, from the dead from a distance. I Prayed with a grandmother over her preborn granddaughter to be delivered and healed from a cancerous spine, and spots on the brain. A week later this little one was declared healed and saved from abortion. And so much more, all from a distance. And I did so by faith in the redemptive work of Jesus, our Savior, Deliver, and Healer.

WHOSE FAITH HEALS THE CENTURION'S SERVANT?

We find the answer to this question in Luke 7:3-10. It is the faith of this controversial figure in this story, the centurion. Why? Because he loves his servant, hears about Jesus, and seeks Him out, recognizing Jesus has greater authority than he does, and simply believes and acts upon this authority.

WHAT CAN WE LEARN FROM THIS TESTIMONY?

From this testimony we can learn that Jesus shows no favoritism. He honors the faith of people we might not be too fond of, as in the case of this centurion who did somehow earn the trust of the Jewish elders but still worked in the enemy's camp. It does not matter to God if we are Jew or Gentile, man or woman, rich or poor, the boss or the worker. He loves us all the same, and honors our faith.

THE RICHES OF JESUS ON DISPLAY

- Jesus is drawn to people of faith.
- He shows no favoritism.
- Jesus wills to save both Jew and Gentile.
- He treats both the rich and the poor alike, with honor.

- Jesus publicly acknowledges people of great faith.
- He takes advantage of every opportunity to teach God's Word.

CRACK THE MIRACLE CODE

Jesus honors faith and it transcends all physical barriers such as distance. As you read Miracle 9, you will discover how to overcome the obstacles that stand in the way of our miracle.

PRAYER OF FAITH

Oh Holy Spirit, I am deeply touched as Jesus is over this man's faith. Help me to grow in the faith that believes not because I see but because I recognize and honor Your authority. And because You say so, I consider it already done. In the precious name of Jesus I pray, amen.

FAITH ASSIGNMENT

Pray that Holy Spirit will lead you to people who are ready and need prayer. Ask them if you can pray for them. If you do this on a regular basis, you will begin to witness miracles.

Questions for Miracle 8: Great Faith

1. Who is the controversial man of power and authority in this story?
2. As controversial as this man is, what does he have?
3. His faith is so great that Jesus does what?
4. What is the Greek word for *marvel?*
5. What does *marvel* in Greek mean?
6. What does this divine healing prove to us?
7. Whose faith heals the centurion's servant?

MIRACLE 9
FORGIVEN AND HEALED

Jesus Heals a Paralytic Man Lowered Down Through the Roof

We begin our next adventure with Jesus and a paralyzed man with his committed friends and a group of offended scribes and Pharisees who meet in an overcrowded house meeting and all witness a life-changing miracle.

> *Now it happened on a certain day, as He was teaching, that there were Pharisees and teachers of the law sitting by, who had come out of every town of Galilee, Judea, and Jerusalem. And the power of the Lord was present to heal them. Then behold, men brought on a bed a man who was paralyzed, whom they sought to bring in and lay before Him. And when they could not find how they might bring him in, because of the crowd, they went up on the housetop and let him down with his bed through the tiling into the midst before Jesus.*
>
> *When He saw their faith, He said to him, "Man, your sins are forgiven you."*
>
> *And the scribes and the Pharisees began to reason, saying, "Who is this who speaks blasphemies? Who can forgive sins but God alone?"*
>
> *But when Jesus perceived their thoughts, He answered and said to them, "Why are you reasoning in your hearts? Which is easier, to say, 'Your sins are forgiven you,' or to say, 'Rise up and walk'? But that you*

may know that the Son of Man has power on earth to forgive sins"—He said to the man who was paralyzed, "I say to you, arise, take up your bed, and go to your house."

Immediately he rose up before them, took up what he had been lying on, and departed to his own house, glorifying God. And they were all amazed, and they glorified God and were filled with fear, saying, "We have seen strange things today!" (Luke 5:17-26)

THE POWER OF THE LORD WAS PRESENT TO HEAL

The atmosphere was ripe for healing. The teaching of God's Word creates an atmosphere of faith for healing and miracles. And Jesus, the Creative Word made visible, was in the house! Everything needed to create healing and miracles was present, but then there was an obstacle that stood in the way of this man's much needed miracle.

OBSTACLE TO THIS MIRACLE

Every life-changing event is met with at least one obstacle, and this divine encounter is no exception. The main obstacle to this miracle is that there is no clear pathway to Jesus. Specifically, there are too many people in the way. You may find yourself in a similar situation, your pathway to Jesus seems cluttered. There are just too many obstacles in the way, but God promises to make a way when there appears to be no way. Isaiah 43:19 (AMPC) says, *"Behold, I am doing a new thing! Now it springs forth; do you not perceive and know it and will you not give heed to it? I will even make a way in the wilderness and rivers in the desert."* I am a firm believer that even when we don't see how God is working on our behalf—He is.

The paralyzed person's friends are an amazing support team, and they are not going to allow this obstacle to stand in the way. So with some creative ingenuity, they come up with a plan to carry him to the rooftop, cut a hole in the roof and lower him down to the feet of Jesus. I love this type of faith; they don't give up. And I believe in the willingness of Jesus to heal, so I believe that He is the One who planted that idea in their minds.

Physically, you may have to wait for a lifesaving operation or procedure. But there are many other candidates on that waiting list before you, so in the natural time is running out. And you may never be called up for this procedure.

But don't be discouraged. Jesus already made a way for you—supernatural healing. There is no waiting line, Philippians 4:6 (AMPC) tells us, *"Do not fret or have any anxiety about anything, but in every circumstance and in everything, by prayer and petition (definite requests), with thanksgiving, continue to make your wants known to God."*

NOTICE WHAT JESUS SEES

Jesus doesn't just see with His physical eyes, He perceives, spiritually discerns the thoughts and the intentions of the hearts of those around Him. And one of the things that He clearly sees in this situation is the faith of this man's friends. And as we witness throughout this work, their faith calls out to the heart of Jesus. Psalm 4:3 (AMPC) says, *"But know that the Lord has set apart for Himself [and given distinction to] him who is godly [the man of loving-kindness]. The Lord listens and heeds when I call to Him."*

Along with the godliness of the faith of this man's friends, He also discerns the evil intentions in the hearts of the scribes and the Pharisees. Jesus was never a fan of these religious leaders. He knew the devious intentions of their hearts toward Him. He always shined the light upon their spiritual darkness. And this situation is no different, where He publicly calls out their hypocrisy of being so spiritually in tune, that they did not recognize Him, the true Messiah, and the power He possessed to forgive sins and to heal this man.

> *But that you may know that the Son of Man has power on earth to forgive sins—He said to the man who was paralyzed, "I say to you, arise, take up your bed, and go to your house"* (Luke 5:24).

Another purpose for healing this man is found in 1 John 3:8 (AMPC):

> *[But] he who commits sin [who practices evildoing] is of the devil [takes his character from the evil one], for the devil has sinned (violated the divine law) from the beginning. The reason the Son of God was made manifest (visible) was to undo (destroy, loosen, and dissolve) the works the devil [has done].*

Jesus came to undo every work of satan.

WHY DID JESUS SAY, "YOUR SINS ARE FORGIVEN YOU"?

At a first glance, Jesus' response to this paralytic man, "Your sins are forgiven you," seems a bit off, but as we ponder upon the situation it makes sense. Back in these times, any type of sickness, disease, or physical malady was directly equated with sin. And while it is true there are sins directly linked to sinful behavior, it's not always the case. Even considering John 5:14, when Jesus heals the man at the pool of Bethesda, He does say to the man, *"See, you have been made well. Sin no more, lest a worse thing come upon you."* But it's not always the case.

Remember, the story of the man born blind who receives his sight from Jesus? Do you remember what His disciples ask Him? *"Rabbi, who sinned, this man or his parents, that he was born blind?"* (John 9:1-3). His response to them is, *"Neither...."* (We will address this miracle later in this work.)

What Jesus is doing in this situation with the paralytic man is proving His deity to the scribes and Pharisees, that He has both the authority and power to forgive sins and to heal by healing this man of paralysis, by addressing sin issues.

WHEN DOES THIS MAN'S MIRACLE MANIFEST?

> *When He saw their faith, He said to him, "Man, your sins are forgiven you."* (Luke 5:20).

This is the key to the timing of this man's healing—when faith is undeniably visible.

REASONS FOR OBSTACLES

I believe this is also why the enemy causes obstacles or distractions in our lives so that we lose our focus and take our eyes off the Healer, Jesus, and look to other things. Whether these obstacles are other means of healing or just plain distractions in our everyday life, we lose our focus of our miracle when we stop focusing on Jesus.

THE POWER OF THE SPOKEN WORD

Besides the power of faith, the power of the spoken word is clearly at play here as well. Jesus being full of faith, speaks a word of authority, which we have seen can cause both positive and negative reactions. At first, as we have discussed, it caused an outburst of false accusations against Jesus, judging Him as being blasphemous. And I warn you, when you begin to declare words of faith and authority, that religious spirit will also speak blasphemously against you.

The Word is clear in Proverbs 18:21 (AMP): "*Death and life are in the power of the tongue, and those who love it and indulge it will eat its fruit and bear the consequences of their words.*" Good or bad, words have power to create or to destroy, and we must learn to wield them correctly. The scribes and the Pharisees ignorantly spoke words that if allowed would kill that man's miracle. But Jesus doesn't back down, He knows His authority and puts that nasty religious spirit in its place—under the submission of His deity.

Then there is another verse in Proverbs 12:18 (AMPC) that says, "*There are those who speak rashly, like the piercing of a sword, but the tongue of the wise brings healing.*" The improper use of words, such as the way these religious leaders rose up against Jesus will obstruct the miraculous power and cause great harm. But we have the supreme example of Jesus' proper use of words, and they not only release forgiveness, deliverance, and healing, they usher in salvation.

THE RICHES OF JESUS ON DISPLAY

- Jesus does not allow a religious spirit to push Him around.
- He does not doubt His deity.
- Jesus is perceptive of the thoughts and intentions of those around Him.
- He does not allow obstacles to obstruct His miraculous work.

CRACK THE MIRACLE CODE

To achieve our miracle, we must move beyond life's obstacles.

As you read Miracle 10, you will learn how hypocrisy and legalism kill a miracle, but grace heals.

Prayer of Faith

Father God, from this message, I have seen the obstacles standing in my way that prevent me from walking in my healing. But like this paralytic man and his friends, I do not want to stop believing. Help me, Holy Spirit, to clear the clutter, and to pick up my mat and walk out this healing for Your glory, and for my good pleasure. In Jesus' name, I pray believing, amen.

FAITH ASSIGNMENT

You need physical healing in your body? Create the atmosphere that ushers in the Healer and welcomes His healing power.

- Pray in faith.
- Eliminate the obstacles, the unnecessary distractions prohibiting you from going to Jesus.
- Declare the healing Scriptures aloud.
- Forgive.
- Love.
- Worship Jesus, your Healer.
- Release His healing power into your body.
- And believe.

If you activate these steps, you will find yourself well on your way to your long-awaited miracle.

Questions for Miracle 9: Forgiven and Healed

1. What was present to heal?
2. Every life-changing event is met with what?
3. Jesus doesn't just see with His physical eyes, but how?
4. What two things does Jesus see in this situation?
5. Why did Jesus say, "Your sins are forgiven you"?
6. What was Jesus proving in the way He handled this man's healing?
7. What do our words possess?

MIRACLE 10

DEFY THE RELIGIOUS SPIRIT AND HEAL

Jesus Heals a Man with Withered Hand on the Sabbath

In this miracle we will witness Jesus defy the religious spirit that lords over the scribes and the Pharisees who are on high alert to catch Him doing something that goes against their legalistic rules, such as healing a man with a withered hand in the temple on the Sabbath. And they do—they catch Jesus red-handed!

Let's read Luke 6:6-11:

> *Now it happened on another Sabbath, also, that He entered the synagogue and taught. And a man was there whose right hand was withered. So the scribes and Pharisees watched Him closely, whether He would heal on the Sabbath, that they might find an accusation against Him. But He knew their thoughts, and said to the man who had the withered hand, "Arise and stand here." And he arose and stood. Then Jesus said to them, "I will ask you one thing: Is it lawful on the Sabbath to do good or to do evil, to save life or to destroy?" And when He had looked around at them all, He said to the man, "Stretch out your hand." And he did so, and his hand was restored as whole as the other. But they were filled with rage, and discussed with one another what they might do to Jesus.*

THE RELIGIOUS LEADERS ARE NOT PLEASED WITH JESUS

As we can see from the negative response by the scribes and the Pharisees, they are not pleased that Jesus heals the man's withered hand. But why aren't they glad that his suffering has come to an end? It's because they are filled with a religious spirit. You might wonder, *What is a religious spirit? And why is Jesus so harsh about it?* This spirit is legalistic, all about appearance, and has nothing to do with compassion and what will truly help and bless people.

JESUS IS NOT KEEN ABOUT THE SCRIBES AND THE PHARISEES

Obviously, Jesus is not too keen about the scribes and the Pharisees, nor does He shy away from calling out their hypocrisy. In Matthew 23 He calls them "hypocrites" seven times. And He has other special titles that reveal what He thinks about their evil intentions such as *"blind guides," "snakes,"* and *"brood of vipers."* He even calls them *"whitewashed tombs"!* (See Matthew 23:16, 27, 33.)

JESUS, THE GOOD SHEPHERD HAS TWO WEAPONS

Jesus, our Good Shepherd, has two weapons that He uses while herding His beloved sheep, His followers. One is His staff that He gently nudges His sheep with to keep them from going astray. His staff has a hook at the end for when we go off the straight and narrow path and He must lovingly be a little more forceful with us and yank us back into the fold. He also has a club to beat off the wolves that are harmful to the sheep. He uses the club most often when dealing with the scribes and the Pharisees, the hypocritical leaders then and now. He takes a righteous stand against their wickedness and issues a list of woes and warnings to them.

EIGHT WOES

This word *woe* is used eight times in Matthew 23. Reader beware: Jesus is driving home a point. He's not pleased with their behavior; in fact, it grieves Him. Let's look at these *woes* listed in Matthew 23:13-33.

The first woe given to the scribes and the Pharisees is found in verse 13, "*For you shut up the kingdom of heaven against men; for you neither go in yourselves, nor do you allow those who are entering to go in."* A religious, hypocritical spirit will do everything within its power to maintain control over others, and hinder people from freely walking in the promises of God. One such example is discouraging God's people from believing for a healing touch from Jesus.

The second woe is in verse 14, "*Woe to you, scribes and Pharisees, hypocrites! For you devour widows' houses, and for a pretense make long prayers. Therefore you will receive greater condemnation.*" This controlling and thieving spirit takes advantage of the vulnerable for profit.

The third woe is found in verse 15, "*You travel land and sea to win one proselyte, and when he is won, you make him twice as much a son of hell as yourselves."*

These woes are not soft rebukes, they are harsh and to the point. Once I was ministering in a church in Tennessee. From the start of the message, I kept getting a word of knowledge about the sexual sins taking place within its members. And the Lord would not release me from warning the people to repent. Little did I know then, but later that year I was told that the pastor of this church had sexual problems and the young men he was mentoring had the same issues. Again, these woes are to protect the people, and to give the corrupt leaders a chance to repent.

The fourth woe is recorded in Matthew 23 verse 16 (AMP), *"Woe to you, blind guides, who say, 'Whoever swears [an oath] by the sanctuary of the temple, that is nothing (non-binding); but whoever swears [an oath] by the gold of the temple is obligated [as a debtor to fulfill his vow and keep his promise].'"* This rebuke is toward those who push an unbalanced message of prosperity. I believe that God's people should be prosperous, but materialistic things cannot purchase true happiness or even health and healing. You can be extremely wealthy financially but be laying on your deathbed alone and friendless. I don't see this as being prosperous. It's best to live God's way and *"Seek first the kingdom of God and His righteousness, and all these things shall be added to you"* (Matthew 6:33).

The fifth woe is listed in Mathew 23:23, and it says, *"You pay tithe of mint and anise and cummin and have neglected the weightier matters of the law: justice and mercy and faith."* This warning is delivered due to priorities being out of order. It is apparent that the weightier matters of the law, justice, mercy, and faith are more important to the Lord than the tithe.

We can read the sixth woe in Matthew 23:25-26, *"You cleanse the outside of the cup and dish, but inside they are full of extortion and self-indulgence. Blind Pharisee, first cleanse the inside of the cup and dish, that the outside of them may be clean also."* Jesus rebukes them for the filthy condition of their hearts. They put on an act and can fool others, but not Jesus. He sees right though the façade and warns them to scrub themselves inside.

Their seventh woe they receive from Jesus is found in Matthew 23:27-28: *"You are like whitewashed tombs which indeed appear beautiful outwardly, but inside are full of dead men's bones and all uncleanness. Even so you also outwardly appear righteous to men, but inside you are full of hypocrisy and lawlessness."* Jesus pretty much hammers the last nail in the coffin for them. He rebukes their superficial behavior and lets them know their act is over. It's time to walk the walk and talk the talk. Get real with God!

The eighth and final woe from Jesus for the scribes and the Pharisees is found in Matthew 23: 29-33, *"Because you build the tombs of the prophets and adorn the monuments of the righteous, and say, 'If we had lived in the days of our fathers, we would not have been partakers with them in the blood of the prophets.' Therefore you are witnesses against yourselves that you are sons of those who murdered the prophets."* Jesus is very harsh with them for He knows the corruption within their hearts and how self-deceived they really are, and that they will do the same as their fathers had done.

The hour is late, and it's time to take these eight woes seriously. Examine your own heart and make sure to repent of any weak areas. God rebukes and warns people because He loves us and obviously sees a pathway forward for us to change—but only if we repent of sin and are authentic with God and with people.

WHY DOES THE MIRACLE TAKE PLACE IN THE TEMPLE?

Jesus is aware of a man with a withered hand in the temple, and He also knows that the scribes and the Pharisees oppose Him. These spiritual vipers want to catch Jesus in the act of doing something that goes against their religious rules. But Jesus will not allow these religious rulers to stand in the way of doing what's right in the sight of Father God and for the good of this man, no matter what day of the week it is.

Jesus came to earth to destroy the works of the devil (1 John 3:8) and He is planting a new seed of freedom from the law of sin and death, and introducing grace. Romans 10:4 (AMPC) explains it like this:

For Christ is the end of the Law [the limit at which it ceases to be, for the Law leads up to Him Who is the fulfillment of its types, and in Him the purpose which it was designed to accomplish is fulfilled. That is, the purpose of the Law is fulfilled in Him] as the means of righteousness (right relationship to God) for everyone who trusts in and adheres to and relies on Him.

Jesus came to free the people from the bondage of a religious spirit, and to demonstrate with bold action that it is good to do good on the Sabbath. After all, the healing of this man's withered hand is part of the plan of redemption (Isaiah 53:4-5).

HOW DOES THIS RESTORATIVE MIRACLE HAPPEN?

Jesus spoke a command with authority: "*And when He had looked around at them all, He said to the man, 'Stretch out your hand.' And he did so, and his hand was restored as whole as the other*" (Luke 6:10). And with Jesus' verbal command and this man's obedience, his hand is instantly restored for the glory of the Lord.

I remember I was preaching this message to the people one Sunday, and I was unaware that there was a man in the congregation that morning who had a withered hand. But Holy Spirit knew, and He knew that this man's faith would be stirred to believe, so He gave me the message for that service. And while I was teaching this healing word, this man's withered hand was healed and made whole.

THE RICHES OF JESUS ON DISPLAY

- Jesus teaches the Word wherever He goes.
- Healing freely flows from Him.
- Jesus proves grace is more important than the letter of the Law.
- He's willing to be criticized by the religious leaders for the restoration of the man's hand.
- Jesus is consistent in doing what is right.

CRACK THE MIRACLE CODE

Hypocrisy and legalism kill a miracle, but grace heals.

As you read Miracle 11, you will learn how the life in Jesus overpowers the death of a widow's son while in his coffin.

PRAYER OF FAITH

Lord Jesus, I see how You stood up against this religious spirit, and how you were willing to be criticized by those were controlled by this spirit to help those who needed to be restored, healed and made whole. Help me, Holy Spirit, to strengthen my faith, to be free to hold true to my convictions about my faith in You and in Your ways. In Your name, dear Jesus, I pray, amen.

FAITH ASSIGNMENT

Challenge your faith and with freedom start to share what you believe with others.

Questions for Miracle 10: Defy the Religious Spirit and Heal

1. Why aren't the scribes and Pharisees glad that this man's suffering has come to an end?
2. What is a religious spirit? And why is Jesus so harsh about it?
3. How many times in Matthew 23 does Jesus call the scribes and Pharisees hypocrites?
4. What other special titles does He call them in Matthew 23:16, 27, 33 that reveal what He thinks about their evil intentions?
5. The word *woe* is used how many times in Matthew 23?
6. Why is this miracle taking place in the temple?
7. How does this restorative miracle happen?

PART TWO
MIRACLES 11-20

Dear Holy Spirit, may our faith burst at the seams as these amazing real-life testimonies from Your Word empowers us to overcome a spirit of death, calm the storms, cast out demons, heal from lifelong physical problems, move into the realm of spiritual multiplication, and learn to overpower the elements of nature. Praise Jesus! Amen.

We begin our study of the miracles of Jesus in Part Two, Miracles 11-20, as we join a funeral processional and witness what happens when the Spirit of Life intercepts death.

MIRACLE 11

LIFE OVERPOWERS DEATH

Jesus Resurrects a Widow's Son from Death

We are going to respectfully join the widow from Nain, and the tragic funeral processional of her only son. But this grievous gathering will transform into a joyous event for all—the resurrection of her only son.

Let's step into this scene in Luke 7:11-17:

> *Now it happened, the day after, that He went into a city called Nain; and many of His disciples went with Him, and a large crowd. And when He came near the gate of the city, behold, a dead man was being carried out, the only son of his mother; and she was a widow. And a large crowd from the city was with her. When the Lord saw her, He had compassion on her and said to her, "Do not weep." Then He came and touched the open coffin, and those who carried him stood still. And He said, "Young man, I say to you, arise." So he who was dead sat up and began to speak. And He presented him to his mother. Then fear came upon all, and they glorified God, saying, "A great prophet has risen up among us"; and, "God has visited His people." And this report about Him went throughout all Judea and all the surrounding region.*

ENCOUNTER WITH THE RESURRECTION AND LIFE

This miracle takes place in the city of Nain, which in Greek means *beauty*,[1] and in Hebrew *pleasant place.*[2] Unfortunately, this initial encounter does not start out as a beautiful and pleasant one. But the grieving widow encounters Jesus, *"the resurrection and life."*

Let's read where this name of Jesus comes from in John 11:25 (NIV): "*Jesus said to her, 'I am the resurrection and the life. The one who believes in me will live, even though they die'"* This is the fifth of seven, *"I am"* statements from the Gospel of John that Jesus declares about Himself.

Why do I share this statement of Jesus here? Because I believe we need to move from being just avid readers of the Bible to living what it says. And amazing as this miracle is about how He raises this widow's only son from the dead, as true disciples we are to raise the bar of our own faith and claim the power of promise for ourselves in our own time of need. The hidden message in this name, "Resurrection and Life," is in plain view. He boldly declares in this name that "He gives us life, because He is Life, and death has no power over Him." Can we give a big shout of praise for this?

Moving forward in time for just a moment, remember the words of the angels to the women who dare enter the empty tomb, *"He is not here; he has risen! Remember how he told you, while he was still with you in Galilee: 'The Son of Man must be delivered over to the hands of sinners, be crucified and on the third day be raised again'"* (Luke 24:6-7 NIV).

These people we read about in the Gospels are like young virgins in the faith, and daily life with Jesus is causing the power of faith to develop within their spiritual wombs. May we each become impregnated with this powerful faith of our Lord Jesus. And if we allow our faith to be consummated with His power—Holy Spirit's power—all limits are off, and its "game on" in this life for us!

In addition to this widow's son, Jesus the Master raises two other people from the dead: Jairus' daughter, whom we will read about in Miracle 15, and His dear friend, Lazarus the brother of Mary and Martha. (See Miracle 33.) These three reveal to us His supreme authority over death— and the hope of resurrection life that we experience through His own death and resurrection.

And again, in the Holy Bible, it is no coincidence that there are three recorded resurrections from the dead before Jesus Himself is raised from the dead. I see it as the oneness of the Trinity. As stated several times throughout this work, we need the Creator, the Creative Word made visible, and the empowerment of Holy Spirit to work a miracle. All three, Father, Son, and Holy Spirit are present and work together in harmony for our miracle.

Let's return to the scene of this divine encounter that happens near the city gate, where the spirit of death is overtaken by the power of Jesus, the Resurrection and Life.

THE MEANING AND CARE OF A WIDOW

In this recorded miracle of Jesus, the grieving mother is also a widow. In the Old Testament, a widow is a married woman whose husband has died, and she remains unmarried—and due to her loss, she is in a vulnerable position, lacking emotional support, and financial provision.[3] And the Bible is clear about the support of a true widow from others: *"Pure and undefiled religion before God and the Father is this: to visit orphans and widows in their trouble, and to keep oneself unspotted from the world"* (James 1:27). This clearly demonstrates another character of our Savior. He's loving and perfectly good, He's omnibenevolent.

THE PROPHETIC NATURE OF THIS COMPASSION

In addition to fulfilling the call of pure and undefiled religion, I believe the compassion Jesus feels for this woman is prophetic. And the deep compassion that Jesus experiences here perhaps is for His mother, Mary, too who will also lose her son, and perhaps will be widowed at the time of great suffering for our Lord or already is a widow. After all, where is Joseph during the crucifixion? He is not mentioned in the Scriptures during this time. His nature is caring and protective of Mary and Jesus. And considering all that they have been through, he would not abandon them in their time of need.

Even before Jesus breathed His last on that painful Cross, Jesus unselfishly goes beyond His own pain and grief and looks to beloved apostle John and commands him to take care of His mother, Mary. (See John 19:26-27.) So I do believe that Joseph has passed before this time. Regardless, I believe much of life's experiences for our Lord call out to Him prophetically about what is to come. The type of compassion that Jesus demonstrates here in Greek is *splagchnizomai,* which highlights a Spirit-wrought emotion in which the whole inner being is stirred toward merciful action (Strong's G4697).

BOLDNESS, FAITH, AND COMPASSION

It takes boldness to tell a grieving mom, who just lost her son, not to weep. But Jesus knows the power of words, and weeping is a form of language, so He forms the right atmosphere for this miracle. And He moves quickly. Faith and compassion are necessary components for this boy's resurrection. And as we read, Jesus has the compassion, love in action. He also has the faith; He now needs the mother to work with Him.

HOW DOES THIS MIRACLE COME TO PASS?

In Luke 7:14-15 we read how this miracle comes to pass.

> *Then He came and touched the open coffin, and those who carried him stood still. And He said, "Young man, I say to you, arise." So he who was dead sat up and began to speak. And He presented him to his mother.*

While their painful hearts are wailing with cries of grief and despair, they hear Jesus command their deceased loved one to arise. They witness Messiah give an order to the dead and the dead responds immediately. Too bad Luke did not record the first words of this young man when he came back to life. I love to witness the first response of those who receive their miracle.

My first words when I raised my infant son, Marcos, from the dead were, "Thank You, Jesus." Another man comes to my mind whom I ministered to during his last breaths. He leaped out of that deathbed and cried out, "I'm healed! And I am going to leave this place and tell everyone that I'm healed!" Another man received Jesus as his Savior. I think of how a mother and her two daughters burst into tears as her other daughter—while her body was shutting down in a coma— suddenly grabbed my arm and turned to me when I told her that she had to choose life and live.

And another response comes to my memory of a young girl on her deathbed, gasping for one last breath with her family at her bedside. As I laid hands on her body, I renounced the spirit of death, released the Spirit of Life, and as I said those words the power of Holy Spirit threw me against the wall and the girl jumped out of her bed. She and her entire Christian family shouted with a loud voice, "Hallelujah!" So, yes, this woman of God wishes Luke would have jotted down the response of this young man, his mom, and those who carried the coffin too.

Imagine the amazement and the fear of this young man's mother, the pallbearers, and the others in attendance, including the disciples. These are normal reactions to stunning miracles. But after the initial fear and shock, then comes great joy.

> *Then he broke through and transformed all my wailing into a whirling dance of ecstatic praise! He has torn the veil and lifted from me the sad heaviness of mourning. He wrapped me in the glory-garments of gladness* (Psalm 30:11 TPT).

The report of this miracle is not meant to cause pain, but it can, especially if the loss is fresh. But instead of inner pain, it is to share encouragement and instruction to the body of Christ what is possible, and what I believe we are to walk in more often than we do.

We never know what tomorrow holds, or when premature death will try to rear its ugly head against our loved ones, or when we will walk into another's critical moment. This is why it's so important to train ourselves in faith before an emergency strikes.

PRAYER OF FAITH TO RAISE THE DEAD

> *In the name of Jesus, I renounce this spirit of death and the cause of it. I release the Spirit of Life to freely flow through this body. I command death out of every cell, tissue, organ, and system, I command (name of person) to choose life, wake up and begin to breathe on your own now in Jesus' name, amen.*

THE RICHES OF JESUS ON DISPLAY THAT BREAK THE CODE FOR THIS MIRACLE

- Jesus cares for the widow.
- He demonstrates great compassion for this grieving mother.
- Jesus has authority over death.
- Even the dead obey Jesus' command.

CRACK THE MIRACLE CODE

The resurrection power of Jesus overpowers death.

When you read Miracle 12, you will find where you have placed your faith —in the storm or in the healing power of your Lord.

PRAYER OF FAITH

> *Dear Jesus, You have walked with me through this miracle of resurrection. And it stirs up faith within me. Holy Spirit, help me to move with this type of bold and courageous compassion for those who have suffered great loss. And may I not be afraid to raise the dead. In your name I pray, amen.*

FAITH ASSIGNMENT

Strengthen your faith in the Holy Scriptures, especially in the arena of joy, not only to endure but to overcome death.

Questions for Miracle 11: Life Overpowers Death

1. What does *Nain* mean in Greek?
2. In Hebrew *Nain* means?
3. Who does this grieving widow and mother encounter?
4. In the Old Testament what is a widow?
5. When we say that Jesus is omnibenevolent, what do we mean?
6. They type of compassion Jesus demonstrates for this widow is called what in Greek?
7. In Psalm 30:11, God turns our mourning into what?

MIRACLE 12

WHERE IS YOUR FAITH?

Jesus Calms a Storm

Let's go for a sail across the lake with Jesus. I'm sure the disciples have a serene picture in mind filled with blue skies and smooth sailing, but it doesn't turn out the way they probably imagined. In fact, they find themselves in a life-and-death situation as their boat fills with water and their hearts fill with fear. And to add to their dilemma Jesus is fast asleep. In their time of immediate need when they wake Him, He rebukes them and questions their faith. Now, either Jesus is out of touch with reality, or the disciples misunderstand reality all together. Which is it? Climb on board to find out.

> *Now it happened, on a certain day, that He got into a boat with His disciples. And He said to them, "Let us cross over to the other side of the lake." And they launched out. But as they sailed He fell asleep. And a windstorm came down on the lake, and they were filling with water, and were in jeopardy. And they came to Him and awoke Him, saying, "Master, Master, we are perishing!" Then He arose and rebuked the wind and the raging of the water. And they ceased, and there was a calm. But He said to them, "Where is your faith?" And they were afraid, and marveled, saying to one another, "Who can this be? For He*

commands even the winds and water, and they obey Him!" (Luke 8:22-25)

This portion of Scripture kicks off with the word *now* and connects us to what previously happens. So let's begin by finding out what happens before this windstorm breaks out. I believe in doing so, we will find out why this storm brews against them in the first place. Yes, there is a reason behind the storm raging against them, and against us as well. I believe this is an eyeopener for us all.

WHY DO BAD THINGS HAPPEN TO GOOD PEOPLE?

Do you ever wonder why bad things happen to good people? Sure you do, we all have. In Miracle 8, under the heading "Myth Breaker," I taught you from John 16:33 where Jesus states the fact that in this world we will have tribulation. In Greek this word *tribulation* means "trouble," but just because someone is facing trouble does not mean they have done something bad. It could be the opposite, they are doing something good and the enemy, the devil, hates and fears them for it. And this is another reason why bad things happen to good people. Because they are doing what's right and shaking the kingdom of darkness to where they enemy tries to stop us from obeying our God and being about Abba Father's business and winning the Lost for His glory.

THE REASON FOR THE STORM

What could be the reason for this storm chasing after the disciples? What good were the disciples up to that would unleash this deadly storm against them? Let's backtrack a little to see what miracles were manifesting and what was going on in between these miracles. Now, I should say first that we can't be 100 percent sure about the exact chronological order of the recorded miracles, but I believe we can be close to the order of how things happen.

As new disciples in Christ, they are feasting on a powerful message that is blowing the scribes and the Pharisees out of the water and exposing their false religious doctrine. Many of the sick are being healed, and those possessed by demons are being liberated, they are baptizing new believers for Jesus, they are discovering that there is no distance in the spirit realm and healing can take place by a word of faith, the filthy plague of leprosy and all the shame that goes with it is being cleansed, they are seeing paralytics walk, and these are just some of the recorded miracles of Jesus.

So, why is the storm chasing after them? It's simple—to steal, to kill, and to destroy them (John 10:10) so they can't complete their mission with Jesus on earth. And it is the same for you too.

FIGHT THE GOOD FIGHT OF FAITH

We are in a spiritual battle, and the forces of Heaven and hell are colliding with one another. There is a full-blown battle for the Lost being fought right before our eyes. And for those engaged in this battle, beware—you have a target on your back and the enemy will try and stop you on all fronts.

Are these battles against us going to stop? Not while we are on earth. Will they lessen in their intensity? No they will not; they will only increase. First Timothy 6:12 tells us to fight the good fight of faith. This refers to spiritual warfare. And not only are we to fight this good fight of faith, and fight it daily, but we are to be victorious with the use of our spiritual weapons He provides for us.

SPIRITUAL WEAPONS

There are many spiritual weapons for us to use, the more predominant ones are: the name of Jesus, the blood of Jesus, the word of God, the power of our words, the power of faith-filled prayer, to name some. But I want to focus on two different ones. As I said there are many more to activate in our lives, but let's look at these two for now: 1) the power of praise and worship and 2) the fear of the Lord.

The power of praise and worship can be underrated, but we have an amazing account of the power it possesses in Acts 16:25-34. Paul and Silas are bound in chains for their ministry work for Christ; but instead of throwing a pity party, they worship God. We see the results in verse 26, *"And suddenly there was a great earthquake, so that the foundations of the prison were shaken; and immediately all the doors were opened, and everyone's chains were loosed."*

Use the spiritual weapon Paul and Silas demonstrate for us, the power of praise and worship. What can happen during the storm raging against us if we praise and worship our God instead of filling ourselves with fear? The chains of bondage will fall off. Lord, help us to remember to praise our way out of the storm.

And speaking of fear, I believe the disciples miss the boat entirely when they choose to fear the storm instead of activating the power of the fear of God against the storm. And this leads to the second weapon of warfare that needs to be operative in our daily life, *the fear of the Lord.*

> *The fear of the Lord is the beginning of wisdom; a good understanding have all those who do His commandments. His praise endures forever* (Psalm 111:10).

Just as the wind and the waves obey His supremacy over them, we ought to have this revelation controlling our hearts and minds that He is the King of kings and the Lord of lords and over all things, including the storms of life. No matter how wicked the wind and the waves appear, they will bow to His wonder-working power working in us, and for us.

Learn to activate both the power of praise and worship with the fear of the Lord and watch the battles and the storms raging against us settle down.

WE ARE NOT ALONE

Just as the disciples were not alone during this dangerous storm, we are not alone either. Joshua 1:9 commands us to be strong and courageous, and not to be afraid or discouraged. Why? Because the Lord our God is with us wherever we go. Even in the middle of a storm Jesus is with us, just as He was with the disciples.

SOS TO JESUS

Okay, the disciples fear the storm will kill them, so they do what they know to do and send out an SOS to Jesus who is with them. Seems like a godly thing to do. Apparently not. But why not?

In Exodus 14, we read of a similar situation with the mighty prophet Moses, who worked such amazing signs and wonders that later just the mention of his name caused the people to faint with fear. The Hebrew slaves were finally released from the bondage of Pharoh but were now being chased by the Pharoh's army and trapped between the enemy and the Red Sea.

What did this mighty man of God do? He held up his staff and declared an amazing declaration of faith: *"Do not be afraid. Stand still, and see the salvation of the Lord, which He will accomplish for you today. For the Egyptians whom you see today, you shall see again no more forever. The Lord will fight for you, and you shall hold your peace"* (Exodus 14:13-14).

But interestingly, he does not receive the immediate response he was expecting from God. Here's what happens in Exodus 14:15-16, *"And the Lord said to Moses, 'Why do you cry to Me? Tell the children of Israel to go forward. But lift up your rod, and stretch out your hand over the sea and divide it. And the children of Israel shall go on dry ground through the midst of the sea.'"*

You see the response that Moses receives here from the Lord is the same type of response that the disciples receive from Jesus. The Lord says to Moses, "Why do you cry out to Me? You do it!" (Yes, I'm paraphrasing to save space.) And this is the same response Jesus gives to the disciples. Jesus is discipling this group of men, and they have been witnessing firsthand what faith can do. And although Jesus is physically with them during this storm, He expects them to activate their faith instead of asking Him to do this for them. It's about growing up in faith and trusting Him enough to do as He does.

NO, YOU DO IT!

This reminds me of a time on the mission field at our children's home in Guatemala. It is during our six-month dry season, and the rain is not due for about two months. So the farmers in the villages begin to prepare the gardens on the mountain hills by slashing and burning. The hills surrounding the children's home are surrounded by wild unattended fires and thick smoke, and everyone is beginning to have difficulty breathing, including me.

Being a woman of courageous prayer, I take the matter to the Lord. I am standing on the balcony overlooking the hills and beginning to pray. I ask the Lord to cause it to rain, and I clearly hear Him say to me, "No, you do it!" A little surprised by His response, I say, "Okay, in Jesus' name I command it to rain." And then I say, "No, no, no, let me do this again." So, with intentional thought, I size up the weather situation, knowing there isn't a cloud in the sky, I declare. "In Jesus' name, I command the winds to blow and bring in thick heavy rain clouds so it rains down hard and clears the smoke out of the air."

My daughter-in-law walks into the house, and I testified to her what had just happened. I kid you not, the winds begin to blow, so much so that dead branches begin to fall out of the trees. My husband and the workers outside stop what they are doing and look up at the sky. I call out to my husband who is working below the balcony and told him what just happened. And low and behold, in come dark rain clouds and the rain begins to fall heavily, cleansing the smoke right out of the air. It was one of those moments of knowing what needed done and asking God to do it, with Him responding, *"No, you do it!"*

WHICH REPORT WILL WE TRUST?

A major lesson we must learn is that Jesus is not moved by tragic circumstances, symptoms, and reports. Isaiah 53:1 asks an all-important question, *"Who has believed our report?"* As lovers and followers of Jesus, we have a choice to make. Are we going to put our trust in a negative report, or will we trust in the promises of God?

WHERE IS YOUR FAITH?

Just like Jesus asked His disciples that day, "Where is your faith?" I believe He is asking us the very same question today. Is our faith in the strength of the storm? Do we believe that sickness or disease is too great for Him to heal? Or do we choose this day to believe in the power of the Lord to calm the storm raging against us? Do we believe in His healing promise?

THE RICHES OF JESUS ON DISPLAY

There are great riches on display in this testimony about how Jesus calms the wind and the waves that break open the miracle code.

- Jesus never leaves us.
- He even goes through the storm with us.
- Jesus remains peaceful even during the storm.
- He doesn't fear death or a deadly report.
- Jesus doesn't question the strength of the storm.
- Even when we are weak, He remains strong.
- Jesus does not respond to our desperate pleas, but to faith alone.
- He expects us to live by faith as He does.

CRACK THE MIRACLE CODE

The storms in life lose their power when we put our trust in Jesus' strength.

When you read Miracle 13, you will learn how even the severely possessed are delivered by the presence of Jesus and a command of faith.

FAITH ASSIGNMENT

Take an honest look at your life. What are you afraid of? Why are you afraid? Do you believe that Jesus is with you? And that He will remain faithful to you? Take these issues to prayer.

PRAYER OF FAITH

Oh, dear Jesus, I must be honest, like the disciples in the boat during that storm, I misunderstood what You desire from me. Faith, not fear. And I see now how You desire for me to grow in the faith and exercise it and create testimonies for Your glory and continue to increase in the realm of faith. Holy Spirit, teach me Your ways, give me opportunities to develop this faith. In Your precious name, Jesus, I pray, amen.

Questions for Miracle 12: Where Is Your Faith?

1. Just because someone is facing trouble does not mean they have done something bad, it could be what?
2. What does 1 Timothy 6:12 tell us to do?
3. What does Joshua 1:9 command us to do?
4. What does Jesus expect the disciples to do during the storm?
5. What is the choice put before us as lovers and followers of Christ?

MIRACLE 13

DELIVERED AND CLOTHED IN HIS RIGHT MIND

Jesus Casts Demons Into a Herd of Pigs

It is time once again to step out of the boat with Jesus, and this time onto the shores of Gerasenes, where He meets a naked man controlled by a legion of demons. Jesus will deliver this man in an unusual but significant way that upsets the people of this land. Let's read to find out what is so unusual about this man's deliverance.

Carefully read the account recorded by the physician, evangelist, and author of the book of Luke, Luke himself:

> *Then they sailed to the country of the Gerasenes, which is opposite Galilee. And when He stepped out onto the land, a man from the city met Him who was possessed with demons; and he had not put on clothing for a long time and was not living in a house, but among the tombs. And seeing Jesus, he cried out and fell down before Him, and said with a loud voice, "What business do You have with me, Jesus, Son of the Most High God? I beg You, do not torment me!" For He had already commanded the unclean spirit to come out of the man. For it had seized him many times; and he was bound with chains and shackles and kept under guard, and yet he would break the restraints and be driven by the demon into the desert. And Jesus asked him,*

"What is your name?" And he said, "Legion"; because many demons had entered him. And they were begging Him not to command them to go away into the abyss.

Now there was a herd of many pigs feeding there on the mountain; and the demons begged Him to permit them to enter the pigs. And He gave them permission. And the demons came out of the man and entered the pigs; and the herd rushed down the steep bank into the lake and was drowned.

Now when the herdsmen saw what had happened, they ran away and reported everything in the city, and in the country. And the people came out to see what had happened; and they came to Jesus and found the man from whom the demons had gone out, sitting down at the feet of Jesus, clothed and in his right mind; and they became frightened. Those who had seen everything reported to them how the man who had been demon-possessed had been made well. And all the people of the territory of the Gerasenes and the surrounding region asked Him to leave them, because they were overwhelmed by great fear; and He got into a boat and returned. But the man from whom the demons had gone out was begging Him that he might accompany Him; but Jesus sent him away, saying, "Return to your home and describe what great things God has done for you." So he went away, proclaiming throughout the city what great things Jesus had done for him (Luke 8:26-39 NASB).

POSSESSED WITH A LEGION OF DEMONS

This lost man is possessed with thousands of demons, the exact number we don't really know, nor does it matter. What's important for us to know is that this man is possessed by a mob of demons and is severely tortured day and night.

WHAT DEMONS ARE IN CONTROL OF THIS MAN?

Looking at the clues given in verse 27, we can detect some of the major demons that are in possession of this man's soul. It says that *"he had not put on clothing for a long time and was not living in a house, but among the tombs."* He is suffering from an unclean spirit (we will study this later in this chapter), he is homeless, so he is struggling with an orphaned spirit, and a spirit of death because he lives among the tombs, just to name a few.

DEMONS RUN TOWARD JESUS, NOT AWAY FROM HIM

It's curious when we read that these demons run to Jesus as He arrives on the shores of Gerasenes instead of running away from Him. This has happened to me while ministering in the Massai land in northern Tanzania. A young man full of demons ran out from the wilderness toward me and knelt at my feet. In perfect English without an accent he cried out to me, "Why have you come to torment us?" And immediately he ran back into the darkness. This situation taught me that demons recognize the authority of Jesus, and when we know our true identity in Him. And just as they fear Jesus when He arrives, they also fear us when we walk in this truth.

Another reason these demons run to Jesus is they know Him. They recognize His true deity, Jesus, Son of the Most High God. And as much as they hate and fear Him, they have no option but to submit to His supremacy. The Word tells us in Philippians 2:10-11 that *"at the name of Jesus every knee should bow, of those in heaven, and of those on earth, and of those under the earth, and that every tongue should confess that Jesus Christ is Lord, to the glory of God the Father."* This is not optional, and one day every human being (past, present, and future) will either willingly bow the knee and confess Jesus is Lord or, like these demons, will bow out of obligation to His holiness.

THE UNCLEAN SPIRIT BEGS JESUS

It's also a bit peculiar that this unclean spirit begs Jesus not to torment him. This word *begs* in the Greek language is *anakrazō,* and it means "to cry out from the depth of one's throat" (Strong's G349). It's not like they portray themselves to unsuspecting humans that they are these nasty terrorists, but this ugly being has no doubt just Who has the power to terrorize who. Jesus clearly has all authority over this unclean spirit and the rest that are working in cahoots with him against this tormented man.

TELLTALE SIGNS OF AN UNCLEAN SPIRIT CONFIRMED

We have several confirmations that this man is under the control of an unclean spirit. *Garments* in the Bible have spiritual significance; and in this case, he did not wear clothing for a long time. This fact is always a telltale sign of an unclean spirit. And verse 29 confirms the major demon in control is an unclean spirit. And this is confirmed again in verse 32 when the demons beg Jesus to allow them to enter the pigs. Why the pigs? Because pigs in the Jewish culture are considered unclean. So, naturally the unclean demon would want to inhabit them as well.

THE UNCLEAN ENTERS THE UNCLEAN

As just mentioned, the unclean spirits enter the unclean pigs, and the pigs go mad and run off the edge of the cliff. The demonic force instantly destroys an entire herd of pigs. How much this man had endured before he met Jesus and was delivered from this mob of demons.

DEMONS WORK TOGETHER

Demons work together to torture their victims; common spirits that run with an unclean spirit include a sexual spirit, spirit of perversion, spirit of shame, a spirit of rejection, an orphaned spirit. He was not living in a house but in among the tombs. This shows us that a spirit of death was in control. This portion of Scripture goes on to say that *"it had seized him many times"* so he was possessed with tormenting spirits. And he would *"be driven by the demon into the desert,"* which shows us that spirits of loneliness, desolation, and hopelessness ruled him too.

SPIRITUAL FORCES

What spiritual forces deliver this man from legions of demons?

1. The presence of Jesus.
2. The command of authority.

We need to operate under the same two spiritual forces to force demons out of people. We need to saturate ourselves with Jesus and make this is an ongoing lifestyle—as we are called to be ready in season and out of season. Jesus isn't a lucky charm we carry in our pocket on Sunday morning, we remain in His presence permanently. We need to train ourselves in the Word concerning our true identity in Christ; and when we know who we are in Him, His authority in our lives automatically operates through us.

AGAIN, THE DEMONS BEG JESUS

In Luke 8:31, we read that the demons, this time the entire lot of them, are begging Him not to command them to go away into the abyss, the fiery lake of hell. The abyss is the bottomless pit, that extra special place God created for the devil and his disgusting demons. And I tell you, we know it's a bad place when the demons beg Jesus not to send them there! When casting demons out of people, I hear them beg not to be sent to hell. I command them to be silent and give them a count to three, and if they do not leave the person, I will send them there. I don't play around with them.

HOPE DELIVERS

Then we have Jesus, the Son of the Most High God, who leaves the circuit (Galilee) to set sail to Gerasenes and delivers this man from a legion of demons. And although it has been many years of spiritual warfare raging against this man, hope arrives on his shores. And the Creative Word made visible—Jesus—delivers the man by a word of authority that has a great reward at the end. And the once naked man, living in the tombs is now found sitting at the feet of the Savior and clothed in his right mind.

CLOTHED IN HIS RIGHT MIND

How beautiful is our Jesus who sets this man free with a command of authority, and the man who had lost control of his mind, emotions, and actions is now clothed in his right mind. No longer is he clothed with an unclean spirit, possessed and controlled by a mob of demons. Now he is clothed with the rich robes of righteousness, forgiveness, and adopted into the family of God. This man's deliverance is such a beautiful testimony about what the love and compassion of our Lord does for those who cry out to Him.

I will sing and greatly rejoice in Yahweh! My whole being vibrates with shouts of joy in my God! For he has dressed me with salvation and wrapped me in the robe of his righteousness! I appear like a bridegroom on his wedding day, decked out with a beautiful sash, or like a radiant bride adorned with sparkling jewels (Isaiah 61:10 TPT).

HE BEGS TO REMAIN WITH JESUS

The Scripture says that *"The man from whom the demons had gone out was begging Him that he might accompany Him."* It doesn't say that he casually asks but begs to go with Jesus. The Greek word for this begging comes from the Greek word, *deomai,* and it means "to desire and long for" (Strong's G1189).

But even though this man is begging, and begging from desperation, his begging is not the same as the demon's begging. The demons are begging from the depth of one's throat, they had possession of a man and did not want to be sent to hell early for it. Whereas this man's begging is different in meaning as it is coming from the voice of a free man who is prayerfully seeking, making supplication, praying earnestly to remain with Him. His motives are from a pure heart, where the demons just desperately want an escape from hell.

PEOPLE BEG WHEN THEY GET DESPERATE

This man has suffered such great horrors that few of us can ever understand. And He finds true freedom, deliverance, safety, and peace in Jesus. I am sure he is fighting fear and terror that these demons might return after He leaves.

Certain characteristics that stand out in my mind concerning severely demonized individuals are that they are terrorized, tortured, they feel lonely, unworthy, unloved, and very vulnerable to demonic attacks. The demons within badger them with insults and self-harming, and very bizarre behaviors. They have no peace, and no rest. So, yes, we can understand why this man begs to go with Jesus.

THE PEOPLE'S RESPONSE

The people's response is not what we would hope for. What they witness fills them with fear, and this fear leads to misunderstanding that they too can be free from their uncleanliness, their sins. As for them, this is the spiritual meaning of the unclean demons entering into the unclean pigs. And they reject the One who can make them clean and whole. And perhaps, they do not recognize their own filthy, sinful nature. And so, instead of rejoicing at this man's dramatic deliverance, they choose to major on the minor, the loss of the herd of pigs.

COMMISSIONED TO TELL

This man suddenly goes from being gravely possessed with a mob of demons to being set free, and even though he begs to go with Jesus, he is denied this request. Not out of cruelty but to be sent out on a mission for Jesus. He was to remain where he was and tell the people what the Lord had done for him.

Let's face it, this man carries a reputation. He's possessed and dangerous. He's not the type of person you want your women and children to be near. And demon-possessed people, no matter their size or age, when in a fit of rage have the supernatural strength of the devil to steal, kill, and destroy (John 10:10). This man is known by the people to be insane.

And now Jesus commissions him to remain with the community of people that shunned and feared him.

I always tell people that if you allow the Lord, He will take your greatest weakness and turn it into your greatest strength. In other words, after you are healed, delivered, transformed by Jesus, He will take what once ailed you and turn it into a testimony for ministry opportunity. And this is what Jesus is doing here with this man.

Jesus no longer wants him to remain hidden but to expose the power of darkness by shining his light and allow the people to witness what the power of the Almighty has done for this man, to encourage them to see what He wills to do for them too.

For the full details of this man's ministry and influence for the Kingdom of God we will have to wait to hear directly from him when we reach Heaven.

So often people think ministry only happens behind the pulpit—but it happens out there with the people in everyday life situations.

Don't beg and plead with Jesus to remain with Him; rather, be vulnerable to His will. Ask Him to send you out among the people and tell them about Jesus—evangelize the people with your very own life.

Isaiah 6:8 (NIV) says, *"Then I heard the voice of the Lord saying, 'Whom shall I send? And who will* go for us?' And I said, 'Here am I. Send me!'" Oh Jesus, may this be our daily prayer, to be sent by the Almighty to tell the people what You have done for us. May we be the real-life testimony so that they cannot deny Your sovereignty.

THE RICHES OF JESUS ON DISPLAY

- Jesus walks in authority.
- He operates with wisdom from on high.
- Jesus does not walk in fear, but in faith.
- He moves with compassion.
- Jesus has a special place in His heart for the untouchables.
- He goes out of His way to reach the Lost.
- Jesus wills for all to be delivered and healed.

THE MIRACLE CODE

The presence of Jesus with a command of faith delivers a reward, healing, and a sound mind.

As you read Miracle 14, you will discover how one special touch of faith heals the unclean, untouchable, and incurable.

FAITH ASSIGNMENT

Do you know someone who is suffering severely? Pray to the Lord to give you a plan of action to help the untouchables. And follow through with the plan He gives to you.

PRAYER OF FAITH

Dear Lord Jesus, much has been revealed in this portion of Scripture. Help me to move in this level of authority, faith, and compassion to reach the Lost for Your glory, amen.

Questions for Miracle 13: Delivered and Clothed in His Right Mind

1. This man was possessed with a legion of demons, but what was the major demon that controlled him?
2. What is one telltale sign of an unclean spirit?
3. Why did the unclean demon beg to enter the pigs?
4. Demons work together to do what?
5. What was the end result in this testimony for this man?
6. What does Gerasenes mean?

MIRACLE 14
A SPECIAL TOUCH

Jesus Heals a Woman with a Blood Issue

Watch what happens to a desperate woman who humbly makes her way to the feet of Jesus and grabs hold of the hem of His garment, and witness what happens next.

> *Now a woman, having a flow of blood for twelve years, who had spent all her livelihood on physicians and could not be healed by any, came from behind and touched the border of His garment. And immediately her flow of blood stopped* (Luke 8:43-44).

UNCLEAN, UNTOUCHABLE, AND INCURABLE

This woman has been slowly bleeding to death for the past twelve years. Her condition makes her unclean and untouchable in society. It says here that she spends all her livelihood. There's nothing left, and I believe it cost this woman her dignity as well. You see the devil is a thief, and Jesus makes it plain in John 10:10 that this robber comes to steal, to kill, and to destroy us. Sickness and disease are mass weapons of destruction that he designs against all people. This suffering lady is no exception to his twisted ways. So, in this verse we find out that this bloody woman is unclean, untouchable, and incurable. As we continue to read her story, we also discover that she is desperate.

A DESPERATE PLAN IS CONCEIVED

Desperate people do desperate things, and within this woman's heart a desperate plan is conceived. She says within herself, *If I just touch the fringe of the hem of His garment, I'll be healed.* Her plan does not consider the obstacle she will face, the crowd. This wild following is out of control. They are thronging to get to Jesus, pulling on Him, and pressing in hard to get a chance to be healed.

She thinks that she will bow low at His feet, hidden by the crowd, reach out and just touch the hem of His garment, and that her touch will go unnoticed. I fully believe this woman in the beginning of her healing adventure is like the rest, she is coming to Jesus for what He has, healing. She does not understand the power of her own faith, let alone the healing virtue that is about to overpower her own being and transform her life.

Like a little child, she doesn't understand the meaning of fire until she touches the flame. And that's a lesson one does not forget, nor will she ever forget what happens to her next.

WHY SECRETLY TOUCH THE HEM OF HIS GARMENT?

Not only does she think her touch will go unnoticed, but I believe she hopes it is inconspicuous too. Why do I think this? It has to do with traditions and beliefs at the time. As stated, the bleeding makes her sociably unclean. And just as it is with the leprous man we talk about in Miracle 7, the people are taught that if she touches them, they too will be unclean. So, this is more than a physical crisis for her, it's a social one too. This is why I share that she is untouchable and unclean.

She's aware that her plan is a risky one. But she believes in her heart that if the religious law does not allow her to touch another person, she will then settle instead to touch the hem of His garment and be healed.

And there is yet another reason that we will discuss in Miracle 21 as to why she might touch the hem of His garment.

UNCLEAN AND UNTOUCHABLE

People often believe they are unclean and untouchable because they feel guilty for a sinful lifestyle, and they need to repent of their sin. Sometimes, many times, people ask Christ to forgive them, but struggle to forgive themselves for past wrongs and struggle to believe that they are forgiven after they asked for forgiveness. Other people have been abused or bullied and believe the lies that were spoken over them, that they don't measure up, and they deserve all the terrible things that happen to them.

If this is you, don't believe the lie. If you have done wrong, confess your sin to Jesus. He is faithful to forgive (1 John 1:9). If you were abused or bullied, you did not deserve this evil that was done against you. The power of the blood of Jesus forgives us of our sin and makes us spiritually clean again. And this same power heals us and makes us touchable and acceptable. It's all about His power and what He has done for us. Believe.

MISPLACED FAITH

You will hear me mention from time to time throughout this work, the term *misplaced faith.* What am I referring to, and why do I bother to bring it up now? This woman is a prime example of someone who has misplaced faith before coming to Jesus with her need. She went from one physician to another, spent all that she had. She tried everything, so she thought, and was not cured. She was not healed until she made the decision to put all her trust in Jesus. I agree, it's a risky decision, but it was not until she came to this place in her faith that she was healed and made whole. *Holy Spirit, minister to our hearts about misplaced faith.*

WHO TOUCHED ME?

> *And Jesus said, "Who touched Me?" When all denied it, and those with him said, "Master, the multitudes throng and press You, and You say, 'Who touched Me?'" But Jesus said, "Somebody touched Me, for I perceived power going out from Me." Now when the woman saw that she was not hidden, she came trembling; and falling down before Him, she declared to Him in the presence of all the people the reason she had touched Him and how she was healed immediately* (Luke 8:45-47).

As mentioned earlier, the crowd is unruly, with people pushing and shoving and in a frenzy. Hey, there's a whole lot of touching going on. This is why Peter and the others respond to Jesus the way they do, "Jesus what do you mean, 'Who touched Me?' *Everybody* here is touching you!" As usual they look at things in the natural and therefore miss the point of what He says. But Jesus overlooks their ignorance and repeats Himself, *"Somebody touched Me, for I perceived power going out from Me."* And this woman who thinks she is going to just grab a little of this healing power for herself, comes to the realization—*He sees me, He notices me.*

A SPECIAL TOUCH

This woman isn't remembered because she did some valiant act of faith, but because of a special touch.

Surely Jesus knows who reaches out and touches Him. He's all knowing, and nothing is hidden from Him. He just doesn't see with His physical eyes but with His heart. He is perceptive and sees into the realm of the Spirit. He knows our every thought and the intentions of our hearts as well. He possesses all knowledge, He's all-knowing, and He's omniscient.

So if Jesus is all-knowing, why does He stop the chaos to publicly confront the woman? Knowing the Law, He knows that due to this woman's issue with blood, she is declared as unclean. And not only does this woman need physical healing, but she needs restoration spiritually, physically, emotionally, as well as restoration back into the community. In this part of the story, Jesus is publicly doing just this, restoring her back into the community, declaring her clean, touchable, and acceptable.

Another reason is that He makes the most of every opportunity to teach and instruct us. Here He teaches that faith is not meant to be private or secret. We are to openly share our faith with others.

If her healing had remained hidden, many people, and possibly us as well, would have missed this important point concerning our faith in Jesus, and that it is our faith in Him that heals us as well.

Perhaps some not familiar with this passage of Scripture think what I say here is blasphemous. It's not, and here's why. The very next verse Jesus says this to this woman, *"Daughter, be of good cheer; your faith has made you well. Go in peace"* (Luke 8:48). Our faith, when placed properly, in the redemptive work of Jesus is very powerful, has no limits, and produces great works—miracles.

SIMILAR SITUATION

Maybe you are in a similar situation like this woman. Perhaps you have even been sick longer than this woman. Because of a disease or ailment you find yourself in a tough spot. You may be financially broke, or you may have spent all you have and are not any better. A wretched health issue makes you feel unclean, untouchable, and they say, "incurable." And more damaging than any of this is that you may feel desperate; you've lost your hope.

I can sense within my spirit that this message speaks to you. If this is you, like this woman, humble yourself before Jesus, and reach out and touch His heart. You do so by faith in Him. Even if you do not understand it all. It's apparent this woman did not understand the power of her faith, or the healing virtue that Jesus possesses, or how being open and honest concerning her faith in Him would transform her life—as it will transform your life too.

Like this woman, when we come into His presence something wonderful happens. We touch Him, we touch His presence, and we become intertwined with Him. *"But the one who is united and joined to the Lord is one spirit with Him"* (1 Corinthians 6:17 AMP). And we are transformed from the inside to the outside. This is where you may need to begin.

PRAYER OF SALVATION

If you need to take this first step of faith and ask Jesus to forgive your sins and ask Him to become your Savior today, then pray this simple prayer of faith from your heart:

> *Dear Lord Jesus, I ask for Your forgiveness for all the bad thoughts, words and deeds I have done. I thank You for forgiving me of my sin. Jesus, I believe that You are who You say You are, the Son of God, who died on the Cross for my sins and rose on the third day from the dead. I believe this with all my heart and confess with the words of my mouth, that Jesus, You are my Savior and Lord. This I pray, amen.*

If you confess with your mouth the Lord Jesus and believe in your heart that God has raised Him from the dead, you will be saved. For with the heart one believes unto righteousness, and with the mouth confession is made unto salvation (Romans 10:9-10).

This Scripture says that we are to believe in our heart. We are to put our trust in Him, and trust is another way to say we have faith. We are also told to confess with our mouth, in other words, we are to tell someone that Jesus is our Savior. This might sound scary to you, but back when I was 18 years old, I prayed a similar prayer in front of about 8,000 to 10,000 people in the Jesus People Church on Hennepin Avenue in Minneapolis, Minnesota. And I tell you the truth, it was the best decision I ever made. This was my beginning with Jesus.

Therefore, if anyone is in Christ, he is a new creation; old things have passed away; behold, all things have become new (2 Corinthians 5:17).

This verse is filled with promise for a future of good things to come in your life.

THE RICHES OF JESUS ON DISPLAY

- Jesus' love for the unclean, untouchable, and incurable is pure and priceless.
- He goes the extra mile to publicly restore those who have been declared unclean and untouchable.
- Jesus heals the incurable.
- He restores hope to the desperate.
- Jesus rewards faith openly.

CRACK THE MIRACLE CODE

No matter what others say about us or about our situation, when faith is properly placed in Jesus, healing happens.

As you read Miracle 15, you will learn how to create and guard the atmosphere of faith for your miracle.

FAITH ASSIGNMENT

Ask Holy Spirit to show you physical ways to demonstrate to the unclean and untouchable people in your community that Jesus really does love and care for them. If you take this to Him, He will give you creative ways; and whatever you do, always do it in the name of Jesus. Get out there and win the Lost for Jesus.

PRAYER OF FAITH

Oh, Father God, as usual Your Word touches the depths of my heart. It convicts yet encourages me at the same time. It is true, this ailment has left me feeling unclean, untouchable, and doubtful about a cure, but more than anything I feel desperate. My faith is not where it should be. At times I have tried to keep it hidden, when I now know that I must be open and proclaim I am a believing believer. Thank You, Holy Spirit, for the revelation about this special touch that I must have with Jesus. And Jesus, I am reaching out and touching Your heart today, amen.

Questions for Miracle 14: A Special Touch

1. This woman's issue of blood makes her what to society?
2. We also discover in this story that this illness is what?
3. What do desperate people do?
4. Does this woman believe she can touch Jesus unnoticed?
5. What does she settle for since the religious law does not allow her to touch another person?
6. What is the realization that this woman comes to?
7. This woman isn't remembered because she did some valiant act of faith, but why?
8. What do we mean when we say Jesus is omniscient?
9. Why was Jesus publicly calling this woman out for touching His garment?
10. According to Luke 8:48, what heals this woman?
11. Our faith, when placed properly, in the redemptive work of Jesus is what?

MIRACLE 15
GUARD THE ATMOSPHERE

Jesus Resurrects Jairus' Daughter from the Dead

We now join Jesus in His return from the region of Gerasenes where He performed mighty miracles and where He is now met by a ruler of the synagogue, named Jairus. What exciting adventure will we witness next?

> *So it was, when Jesus returned, that the multitude welcomed Him, for they were all waiting for Him. And behold, there came a man named Jairus, and he was a ruler of the synagogue. And he fell down at Jesus' feet and begged Him to come to his house, for he had an only daughter about twelve years of age, and she was dying.*
>
> *...While He was still speaking, someone came from the ruler of the synagogue's house, saying to him, "Your daughter is dead. Do not trouble the Teacher." But when Jesus heard it, He answered him, saying, "Do not be afraid; only believe, and she will be made well." When He came into the house, He permitted no one to go in except Peter, James, and John, and the father and mother of the girl. Now all wept and mourned for her; but He said, "Do not weep; she is not dead, but sleeping." And they ridiculed Him, knowing that she was dead. But He put them all outside, took her by the hand and called, saying, "Little girl, arise." Then her spirit returned, and she arose immedi-*

ately. And He commanded that she be given something to eat. And her parents were astonished, but He charged them to tell no one what had happened (Luke 8:40-42, 49-56).

A SPIRITUAL ATMOSPHERE REPORT UPON HIS ARRIVAL

Permit me to begin with a report about the spiritual atmosphere upon the arrival of Jesus. Scriptures report, *"So it was, when Jesus returned, that the multitude welcomed Him, for they were all waiting for Him."* One could not ask for a more beautiful welcome than this. His followers are not only welcoming, but they are all waiting for His arrival. This means they are waiting with expectancy. And the result behind this expectancy produces miracles—because faith impregnates their souls.

As I picture this greeting in my mind's eye, it reminds me of a very sweet greeting that embedded itself upon my heart. Back in the fall of 2002, I enter a village in southern Tanzania. As my prayer intercessor and I step out of the safari vehicle, the villagers are there to welcome us. I will never forget the sweetness of these precious people; to show honor for their guest ministers, they sing beautiful songs and throw pretty, little white flowers down at our feet.

Why do I share this memory with you? Because the honor that these beautiful people bestowed on us opened the hearts of all present to give and receive what the Lord had in store for us. We did not have to fight against a haughty religious spirit, there was just friendly fellowship with one another, and the freedom for Holy Spirit to reign. When we create the right atmosphere where we welcome our Lord, we can wait expectantly for our miracles to manifest.

A RULER OF THE SYNAGOGUE AT THE FEET OF JESUS

After all the negative response by the rulers of the synagogue toward Jesus, I find it refreshing that this ruler, Jairus, probably a Pharisee, throws himself at the feet of Jesus. It shows me that all the teaching and demonstrating of miraculous power does not fall completely on deaf ears. God's Word does not return void as the Scripture says in Isaiah 55:11. Someone in that hard-hearted group of religious leaders pays attention to Jesus' spiritual truths. *"He who has ears to hear, let him hear!"* (Matthew 13:9).

I have found in all my years of ministering in this healing ministry, the most difficult group to reach are those with a religious spirit. And unfortunately, the Church is full of them.

Dear Holy Spirt, may we forever have our spiritual ears wide open and ready to receive all that You say to us. In the name of Jesus, I pray, amen.

Although, Jairus is part of the group called scribes and Pharisees that fights against Jesus, when this man has a serious need for the health and well-being of his daughter, he humbles himself and throws himself at the feet of Jesus.

This Bible version translates that Jairus *begs* Jesus to come to his home. This word *begs* in Greek language translates as *parakaleō,* and it means "to beseech, call to one's side" (Strong's G3840). Again, we read of another who begs Jesus for help. We can ascertain from this situation that all the religious acts in the world do not prepare us for an encounter with Jesus. And thanks be to our God, this is not what He desires from us—we follow Him with a loving and humble heart for Him. He wants us to be authentic and real with Him, not someone who pretends to be perfect.

TWELVE YEARS, LONG OR SHORT?

Jairus' need is for his daughter, his only daughter who is about 12 years of age. It's apparent that Jesus has a different view concerning age and time; while it means a lot to us, it doesn't so much for Him. Permit me to explain my thoughts about this. Jairus' daughter is on her deathbed, she's about to die and she is young. In other words, she has been alive only for a short time, and she's too young to pass. And I wholeheartedly agree, this is too young to die.

But remember in the beginning of this healing adventure between verses 42 and 49, in verse 43 of this same chapter of Luke, Jesus meets an older woman who suffers from a grave bleeding issue. She bleeds for 12 years, as long as this little girl has been alive. But for this unnamed woman, her view of the past 12 years differs from how Jairus feels about that amount of time.

While Jairus believes he is being robbed of time with his little girl, and again, I agree with him, this woman with the issue of blood, believes she is being robbed of life as the past 12 years of suffering have been long and hard, and unfair to her. And you know what? She's right too. Both Jairus and this suffering woman look at the past 12 years through differing lenses, both views are correct, and matter to Jesus.

DOES JESUS SHOW PREFERENCE?

We have an interesting situation here, first Jesus meets a man, no ordinary man, but one of the most influential men in his community. He is a rich ruler of the synagogue, probably a Pharisee. He teaches in the synagogue. And we find this influential leader prostrate, face down at the feet of Jesus, and hear him beg Jesus to come to his home because his little girl is dying and needs an urgent miracle.

And along comes a poor woman who is less than ordinary, she's an outcast from society. She is ceremonially unclean, not allowed to enter into Jairus' synagogue. She's not to even speak to this ruler. Interestingly, we do not find her begging for healing, instead she goes in and grabs it for herself, and her bold and outlandish act of faith gets her healed, while Jairus' daughter dies.

And if we remember from the last recorded miracle of Jesus we studied, Miracle 14, this outcast of a woman not only grabs the hem of His garment, but her faith grabs hold of His heart. And her faith stops Jesus, the wild crowd, and Heaven in their tracks. And her faith is honored for eternity.

So we can plainly see that Jesus does not show preference between people according to position or wealth—His love extends to all equally.

JESUS IS NOT MOVED BY URGENCY

As we walk alongside Jesus and view both these miracles, we see that Jesus is not moved by urgency, but by faith, and faith alone. Why is this? Because Jesus is a faith being, and He created people in His image, faith creatures. And one of the main reasons, along with redeeming us from our sin, is to live on earth as a human being, leaving all God-powers behind in Heaven to demonstrate to us how to live by faith daily.

And our faith has nothing to do with feelings, timing, or urgency. Faith is trust in the greatness of our God. So, no, Jesus is not moved by the urgency of the situation with Jairus' daughter, but clearly by faith.

For we walk by faith, not by sight (2 Corinthians 5:7).

DO NOT TROUBLE THE TEACHER

Jairus' servant delivers a bad report, "Your daughter is dead. Do not trouble the Teacher." For one, the belief that we are a bother to our Lord stems from a harsh religious perspective. But presenting our need to Jesus is never a bother to Him. His will is to heal us and our families too.

> *Let us therefore come boldly to the throne of grace, that we may obtain mercy and find grace to help in time of need* (Hebrews 4:16).

We are not to be intimidated or fearful, but confident that He loves and cares for us, especially in time of great need.

THE PEOPLE RIDICULE JESUS FOR HIS FAITH

> *Now all wept and mourned for her; but He said, "Do not weep; she is not dead, but sleeping." And they ridiculed Him, knowing that she was dead* (Luke 8:52-53).

This situation Jesus finds Himself in is not unique to Him only. Whenever we exercise great faith, as He always does, we receive the same type of response from those who do not understand faith. And this leads us to the main point of this miracle, *guarding the atmosphere.*

GUARD THE ATMOSPHERE

In Luke 8:51 we are told the steps Jesus takes to guard the atmosphere: "*When He came into the house, He permitted no one to go in except Peter, James, and John, and the father and mother of the girl.*" Why did He restrict others from going in? Because the mourners are mourning, and the ridiculers are ridiculing, and both these activities destroy faith. Jesus must create and maintain an atmosphere of faith to work this miracle.

Proverbs 28:21 (AMPC) tells us something about the power of our words, *"Death and life are in the power of the tongue, and they who indulge in it shall eat the fruit of it [for death or life]."* Both mourning and ridiculing are forms of language that produce doubt and unbelief, and Jesus must spiritually cleanse that atmosphere.

HOW DOES JESUS WORK THIS MIRACLE?

After Jesus cleanses the atmosphere from doubt and unbelief, He creates and maintains an atmosphere of faith. There are only seven individuals permitted in this room: Jesus, the Healer, Peter, James, John, His inner circle who are among His 12 disciples, the young girl's parents who are her legal and spiritual authority, and the little dead girl herself. After an atmosphere of faith is established, Jesus then takes the little girl by the hand. Healing virtue is being transmitted via the touching of hands, and then He dispatches a verbal command to Jairus' daughter, *"Little girl, arise!"* And she obeys His command of faith and authority, she lives.

Jairus and his wife are astonished. This word *astonished* in the Greek language is *eksístēmi,* and it means "to amaze, to astonish, to be beside oneself, to be out of one's mind, or to be flabbergasted" (Strong's G1839). This Pharisee, Jairus, along with his wife, are absolutely flabbergasted by the miracle-working power of Jesus over their daughter.

THE RICHES OF JESUS ON DISPLAY

- Jesus does not play snooty religious games of favoritism for the rich and famous. No, He treats everyone the same, with love and respect.
- He does not fear death.
- Jesus knows He has authority over death.
- He shows great compassion for those shunned by society.
- Jesus' faith is steady, never wavers, even during emergencies.

CRACK THE MIRACLE CODE

We must create and maintain an atmosphere of faith for the manifestation of our healing.

When you read Miracle 16, you will learn to call upon Him and His mercy for your healing.

FAITH ASSIGNMENT

Create the right atmosphere of faith for your miracle. Surround yourself with people of faith, and do not allow mourners and ridiculers into the same room as you. Declare words of faith and put physical action behind those actions.

PRAYER OF FAITH

Dear Father God, this lesson has been a real eyeopener for me. Show me how to operate as You do, no favoritism, just love and respect for all. Help me, Holy Spirit, to have the eyes of a hawk and carefully guard the spiritual atmosphere. If I do not already know, reveal to me the mourners and the ridiculers, and grace me with the words to ask them to leave when they choose not to cooperate with my faith in You for a miracle. In Your name I pray, sweet Jesus, amen.

Questions for Miracle 15: Guard the Atmosphere

1. How are we to be waiting for our miracle?
2. What does Isaiah 55:11 say about God's Word?
3. What does the Greek word *parakaleō* mean?
4. For Jairus concerning his daughter, what did 12 years mean to him?
5. For the unnamed woman with the blood issue, what did 12 years mean to her?
6. Who does this woman's faith stop?
7. According to 2 Corinthians 5:7, how are we to walk?
8. According to Hebrews 4:16, how are we to approach the throne of grace?
9. What do mourning and ridiculing produce?
10. According to Proverbs 18:21, what does the tongue possess?
11. In the Greek language, what does the word *eksistēmi* mean?
12. The Pharisee Jairus and his wife are flabbergasted about what?

MIRACLE 16
HAVE MERCY ON US

Jesus Heals Two Blind Men

We are about to join two blind men and receive a new perspective about a well-known verse that declares, *"Blessed are those who have not seen and yet have believed"* (John 20:29). This should knock any residue of the spirit of doubting Thomas right out of us!

Let's begin with our text for Miracle 16 in Matthew 9:27-31:

> *When Jesus departed from there, two blind men followed Him, crying out and saying, "Son of David, have mercy on us!" And when He had come into the house, the blind men came to Him. And Jesus said to them, "Do you believe that I am able to do this?" They said to Him, "Yes, Lord." Then He touched their eyes, saying, "According to your faith let it be to you." And their eyes were opened. And Jesus sternly warned them, saying, "See that no one knows it." But when they had departed, they spread the news about Him in all that country.*

WHERE IS THERE?

This portion of Scripture begins with the words, *"When Jesus departed from there,"* but where is there? In Matthew 10:23-26 we read that Jesus raises

Jairus' only daughter from the dead, and a few verses before that we read how His healing virtue was released and the woman with the issue of blood was healed. And now in verse 27 these two blind men follow Him. He's either had a super busy day healing people or there are sick people everywhere he goes. I believe the latter as, unfortunately, there is no shortage of sick people back then or now. Open your eyes and see through the eyes of Jesus. They are everywhere.

THEY RECOGNIZE JESUS

Even though these men are blind, they perceive truthfully that Jesus is indeed the *"Son of David."* They have the inner witness within them testifying that Jesus is the true Messiah, the fulfillment of the Old Testament prophesies who is walking and beathing among them.

JESUS REFERRED TO AS THE "SON OF DAVID"

Along with the reference by these two blind men to Jesus as the "Son of David" in Matthew 9:27, there are more references to Jesus being the "Son of David," the long-anticipated Messiah in the book of Matthew. In Matthew 1:1 we can read the record of the genealogy of Jesus, the Messiah, *the son of David*, the son of Abraham. And in 12:23, Matthew records the crowds are amazed and are questioning, *"Could this be the Son of David?"* In Matthew 15:22, a Canaanite mother cries out on behalf of her demon-possessed daughter, *"Have mercy on me, O Lord, Son of David."* And later, the crowds are going ahead of Him waving palm branches and shouting, *"Hosanna to the Son of David! Blessed is He who comes in the name of the Lord! Hosanna in the highest!"* (Matthew 21:9). And we read again in 21:15 that the chief priests and scribes are indignant as they see the wonderful things Jesus does, and hear the children cry out in the temple *"Hosanna to the Son of David!"*

Matthew refers to the name of our Lord Jesus being cried out by the people on six different occasions as *"Son of David."* His use of this name is unique in comparison to the other Gospels. First, the number 6 in the Bible symbolizes man and human weakness.[1] Is it a coincidence or a divine inspiration of Holy Spirit that the people and their human weakness call out to Jesus, as "Son of David" in six different occasions in the book of Matthew? I believe this to be a divine inspiration of Holy Spirit uniquely recorded for us in the book of Matthew.

WORD STUDY FOR JESUS, SON OF DAVID, AND MESSIAH

We will do a little study of words in Matthew 9, verse 27, to have a deeper understanding of its meaning for them and for us. *Jesus* means "Jehovah is salvation,"[2] and they are crying out, "Son of David," which is more than connecting Him to His genealogy of the King of David, but publicly acknowledging His real identity, "Messiah." *Messiah* comes from the Hebrew word *mashiach* and means "anointed one" or "chosen one." The Greek equivalent is the word *Christos* or, in English, *Christ*. The name "Jesus Christ" is the same as "Jesus the Messiah." In biblical times, anointing someone with oil was a sign that God was consecrating or setting apart that person for a particular role. Thus, an "anointed one" was someone with a special, God-ordained purpose.[3]

HAVE MERCY ON US

Again in Matthew 9:27, these two blind men call out to Jesus to have mercy on them. *Mercy* is an action word, in Greek it's *eleeō,* and means "to help the afflicted" (Strong's G1653). And our ever-caring Jesus extends His hand of mercy and delivers them from their affliction.

INSIDE THE HOUSE

In Matthew 9:28 we see the place where Jesus heals them: *"And when He had come into the house, the blind men came to Him."* He leads them to a private place, inside a house.

So many people feel they must stand behind a pulpit to minister. I often have requests about this. And I say to them what I share with you now. You do not need a pulpit to minister. Look around you, there are infirmed people all around us. Be the hands and feet of Jesus, and voice-activate healing into their body in the name of Jesus.

Oftentimes, we read about Jesus healing the sick outside the walls of the temple. Wherever He goes, He heals the sick. And where is He now? Inside a private home.

DO YOU BELIEVE?

Lovers and followers of Jesus tend to take offense when we ask them if they believe. But Jesus asks these two blind men who have been following Him if they believe. Are they offended? No. Then why should we be offended? He asks them, *"Do you believe that I am able to do this?"* In the affirmative, they answer, *"Yes, Lord."*

ACCORDING TO YOUR FAITH

In Matthew 9:29-30 we read Jesus' response to these two blind men who ask for Him to have mercy upon them. How does He respond? *"Then He touched their eyes, saying, 'According to your faith let it be to you.' And their eyes were opened."* They are asking Messiah, the Anointed One for mercy. And they have His mercy.

But He takes this mercy a step further. These men out of necessity are accustomed to follow, but Jesus puts them in the lead, or in charge of their own miracle now. He challenges them with these words, *"According to your faith let it be to you."* I believe not only do the men need physical healing of their eyes, but there is also a need for internal healing of the soul (mind and emotions) that needs to take place. He restores what this infirmity stole from them, independence. They are now capable of leading, not just following, beginning now with their healing.

THE HEALING PROCESS

In verses 29-30 we see the healing process that Jesus administers: "*Then He touched their eyes, saying, 'According to your faith let it be to you.' And their eyes were opened.*" By the power of their passionate request, "*Son of David, have mercy on us!*" He releases healing virtue via the power of touch.

WHOSE FAITH HEALS?

These men, before the healing of their eyes manifests, demonstrate great faith in that even without witnessing with their physical eyes miracles, signs, and wonders, they believe that Jesus is the long-awaited Messiah. And because they believe in who He is, they readily follow Him. And when Jesus ministers healing to them, He declares, *"According to your faith let it be to you."* So whose faith heals their blind eyes? The two blind men's faith.

> *Blessed are those who have not seen and yet have believed* (John 20:29).

THE RICHES OF JESUS ON DISPLAY

- Jesus doesn't just heal; He makes people whole.
- He treats these blind males as mature men, not little boys.
- Jesus challenges faith.
- His mercy is great.

CRACK THE MIRACLE CODE

We must call upon Him and His mercy for our healing.

While you read Miracle 17, you will learn how demons cannot resist the irresistible force of Jesus—demons must submit to Him.

FAITH ASSIGNMENT

Get real with yourself, and ask, *Do I believe Jesus can heal me even when I do not see it physically? Am I willing to do whatever it takes to get to this spiritual place of mature faith?* If so, write down steps of faith to take.

PRAYER OF FAITH

> *Dear Holy Spirit, as always, Your words bring deep conviction to my soul. I do not want to take offense when asked if I believe. If I know I do, I praise You, Jesus! If I know I am not quite to that place where I can believe, then I humbly ask for Your help now to ready me to believe. In Your name, dear Jesus, I pray, amen.*

Questions for Miracle 16: Have Mercy on Us

1. These two blind men correctly perceive that Jesus is who?
2. What do these two men have an inner witness about concerning Jesus?
3. What does the number 6 in the Bible symbolize?
4. Is it a coincidence or a divine inspiration of Holy Spirit that people in their human weakness call out to Jesus as "Son of David" in six different occasions in the book of Matthew?
5. What does the name of *Jesus* mean?
6. What does *Messiah* mean?
7. What is the Greek word for *mercy?* And what does it mean?
8. Whose faith heals these two blind men?

MIRACLE 17
IRRESISTIBLE FORCE

Jesus Heals a Mute Man

Today we witness Jesus exercise the spiritual act of deliverance from demon possession. Jesus will rescue a man under the power of a demon who stole his voice and literally silenced him. But then what happens when this mute man meets Jesus, the Creative Word made visible, is truly marvelous to behold.

Matthew 9:32-34 shares this man's amazing story with us:

> *As they went out, behold, they brought to Him a man, mute and demon-possessed. And when the demon was cast out, the mute spoke. And the multitudes marveled, saying, "It was never seen like this in Israel!" But the Pharisees said, "He casts out demons by the ruler of the demons."*

UNDER THE POWER OF A DEMON

Matthew 9:32 makes it clear that this man is demon-possessed. The Greek word for this spiritual infirmity is *daimonizomai,* and it means "to be under the power of a demon" (Strong's G1139). This demon is an agent of the devil, and it has to go!

What's so disturbing about the evil actions against this man is that it stole his voice; as mentioned in the introduction of this miracle, this demon silenced the man. Spiritually speaking, this is a serious crime. Why? Why do I say this?

Because our Lord empowers us with the law of the spoken word. This is how our God operates. (Read Genesis 1.) He instructs us in Proverbs 18:21 that we possess the power of life and death in our words. And by the power of spoken words, we can command and overcome the mountains in our life. Mark 11:23 (AMPC) says it like this, *"Truly I tell you, whoever says to this mountain, Be lifted up and thrown into the sea! and does not doubt at all in his heart but believes that what he says will take place, it will be done for him."* Romans 4:17 teaches us to call things that do not exist as though they already do.

So by stealing this man's voice, his ability to speak, this demon steals one of his greatest spiritual weapons to live victoriously on earth. But glory to God, the man is about to personally meet the One who will hit the unmute button in his life.

MUTE AND ITS MEANING

The study of words reveals many details in Scripture that we might not otherwise know. For instance, take this word *mute*, the Greek word for this is *kōphos* and means he had a "lame tongue," but this Greek word also implies deafness. It is very probable that the man was also deaf, or partially deaf. Many times, I have released the healing power of Jesus into someone who was deaf and unable to speak, and instantly they can both hear and speak with clarity.

> *He who has ears [to hear], let him be listening and let him consider and perceive and comprehend by hearing* (Matthew 13:9 AMPC).

AN IRRESISTIBLE FORCE

This demon is no match for Jesus, an irresistible force. In verse 33, this man's bondage is broken, *"And when the demon was cast out, the mute spoke."* phrase *cast out* in Greek is *ekballō,* and it means "to lead one forth or away somewhere with a force which he cannot resist" (Strong's G1544). So we must set the stage for deliverance with an irresistible force that this demon cannot resist—Jesus. And how do we do this?

SET THE STAGE FOR DELIVERANCE

How do we set the stage or prepare for deliverance? We need to bring in the power of Jesus onto the scene of this spiritual crime.

1. We need to build up our faith in Jesus. Jude 20 (AMPC) says it like this, "*But you, beloved, build yourselves up [founded] on your most holy faith [make progress, rise like an edifice higher and higher], praying in the Holy Spirit.*"
2. Recognize our authority as a believer in Yeshua. "*You are of God, little children, and have overcome them, because He who is in you is greater than he who is in the world*" (1 John 4:4).
3. Cast out the demon in Jesus' name. "*And these signs will follow those who believe: In My name they will cast out demons; they will speak with new tongues; they will take up serpents; and if they drink anything deadly, it will by no means hurt them; they will lay hands on the sick, and they will recover*" (Mark 16:17-18).

WARNING TO DELIVERANCE MINISTERS

I have witnessed a lot of dangerous practices in the ministry by people who claim to walk in the ministry of deliverance. This is not a game; someone's life is at stake. The following are a few issues that we must bring correction for the sake of the one being delivered, and those conducting the service of deliverance.

A LIFESTYLE OF PRAYER AND FASTING

You must practice a lifestyle of prayer and fasting. This is why Jesus was so successful, He often spent time alone away from the people to be with the Father to pray. And during these times with the Father, we never read about Him packing a lunch to take along. He spent much time in prayer and fasting. (Check out the following nine passages of Scriptures that record His private getaways with the Father. See Matthew 14:13; 15:29, Mark 1:12,35,45; 3:13; 6:31-32, 46; 14:32.)

As we read through these verses, we see that Jesus departed by boat to a deserted place by Himself to pray. He went up to the mountain to sit. The

Spirit of God drove Him out into the wilderness. On another occasion in the morning He went to a solitary place to pray. We read He went out to deserted places, and again He went up to the mountain, and another time He departed to a deserted place by boat. On another time after He sent His disciples away, He departed to the mountain to pray. And during His most difficult trial, He went to the Garden of Gethsemane with His disciples to pray.

And remember, Jesus said concerning some demons in Mark 9:29 that *"This kind can come out by nothing but prayer and fasting."*

DO NOT ENTERTAIN AND CONVERSE WITH DEMONS

Shocking but true, I have met people in the deliverance ministry who brag about how they entertain and converse with demons. One has a special room in the house where individuals who are either oppressed or possessed by demons come and sit, and she spends her time talking to the devils. Jesus does not instruct us to entertain these fallen angels but to cast them out of people. Interacting with demons is both dangerous and foolish. I believe that yes, we are to have our spiritual ears open, but not to listen to lying spirits that fill our heads with falsehoods, or evils that they commit against people.

While ministering to oppressed or possessed people, the Spirit of the Lord will show me visions of what has happened. As I see into the spirit realm of this person's life, I will then ask the person, not a demon, *"Did this happen to you?"* And the hurting person will answer me. But never do I carry on a conversation with a demon. It is ludicrous to think demons will lead us to the truth. Their desire is to remain within the person so they can continue to torment them, not to disclose devious secrets to help you clear them out of the person. The guidance of Holy Spirit is the only One we need to speak to during deliverance. "*The Spirit of Truth, Whom the world cannot receive (welcome, take to its heart), because it does not see Him or know and recognize Him. But you know and recognize Him, for He lives with you [constantly] and will be in you"* (John 14:17 AMPC).

CAST THEM OUT IN JESUS' NAME

And last, we are to follow the example of Jesus and exercise His authority that He so graciously gave to us over the devil and his demons and cast them out in Jesus' name.

> *Behold! I have given you authority and power to trample upon serpents and scorpions, and [physical and mental strength and ability] over all the power that the enemy [possesses]; and nothing shall in any way harm you* (Luke 10:19 AMPC).

HIS LIFE CHANGED

One encounter with Jesus, the Miracle Worker, and the man's life is forever changed. For many years he was unable to legibly express his thoughts, wants, and needs—but one moment with Jesus and he's no longer silent, he speaks. And I'm sure he will have a lot to say to us in Heaven about the day Jesus delivered him and gave him a voice.

THE RICHES OF JESUS ON DISPLAY

- The ability to speak is indeed very important to Jesus.
- Jesus wills for us to use the power of the spoken word.
- His compassion runs deep for those oppressed or possessed by demons.
- Jesus will not tolerate a demon's torment of a person in His presence.
- He delivers, heals, and makes people whole again.

CRACK THE MIRACLE CODE

In matters of deliverance, we need to usher in the irresistible force of Jesus that demons cannot resist.

When reading Miracle 18, you will learn how to make no more excuses, take responsibility for your miracle, and put your faith in action and be healed.

FAITH ASSIGNMENT

I challenge you to begin to spend alone time with Jesus. A special time away from other people, and the distractions of this life. Just you and Jesus, your Bible, a listening ear, and something to write down what He speaks to your heart about. Spend time praying in the Spirit, and then just be silent and let Him speak to your heart. And please note, He will do most of the talking.

PRAYER OF FAITH

I give You thanks, Lord Jesus, that You are the irresistible force in my life who drives all evil away from me. I know now that oppressive and possessive powers of darkness cannot resist an eviction notice given by faith in Your name, amen.

Questions for Miracle 17: Irresistible Force

1. What is the Greek word for *demon-possessed?*
2. What does *daimonizomai* mean?
3. What is the Greek word for *mute?*
4. What does the Greek word for *mute* mean?
5. What also does the Greek word for *mute* imply?
6. What is the Greek word for the phrase *cast out?*
7. What does the Greek word for the phrase *cast out* mean?
8. What type of lifestyle must a deliverance minister practice?
9. Whose guidance do we need during deliverance?
10. What are we to do with demons?

MIRACLE 18

DO YOU WANT TO BE MADE WELL?

Jesus Heals an Invalid at Bethesda

Let's travel to the pool of Bethesda, where perhaps if we're lucky we will be visited by an angel. And if we're quick enough we will be the first one in the water and the blessed one to be healed. I wonder what will happen at the pool today.

> *After this there was a feast of the Jews, and Jesus went up to Jerusalem. Now there is in Jerusalem by the Sheep Gate a pool, which is called in Hebrew, Bethesda, having five porches. In these lay a great multitude of sick people, blind, lame, paralyzed, waiting for the moving of the water. For an angel went down at a certain time into the pool and stirred up the water; then whoever stepped in first, after the stirring of the water, was made well of whatever disease he had. Now a certain man was there who had an infirmity thirty-eight years. When Jesus saw him lying there, and knew that he already had been in that condition a long time, He said to him, "Do you want to be made well?" The sick man answered Him, "Sir, I have no man to put me into the pool when the water is stirred up; but while I am coming, another steps down before me."*
>
> *Jesus said to him, "Rise, take up your bed and walk." And immedi-*

ately the man was made well, took up his bed, and walked. And that day was the Sabbath. The Jews therefore said to him who was cured, "It is the Sabbath; it is not lawful for you to carry your bed." He answered them, "He who made me well said to me, 'Take up your bed and walk.'" Then they asked him, "Who is the Man who said to you, 'Take up your bed and walk'?" But the one who was healed did not know who it was, for Jesus had withdrawn, a multitude being in that place. Afterward Jesus found him in the temple, and said to him, "See, you have been made well. Sin no more, lest a worse thing come upon you." The man departed and told the Jews that it was Jesus who had made him well (John 5:1-15).

THE POOL OF BETHESDA

First, Bethesda means "house of mercy" or "flowing water" and is known for its angelic visits and waters with curative powers (Strong's G964). This is why we often see a great multitude of sick people, the blind, the lame, and the paralyzed, waiting and hoping for a miracle.

DO YOU WANT TO BE HEALED?

What a direct question this is from the mouth of Jesus, *"Do you want to be healed?"* It aims right to the heart of the matter, the will of the person. I ask this question often, and sometimes the answer stuns me. To my surprise, there are those who would rather remain ill, or hold on to the title of "Disabled" so they can receive a check from the government for monthly support. There is a time and a place for this assistance, but as true followers and lovers of Jesus, it should not become our daily source. Jehovah Jeriah is our Provider. I don't believe this is God's best, nor will I align my faith with such a request for prayer. I believe God wants His people strong, healthy, and healed so that we can be about our heavenly Father's business and win people to Jesus.

WHAT'S YOUR EXCUSE?

Notice when Jesus asks this man if he wants to be healed, instead of giving a definitive answer, he makes excuses about why he can't be healed. *"Sir, I have no man to put me into the pool when the water is stirred up; but while*

I am coming, another steps down before me." Well, I am sure there is truth to his excuses, but if this is all we see, then we miss the main point of the story.

We make excuses all the time to the Lord about why it is someone else's responsibility, even God's responsibility, for our healing. Anybody else's responsibility, but not our own. And unknowingly we make excuses about why we can't be healed such as, "It's stage 4 cancer," "The test results show the tumor is bigger than it was before," "I've had this disease all my life," "I'm a terrible person, I had an abortion…." And this list of excuses as to why we think we cannot be healed is inexhaustible.

But as it is for this man, it is for us too, Jesus doesn't put a lot of importance in our excuses. He wants results. And if we remain in a negative funk of making excuses and blaming others, we will never get up and walk in our promised healing.

HE DOES NOT RECOGNIZE JESUS

Do you realize that this man does not recognize Jesus? Why is this? Unfortunately, the man is so wrapped up in himself and his human reasoning about why it's not possible for him to be healed. He's bound up so tightly with negativism that he doesn't even recognize the Miracle-Worker in his presence.

ENCOURAGEMENT NOT PITY

People like this man do not need our pity, they have enough of it for themselves, and even more to spare. But they do need our words of encouragement to trust and believe for their miracle. They need us to be their support group and confess words of faith over them, encourage them to put their faith in action as Jesus did with this man.

THE PROGRESSION OF THIS MAN'S MIRACLE

First, this man must wait for an angel to make an appearance and *"stir the water."* Then this paralyzed man who has been infirmed for 38 years now has to hope that he will be able to get into the water before anyone else. For a man in his condition the stakes are stacked against him. His hope for healing is rather dim.

THEN FAITH ARRIVES

Then one day, faith arrives at the house of mercy, Bethesda. But Jesus does not give this man pity, He give him a challenge to put his faith into action, and a command of faith to pick up his bed and walk.

A BETTER COVENANT

We have a much better covenant that does not involve chances, but faith. And this covenant can be activated at any time, and for anyone. It doesn't involve the appearance of angels or our speediness to respond—only that we do respond with faith in what Jesus has already accomplished for us.

> *For if that first covenant had been without defect, there would have been no room for another one or an attempt to institute another one. However, He finds fault with them [showing its inadequacy] when He says, Behold, the days will come, says the Lord, when I will make and ratify a new covenant or agreement with the house of Israel and with the house of Judah* (Hebrews 8:7-8 AMPC).

We can compare the old covenant to this man's inability to make it to healing pool before anyone else. As amazing as angel stories can be, this one is a bit faulty as those with the greatest needs were unable to obtain their healing. The requirements were next to impossible to fulfill. Like the old covenant, the requirements were nearly impossible to live by and had no mercy, no grace.

> *But as it now is, He [Christ] has acquired a [priestly] ministry which is as much superior and more excellent [than the old] as the covenant (the agreement) of which He is the Mediator (the Arbiter, Agent) is superior and more excellent, [because] it is enacted and rests upon more important (sublimer, higher, and nobler) promises* (Hebrews 8:6 AMPC).

THE DIFFERENCE BETWEEN HOPE AND FAITH

The difference between hope and faith is not difficult to understand. Hope is like a wish. Allow me to share a story that comes to my mind as I write about the difference between hope and faith.

I learned this lesson from one of my brothers back when I was a little girl traveling in the camper with my family one summer. While we are traveling down the highway under a bridge, I held up my index finger in the air and said a wish from my heart aloud, "I hope Grandpa gets well." My brother Tom then says to me, *"Becky, you don't make a wish under a bridge for Grandpa, you pray to God for him."* It is one of those little life lessons that will forever be imprinted upon my heart. And what he said to me is true. We don't wish for someone to get better. We have faith that they will.

So if we remain in the realm of hope for healing, it will never happen. Why not? Because there is an element of unsurety with hope. We must take it a step further and accept responsibility for that wish and add a measure of faith to that desire.

We reside in the desert of Arizona, where temperatures reach triple digits during the summer months. And the little bit of greenery we have in our yards will shrivel and die unless we do something—unless we water the plants daily.

Faith works the same way, if we want to move from hope to the spiritual arena of faith—we have to do something. James, the brother of Jesus and a leader in the early church explains it this way, *"So also faith, if it does not have works (deeds and actions of obedience to back it up), by itself is destitute of power (inoperative, dead)"* (James 2:17 AMPC).

And sometimes the battles in life that we face intensify, like the hot Arizona desert, and it's a fight to keep the plants alive. This is when we need to turn up the heat of our faith and fight the good fight of faith.

> *Fight the good fight of the faith; lay hold of the eternal life to which you were summoned and [for which] you confessed the good confession [of faith] before many witnesses* (1 Timothy 6:12 AMPC).

In the Greek, this word *fight* is *agōnizomai* and means "to contend with adversaries" (Strong's G75). And we do have an adversary, the devil (1 Peter 5:8), and we must not give him an opportunity to hit us. The only way to prevent this is for us to put on our spiritual boxing gloves and fight the good fight of faith.

This is the difference between hope and faith. Hope is about wishing, and whatever happens, happens. While faith is willing to enter the ring and contend for the prize of the high calling (Philippians 3:14).

A RELIGIOUS SPIRIT RISES AGAINST PEOPLE OF FAITH

And again, we see the religious spirit rise against faith and miracles. This legalistic spirit kills both, and its harshness stems from jealousy and a need to be in control of others, no matter the cruel suffering it inflicts.

FAITH ANGERS A RELIGIOUS SPIRIT

Faith is simple and uncomplicated. It trusts and stems from the heart. It's founded in the riches of God's grace and mercy. Whereas religion is all about fulfilling the letter of the law, mandating strict rules and regulations on others that they themselves do not adhere to. And it lacks grace, mercy, and understanding.

THE RICHES OF JESUS ON DISPLAY

- Jesus activates compassion, love in action.
- He overlooks excuses.
- Jesus is not afraid to ask the hard questions.
- He always goes to the heart of the matter.
- Jesus extends mercy.

CRACK THE MIRACLE CODE

Make no more excuses, put your faith in action and be healed.

As you read Miracle 19, you will see how supernatural protection belongs to those who are called and committed to Christ.

FAITH ASSIGNMENT

Ask yourself the hard question, *Do I want to be healed?* Why or why not? According to your answer, move forward to the next step and activate your faith for that miracle.

PRAYER OF FAITH

Dear Holy Spirit, I accept the challenge of no longer making excuses and will activate my faith for my miracle. I ask for Your guidance and encouragement along the way to cooperate with the will of Your Word and believe and act on the trust I have in You. In Jesus' name I pray, amen.

Questions for Miracle 18: Do You Want to Be Made Well?

1. What does *Bethesda* mean?
2. What is *Bethesda* known for?
3. Who is Jehovah Jireh?
4. What do people need from us?
5. What don't people need from us?
6. What is the Greek word for fight?
7. What does the Greek word for fight mean?
8. Who is our enemy?
9. Does Jesus pay attention to our excuses?
10. Explain faith.

MIRACLE 19
SPIRITUAL MULTIPLICATION

Jesus Feeds 5,000 Plus Women and Children

For an undetermined time, Jesus has been traveling with His disciples doing Kingdom business, teaching and preaching the Good News with signs and wonders following. Afterward, He crosses over the Sea of Galilee and hikes up the mountain where we find Him sitting with His disciples. Jesus looks up and sees coming toward Him a great multitude of 5,000 men plus women and children who have been following Him.

FEEDING THE MULTITUDE

> *After these things Jesus went over the Sea of Galilee, which is the Sea of Tiberias. Then a great multitude followed Him, because they saw His signs which He performed on those who were diseased. And Jesus went up on the mountain, and there He sat with His disciples. Now the Passover, a feast of the Jews, was near. Then Jesus lifted up His eyes, and seeing a great multitude coming toward Him, He said to Philip, "Where shall we buy bread, that these may eat?" But this He said to test him, for He Himself knew what He would do. Philip answered Him, "Two hundred denarii worth of bread is not sufficient for them, that*

every one of them may have a little." One of His disciples, Andrew, Simon Peter's brother, said to Him, "There is a lad here who has five barley loaves and two small fish, but what are they among so many?"

Then Jesus said, "Make the people sit down." Now there was much grass in the place. So the men sat down, in number about five thousand. And Jesus took the loaves, and when He had given thanks He distributed them to the disciples, and the disciples to those sitting down; and likewise of the fish, as much as they wanted. So when they were filled, He said to His disciples, "Gather up the fragments that remain, so that nothing is lost." Therefore they gathered them up, and filled twelve baskets with the fragments of the five barley loaves which were left over by those who had eaten. Then those men, when they had seen the sign that Jesus did, said, "This is truly the Prophet who is to come into the world" (John 6:1-14).

TESTING PHILIP'S FAITH

I can imagine Jesus with a smile on His face, kind of chuckling to Himself, saying to Philip, *"Where shall we buy bread, that these may eat?"* Jesus is not inquiring of Philip for the address of the local baker. He already knows what He plans to do. So what's He up to? He is testing Philip's faith.

Philip has been training with boots on the ground with Jesus, and now it's time for some testing. Let's examine how he does. I would think by now, Philip has witnessed so many amazing signs and wonders, healings, and miracles that his faith is absolutely soaring high. How does he respond to Jesus? Philip answers Him, *"Two hundred denarii worth of bread is not sufficient for them, that every one of them may have a little."* I think we would agree that this is the wrong answer. I'm sure Jesus is hoping for an answer of faith, but He does not receive it at this time.

And then things get a little more hopeful with Andrew, Simon Peter's brother, when he reports, *"There is a lad here who has five barley loaves and two small fish."* Oh, just maybe Andrew is going to ace the test, but then finishes his statement of faith with these faithless words, *"but what are they among so many?"* And again, I can imagine Jesus shaking His head and saying to Himself, *Oh ye, of little faith!*

WHY THE TESTING?

Testing Philip and Andrew's faith reveals what they have learned thus far in their times of ministry together. And at least in this test, they fail to see the possibility of faith. God also uses tests to show us what's hidden within our heart. These tests reveal our strengths and weaknesses and are a normal part of spiritual growth. When we fail to pass a test, rest assured that God will bring another similar test our way so we learn from our failures.

THE LITTLE BOY GIVES WHAT HE HAS

While Philip and Andrew fail their time of testing, I love how a little boy freely gives up his lunch of five barley loaves and two small fish to help Jesus feed the multitude. And boy, oh boy, does this young lad have a story to tell for generations to come.

There are rich lessons of faith to glean from this boy's testimony. First, he hears of the need to feed the hungry people, including his own belly. And although he doesn't have enough to feed all, he freely gives what he does have. Jesus has a special place in His heart for children and the power of their simplistic faith. And it's this childlike, not childish, faith that Jesus taps into to reveal faith lessons for ages to come, important lessons such as with Jesus there is no such things as lack of provision.

But it all begins with a willing heart that's not afraid to give it all away, if need be, for the process of spiritual multiplication to take over and produce supernaturally what's not there physically, just as we see with the five barley loaves and two small fish. All were happy and well fed by the innocence of a child's faith to give what he had to help Jesus.

It also clears up wrong thinking in giving. If given with a pure heart of faith, a little with Jesus goes a long way.

SYMBOLISM OF THE BREAD AND THE FISH

The bread and fish that we read about in the feeding of the 5,000 men plus the women and children is rich in symbolism. Bread prophetically testifies of Jesus from the time of His birth, born in a stable and for His crib, a feeding trough (Luke 2:7). Jesus declares of Himself in John 6:35 (AMPC), *"I am the Bread of Life. He who comes to Me will never be hungry, and he who believes in and cleaves to and trusts in and relies on Me will never thirst any more (at any time)."*

When Jesus says of Himself, *"I am the Bread of Life,"* not only is He declaring His deity as their Messiah, but that He is a staple, their sustenance for daily life, and more importantly for their eternal life. And during the Last Supper, we read in Matthew 26:26 (AMPC), *"Now as they were eating, Jesus took bread and, praising God, gave thanks and asked Him to bless it to their use, and when He had broken it, He gave it to the disciples and said, Take, eat; this is My body"* (AMPC).

When it comes to the spiritual meaning of the fish, we could say, "Jesus is going fishing!" But not for the type of fish we eat. Rather by sharing in word and demonstrating by miracles, signs, and wonders that He is reeling in disciples, followers (Matthew 4:19).

PASSOVER WAS NEAR

Passover is an important Jewish holiday that celebrates the Israelites' liberation from Egypt and from the bondage of slavery. It's not a coincidence, In this portion of Scripture, that the timing of the Passover is near, and we are about to read the supernatural feeding of the 5,000 men plus women and children. Jesus not only feeds these hungry people spiritual food with His Kingdom teachings, He also concerns Himself with their need for physical nourishment.

Regarding the Passover, from the book of Exodus we read how God sends ten plagues because Pharaoh refuses to "Let My people go!" Before the final plague, the death of the firstborn, God instructs Moses and Aaron to instruct the Israelites to paint their doorposts with the blood of a lamb. That way the spirit of death would pass over their homes and spare the life of their firstborn.

A major event is just around the corner for Jesus. He is fully aware that His time on earth as a human being is coming to an end, where He will give His life willingly and become our sacrificial Lamb (John 1:29) who takes away the sin of the world. (Read John chapters 12–21.)

THE RICHES OF JESUS ON DISPLAY

- Jesus cares about both our spiritual needs and our physical needs.
- He's a spiritual mathematician.

- Jesus uses every opportunity to declare the Good News about Himself.
- He uses the faith of a child to minister to the needs of the multitudes.
- Jesus tests our faith to reveal to us what's in our hearts.

CRACK THE MIRACLE CODE

A willing heart plus courage to give it all away allows spiritual multiplication to take over and produce what's not there physically.

As you read Miracle 20, you will see how supernatural protection belongs to those who are called and committed to Christ.

FAITH ASSIGNMENT

Ask Abba Father what He would have you do for Him today, and be willing to give what you have, even if it means to give it all away and watch God's process of spiritual multiplication take over and produce the provision for the need.

PRAYER OF FAITH

Dear Jesus, this young lad's faith to give what he had to help Your Kingdom work challenges me. Help me to see and hear when You present a need. I desire to be part of Your process of spiritual multiplication.

Questions for Miracle 19: Spiritual Multiplication

1. What is Jesus up to when He says to Philip, *"Where shall we buy bread, that these may eat?"*
2. Did Philip pass this test?
3. Did Andrew pass this test?
4. Who passed this test?
5. What type of faith can Jesus tap into?
6. With Jesus there is no such thing as what?

7. How does the process of spiritual multiplication begin?
8. If given with a pure heart, what goes a long way with Jesus?
9. In John 6:35, what does Jesus declare about Himself?
10. How does Jesus reel in disciples?
11. According to John 1:29, what is Jesus?

MIRACLE 20

RESCUED FROM THE STORMS OF LIFE

Jesus Walks on Water

Let's go for a walk on the water with Jesus, out to where the disciples are in their boat, and find out where this miraculous adventure takes them, and how.

JESUS WALKS ON WATER

Unless otherwise stated, in this work all Scriptures are from the New King James Version of the Bible, but for this portion of Scripture, John 6:16-21, I prefer the way it reads in *The Passion Translation:*

> *After waiting until evening for Jesus to return, the disciples went down to the lake. But as darkness fell, He still hadn't returned, so the disciples got into a boat and headed across the lake to Capernaum. By now a strong wind began to blow and was stirring up the waters. The disciples had rowed about halfway across the lake when all of a sudden they caught sight of Jesus walking on top of the waves, coming toward them. The disciples panicked, but Jesus called out to them, "Don't be afraid. You know who I am." They were relieved to take him in, and the*

moment Jesus stepped into the boat, they were instantly transported to the other side!

WAITING FOR JESUS

> *After waiting until evening for Jesus to return, the disciples went down to the lake. But as darkness fell, He still hadn't returned, so the disciples got into a boat and headed across the lake to Capernaum* (John 6:16-17 TPT).

Have you ever been in a situation where you feel like Jesus is late, so you head out on your own without Him? Sure you have, we all have. But getting ahead of Jesus can lead us right into the midst of a bad storm.

"Wait on the Lord; be of good courage, and He shall strengthen your heart; wait, I say, on the Lord!" (Psalm 27:14). King David often wrote psalms such as this one during times of personal tribulation. And I should note that when he encourages us to wait on the Lord, he is saying to us to wait with faith.

There is a big difference when we wait in faith, instead of frustration. Nothing good comes from frustration. In fact, when we allow ourselves to cross into the territory of frustration, we no longer are in faith, but full of doubt and unbelief. Our mind screams failure, our attitude is crabby, our words are negative and can even become blasphemous, and our actions toward God and others are nasty. Combine all of these acts of frustration and we have disaster.

What does it look like when we wait in faith? For one, our soul (mind and emotions) will be at peace. We might not know how He is going to turn the situation around for us, but we have the assurance that He will. So the next time we find ourselves in the middle of a storm, and we have to wait on Jesus, it would be best, and I believe help speed up the process, if we pray a prayer of faith.

I often talk like this to the Lord,

> *Dear Jesus, I don't know how You are going to bring the answer about, but I know that You will. And by faith, I thank You, Jehovah Rapha, in advance that my every need is met, the bills are paid, there's food on our table, and my family is strong and healthy. I trust in You and Your faithfulness to me, amen.*

STORMS OF LIFE

The storms of life include disastrous weather, sickness and disease, unemployment, financial trouble, relationship issues, persecution for our faith, and the list goes on and on. There's no shortage of troubles on earth. The key is to have Jesus with you as you pass through them.

The prophet Isaiah reminds us in Isaiah 43:2 (AMP), *"When you pass through the waters, I will be with you; and through the rivers, they shall not overflow you. When you walk through the fire, you shall not be scorched, nor will the flame burn you."* Such an outstanding passage of protection and rescue.

Concerning the storms of life that we find ourselves in, no matter how we arrive there, it gives comfort to know that our Redeemer is always with us.

The cause of the storm is found in John 6:18, *"a strong wind began to blow and was stirring up the waters."* And this is where the disciples find themselves in the center of a dangerous storm.

Would they have been in this storm had they exercised patience and waited for Jesus? We don't know. Jesus does tell us in John 16:33 that in this world we will have tribulation, personal difficulties.

FEAR NOT

Contrary to popular belief, the Bible does not say, "Fear not" 365 times. But it is a reoccurring theme throughout the Bible, so we know it is important. With a heart of gratitude, David pens this psalm, *"I sought (inquired of) the Lord and required Him [of necessity and on the authority of His Word], and He heard me, and delivered me from all my fears"* (Psalm 34:4 AMPC). May this psalm become a spiritual song that we sing with a heart full of thanks to our Savior too.

The Holy Spirit pens through the writer in John 6:20 these words of Jesus, *"Don't be afraid. You know who I am."* Wow! This statement Jesus spoke is a sermon onto itself. How many times do we fear something new or different—like when the disciples see Jesus walk on the water toward them?

Supernatural occurrences are astounding and puzzling at first as we try to discern what we are witnessing. And oftentimes the initial reaction is fear. But repeatedly, these calming words are declared over God's people, *"Fear not."* And quite frankly, we should not fear anything because we know who Jesus is.

THREE REASONS WE NEED NOT FEAR

1. Nehemiah 4:14 tells us that our God is great and awesome, and He fights for His people.
2. God never sleeps or slumbers and He preserves us from evil, according to Psalm 121:4,7.
3. Psalm 91 is filled with God's promise to protect us.

JESUS RESCUES THE DISCIPLES

How many times does Jesus rescue the disciples from the storms on the sea? Jesus rescues them on two separate occasions. We can read about the first time in Mark 4:35-41, and then again when Jesus walks on the water to deliver them from the storm in Matthew 14:22-23. I don't know about you, but I always want Jesus to be with me, especially when a storm is brewing in my life.

From prison the apostle Paul writes this letter to the believers in Philippi:

> *Do not fret or have any anxiety about anything, but in every circumstance and in everything, by prayer and petition (definite requests), with thanksgiving, continue to make your wants known to God. And God's peace [shall be yours, that tranquil state of a soul assured of its salvation through Christ, and so fearing nothing from God and being content with its earthly lot of whatever sort that is, that peace] which transcends all understanding shall garrison and mount guard over your hearts and minds in Christ Jesus* (Philippians 4:6-7 AMPC).

Jesus will always come to our rescue.

SEARCH AND RESCUE

This testimony gets more exciting with every word. Not only does Jesus walk on the water to perform a search and rescue for His disciples, but He does something even more astounding. Let's read John 6:21 (TPT) again: *"They were relieved to take him in, and the moment Jesus stepped into the boat, they were instantly transported to the other side!"* Did you catch that? The moment Jesus stepped into the boat, remember He was supernaturally strolling on the water in the midst of the storm, Jesus, along with the disciples and the boat, were instantly translated to the other side of the lake!

What happens to them is described by a Greek word *harpazó* (Strong's G726), which means "to catch (away, up), pluck, pull, take (by force)." The supernatural power of God plucked or pulled (translated) them from one place of danger to an immediate place of safety on earth, supernaturally.

I have experienced this one time in my life with my son, Aaron, as we were about to either have a head-on collision with a semitruck, smashed by a demon-possessed man in another large truck to our right (who was trying to cause our death), or be run off the cliff to our left while driving through Mexico to Guatemala where we were full-time missionaries for 25 years. There was literally no way of escape for us in the natural realm, and by God's grace and mercy He plucked us up and the car and translated us out of the situation and safely out of the death trap the devil had created for us. It happened in an instant. I only remember the horrific possibility that was about to happen, and a flash of the brightest light I have ever seen, then being in a place of safety. I can imagine how the disciples felt about their miracle. I know I spent a long time reliving this miracle in my mind.

From this supernatural intervention in my life, I know without a shadow of a doubt when you are called and committed to Christ, as the disciples were, there is nothing and no one, including the devil, that can take you before your time.

The devil will devise wicked storms against us, but with Jesus we win!

THE RICHES OF JESUS ON DISPLAY

- Jesus spends private time with the Father.
- He loves to go for a stroll on the water.
- Jesus has total authority over the storms of life, and He knows it.
- He knows no fear.
- Jesus protects those called and committed to the cause of Christ.
- He is totally supernatural!

CRACK THE MIRACLE CODE

Supernatural protection belongs to those who are called and committed to the cause of Christ.

When reading Miracle 21, you will come to grips with the fact that when you finally do understand who Jesus really is, your healing is unstoppable.

FAITH ASSIGNMENT

Take this message to heart, spend time like Jesus does with the Father. Ask Holy Spirit to reveal to you His call and purpose for your life. Keep in mind, it is not too late to be about your heavenly Father's business and win people to Jesus.

PRAYER OF FAITH

Dear Jesus, again, Your Word convicts and woos me to the power of Your greatness. I see there is no reason to fear the storms of life, because You are nearby. And I see how capable and willing You are to move Heaven and earth to protect those who are called and committed to Your cause. Holy Spirit, prepare me for this work in these latter days. In Your name, I pray, amen.

Questions for Miracle 20: Rescued from the Storms of Life

1. How are we to wait on the Lord?
2. What is the key to passing through the storms of life?
3. What does John 16:33 tell us we will have?
4. In verse 21, why does Jesus tell the disciples not to be afraid?
5. How many times does Jesus rescue the disciples from the storms on the sea?
6. What does the Greek word *harpazó* mean?
7. Supernatural protection belongs to those who are what?

When reading Numbers [illegible]
[illegible]

[illegible]

[illegible]

[illegible]

Questions on Numbers [illegible] from the [illegible]

1. [illegible] the Land?
2. [illegible]
3. What [illegible]
4. [illegible]
5. How many [illegible]
6. [illegible]
7. [illegible]

PART THREE
MIRACLES 21-30

Dear Holy Spirit, lead us and guide us into the deep and profound revelation of Your Word in such a profound manner that our hearts are forever changed, never to be faithless again. In the precious name of our Lord and Savior Jesus, we believe and pray, amen.

We will begin Part Three, Miracles 21-30 with Miracle 21 and witness the healings of all those who reach out and touch the hem of His garment.

MIRACLE 21
HEALING IN HIS WINGS

Jesus Heals Many Sick as They Touch His Garment

Let's step out of the boat again with Jesus and His disciples and find out what all the latest craze about His garment is about, and why the people rush to touch the hem of His garment.

LET US TOUCH THE TASSEL OF YOUR PRAYER SHAWL

We read in Mark 6:53-56 (TPT) that:

> *They made landfall at Gennesaret and anchored there. The moment they got out of the boat, everyone recognized that it was Jesus, the healer! So they ran throughout the region, telling the people, "Bring all the sick—even those too sick to walk and bring them on mats!" Wherever he went, in the countryside, villages, or towns, they placed the sick on mats in the streets or in public places and begged him, saying, "Just let us touch the tassel of your prayer shawl!" And all who touched him were instantly healed!*

NEWS SPREADS ABOUT THE MIRACLE WORKER

Not only is news spreading about this Miracle Worker, but also the testimonies of the individuals who are healed, and how they are healed. If we hear about a woman with an issue of blood healed by the simple act of faith of touching the hem of His garment (read Miracle 14), I'm sure many more of us would be chasing after Jesus to touch the border of His cloak too, just like the people do here and elsewhere.

HEALED BY TOUCHING THE HEM OF HIS GARMENT

The healing virtue is released through the hem of Jesus when the woman with the issue of blood for 12 years believes in her heart and grabs hold of it in Matthew 9:20-22; Mark 5:25-34; and in Luke 8:43-48. But this is not the only one whose healing manifests from touching the hem of His garment. In Matthew 14:34-36, we discover that when Jesus and His disciples land by boat at Gennesaret and the men of that place recognize Jesus, they send word throughout that land and bring to Him all who are sick. And as many as touch the hem of His garment are healed. In this portion of Scripture (Mark 6:53-56) they beg Him to allow them to touch the tassel of His prayer shawl—when they do, they are healed too.

ANOTHER REASON TO TOUCH THE HEM OF HIS GARMENT

Another reason for people begging to touch the hem of His clothing is because the way in which they dressed back then, and the significance of their articles of clothing, such as in this case.

The woman with the issue of blood, and these people in this portion of Scripture as well, want to touch the hem of His garment. But why? What's so special about the hem of His garment?

To answer this question, we need to search out the definitions of a few words and look at the traditional clothing of the time. Most of us are familiar with the tunic, the undergarment, and the cloak, the outer garment that they wear, but perhaps there are some who do not understand the reason and beliefs about the clothing, and the significance of Jesus' apparel.

THE MEANING BEHIND JESUS' GARMENTS

The meaning behind the typical clothing for a man during the time Jesus walks the earth in human form is misunderstood in today's world, especially by Gentiles. This is why searching for more depth and the meaning of cultural dress leads to a deeper understanding. "In Jewish culture, the hem or fringe of a garment, known as the 'tzitzit,' held religious significance as a reminder of the commandments of God" (Numbers 15:38-39).[1]

> *Speak to the children of Israel: Tell them to* ***make tassels on the corners of their garments*** *throughout their generations, and to put a blue thread in the tassels of the corners. And you shall have the tassel, that you may* ***look upon it and remember all the commandments of the Lord*** *and do them, and that you may not follow the harlotry to which your own heart and your own eyes are inclined* (Numbers 15:38-39).

Because of what we read in Numbers 15:38-39, Jewish men always wore tassels on the corners of their tallit. The tassels were called *tzitzit.* There were to be four tzitzit, one on each corner of your robe, and each tassel[2] was to have a blue cord, representing royalty. The tassels were to be a visual reminder of God and His commands and His authority. The corner of the robe with the tassels on it was called, *kanaf.* This Hebrew word also meant "wing" and *kanaf* is the same word used to describe the word for *wing* in Malachi 4:2. Let's continue.

Because of this prophecy in the book of Malachai 4:2, it is believed that the woman with the issue of blood should have recognized Jesus as the true Messiah. We can't be 100 percent sure of this, but she very well could have. But if she did not recognize Him before she set out into an unruly crowd, then when she met Him face to face, she knew. Here is the prophecy, *"But to you who fear My name The Sun of Righteousness shall arise with healing in His wings; and you shall go out and grow fat like stall-fed calves"* (Malachi 4:2). *Wing* in Hebrew is *kānāp̄,* and means "corner of garment" (Strong's H3671).

As mentioned earlier, news is spreading about this Miracle Worker, and how the people are being healed. Excitement is building about the possibility of this Man being the long-awaited-for Messiah. This woman's healing takes place as she touches the hem, *kanaf* of His garment. For those who keep up with the local news, they can't help but to run all over the territory and gather up their sick, even if they must carry them on their sickbeds, so they can touch the hem of His garment.

So, yes, the garments that Jesus is wearing, along with the many fascinating healings, miracles, signs, and wonders taking place everywhere He goes is opening the eyes of the people about His true deity—the Messiah!

This is why His garment is so special and why the people are rushing to touch it.

PEOPLE RESPOND WHEN THEY RECOGNIZE HIM

Do you notice how excited the people are when they recognize Jesus? They send word or run throughout their entire region to tell the people He's arrived, and invite the people to come, to bring their sick, even carry them on their sickbeds if need be. And the joyous reward they receive as they exhibit their faith in Him. And did you notice throughout this work how they are in a rush to get to Him, but not in a hurry to leave. What a pleasing response this is to Jesus when they recognize Him. And some recognize Him as soon as He arrives.

I pray that you, the one holding this book right now, will have supernatural eyes to see, and ears to hear the message that is being presented to you. That you would return to your first love, Jesus, and tell everyone you know about our wonderful and amazing Lord. And you will shake off spiritual slothfulness and get on the move and bring the people to Jesus in your arena of life. In Jesus' name, I pray this for you, amen.

THE RICHES OF JESUS ON DISPLAY

- Jesus wills for the people to know the truth.
- Healing virtue resonates from His entire being.
- Jesus wants everybody to be healed.

CRACK THE MIRACLE CODE

When we recognize who Jesus really is, our healing is unstoppable.

While you read Miracle 22, you will learn the power behind unrelenting faith.

FAITH ASSIGNMENT

Be on the lookout for Jesus in your life. You should be able to recognize Him immediately because He promises to never leave us. So, make a conscious effort to live life in such a manner that yes, you do see and recognize His Spirit all around you. And may the people in your arena of influence see and recognize Him in you too.

PRAYER OF FAITH

> *Bravo and thanks to You, dear Jesus, for what You have done, are doing, and will continue to do in my life. Holy Spirit, You are a breath of fresh air to me. May I be so on fire for You that everywhere I go Your power is evident and operating in my life for Your glory, amen.*

Questions for Miracle 21: Healing in His Wings

1. In Miracle 21 how are the people healed?
2. What is the inner garment Jesus wore called?
3. What is the outer garment Jesus wore called?
4. In Hebrew what does *kānāp̄* mean?
5. What are the tassels on the *tallit* called?
6. What were people beginning to recognize about Jesus by His garments and the healings, miracles, signs, and wonders?

MIRACLE 22
UNRELENTING FAITH

Jesus Heals a Gentile Woman's Demon-Possessed Daughter

We will now travel with Jesus into Tyre and Sidon, two cities of Lebanon, a non-Jewish region where we read in this portion of God's Word that Jesus delivers a Gentile woman's daughter. But more is happening here than the young girl's liberation from demon possession. Let's read on to find out more.

> *Then Jesus went out from there and departed to the region of Tyre and Sidon. And behold, a woman of Canaan came from that region and cried out to Him, saying, "Have mercy on me, O Lord, Son of David! My daughter is severely demon-possessed."*
>
> *But He answered her not a word.*
>
> *And His disciples came and urged Him, saying, "Send her away, for she cries out after us."*
>
> *But He answered and said, "I was not sent except to the lost sheep of the house of Israel."*
>
> *Then she came and worshiped Him, saying, "Lord, help me!"*
>
> *But He answered and said, "It is not good to take the children's bread and throw it to the little dogs."*
>
> *And she said, "Yes, Lord, yet even the little dogs eat the crumbs which fall from their masters' table."*

Then Jesus answered and said to her, "O woman, great is your faith! Let it be to you as you desire."

And her daughter was healed from that very hour (Matthew 15:21-28).

Let's begin. Jesus is traveling in a non-Jewish region. My question to you concerning this journey, "Is this by mistake or does He have a purpose?" I believe the latter, He has a reason for being here.

We read, *"a woman of Canaan,"* a Canaanite refers to a non-Jewish person who lives in Canaan. This non-Jewish woman cries out to Jesus, *"Have mercy on me, O Lord, Son of David!"* As discussed previously in this work (see Miracle 16), this title, "Son of David," alludes to the facts about Jesus' earthly heritage. She gives recognition to Jesus as the fulfillment of Old Testament prophecies and declares His identity as the Messiah.

Already we see something that many tend to overlook, this woman believes in her heart that Jesus is the *"Son of David,"* and she publicly acknowledges His deity. She also takes another step and humbles herself before Him and calls Jesus, *"Lord"* and worships Him. You cannot publicly fling yourself at the feet of Jesus and call Him Lord unless You believe He is the Anointed One. And what does the Holy Bible instruct us about salvation?

Luke, who authors the books of Luke and Acts, writes to the lovers of God in Acts 2:21, *"And it shall come to pass that whoever calls on the name of the Lord shall be saved."*

What is this Canaanite woman doing? She is calling on the name of the Lord, *"Son of David."* And she is calling on the only One who can help her daughter, *"Have mercy on me!"* This is an amazing oversight of many—Jesus is spiritually healing this woman, remaining silent, and granting her mercy, giving her time to call upon His name for salvation. And it does not matter to Him that she is a Gentile.

Oh, but you think to yourself, *Well, what do you have to say about Jesus' response to His disciples' request to send her away?* Plenty.

BUT THEY'RE NOT LIKE US

We might not care for the type of people who are calling out to Christ. We might feel uncomfortable about the way they look, their present lifestyle, and a host of other reasons. But this I know, Jesus came to save the Lost. The beloved apostle John pens in John 3:17 the reason our Lord came to this world, *"For God did not send His Son into the world to condemn the world, but that the world through Him might be saved."* The disciples did not care for this woman because she was a Gentile and a woman. She did not live by the Jewish customs. She was not like one of them. They want Jesus to send her away.

We must remind ourselves that just as it was back then, we too are living amid a mighty revival. The hour is late, time is short, and the Lost are many, but great is His love, and His mercy abounds to all who will call upon His name.

> *Dear Lord Jesus, may we take care not to send people away because they are not like us, but may we operate with the wisdom of Your grace and remember You came to save all people from the clutches of the devil. In Your name, I pray, amen.*

THE JEW VERSUS THE GENTILE DEBATE

What is happening in Matthew 15:24-27?

> *But He answered and said, "I was not sent except to the lost sheep of the house of Israel." Then she came and worshiped Him, saying, "Lord, help me!" But He answered and said, "It is not good to take the children's bread and throw it to the little dogs." And she said, "Yes, Lord, yet even the little dogs eat the crumbs which fall from their masters' table."*

With Jesus it is always "boots on the ground" training. He uses real-life situations to teach about the policy of His grace and mercy and to institute everlasting change. Part of His mission is to extend the bridge of salvation to the Gentile population.

Jesus allows all sides to be heard. He hears the disciples say, "Send the Canaanite woman away," and the Gentile woman's plea, "Lord, have mercy on me!"

This woman is fully aware of their differences, and yet a boldness arises within her to pursue the loving nature of Jesus on behalf of her daughter. And she is not willing to allow their differences to stand in the way.

It is not the intent of Jesus to deny her request, but to allow this much-needed conversation. It's time to allow the Gentiles into the family of God. But His disciples who will carry on His work need to see and hear the Father's heart for the Lost.

She acknowledges that the race war between the Jews and the Gentiles is real. And in this situation, she, the Gentile is the little dog, and the Jews are the children of God. But this is not going to stop her from receiving crumbs from her Master's table. Her faith in the Messiah is fully engaged.

And it's her faith in the justice of Jesus that activates His mercy for her daughter and teaches the disciples exactly what Jesus needs them to understand.

And for those of us that need clarity in today's world. He is not calling the Gentiles to be Jews, or the Jews to be Gentiles, but to become His disciples—lovers and followers of Him.

God's Holy Word is clear, *"There is neither Jew nor Gentile, neither slave nor free, nor is there male and female, for you are all one in Christ Jesus"* (Galatians 3:28 NIV).

THE RESULTS OF UNRELENTING FAITH

This woman's unrelenting faith in Jesus highlights the results of strong faith. In Matthew 15:28, from *The Passion Translation*, Jesus has this to say to her about it: "'*Dear woman, your faith is strong! What you desire will be done for you.' And at that very moment, her daughter was instantly set free from demonic torment."*

This woman must fight off incorrect religious theology and cultural bias. She must contend for her daughter's freedom from the devil's torment—and not allow anyone or anything to stop her from receiving what Jesus freely gives.

WHAT DO YOU DO?

You might find yourself facing incorrect religious doctrine from people in authority. Perhaps they don't believe Jesus heals today, or that disease is from God, or what you desire from the Lord is impossible. What do you do?

- Stay focused on the healing promises of God.
- Be bold and unrelenting in your faith.

- Don't allow the devil to boss you around.
- And sometimes, you need to find a new place of worship where people *do* believe and practice God's supernatural healing power.

THE RICHES OF JESUS ON DISPLAY

- Jesus is willing to confront the hard issues between people.
- His justice.
- Jesus' desire to draw all people to Himself.

CRACK THE MIRACLE CODE

Unrelenting faith is strong and bold, and it delivers.

While you read Miracle 23, you will learn to activate God's creative power and words of faith to produce miracles.

FAITH ASSIGNMENT

Examine your situation according to the Word of God concerning healing and deliverance. Write down the opposition rising against your desire for healing. In the Bible, find 1-3 promises of God concerning healing to stand on in times of opposition. Choose to stand on God's healing promise; and no matter how long it takes, never give up. The miraculous results of strong faith are worth the fight.

PRAYER OF FAITH

Dear Holy Spirit, as always, Your Word continues to challenge my faith. Sometimes I feel a tinge of pain in my spirit due to Your conviction, but I desire to press through the challenges and move forward into the territory of strong faith. I thank You for Your help in this. In Your name, dear Jesus, I pray, amen.

Questions for Miracle 22: Unrelenting Faith

1. What is a Canaanite?

2. When this woman calls out to Jesus, *"Son of David,"* what is she recognizing?
3. What is something that many tend to overlook with this woman's testimony?
4. What is the next step she takes?
5. What is Jesus doing for this woman?
6. Does it matter to Jesus that this woman is not a Jew?
7. Who did Jesus come to save?
8. In this situation, why does Jesus use real-life situations?
9. In this situation, what is part of His mission?
10. What is this woman not willing to do?
11. In verse 26 who are the dogs?
12. Who are the children of God in verse 26?
13. Is Jesus calling the Gentiles to be Jews, or the Jews to be Gentiles?
14. What is He calling us to be?
15. What is the result of this woman's strong faith?

MIRACLE 23
SPITTLE AND A COMMAND OF FAITH

Jesus Heals a Deaf and Mute Man

Join Jesus as He travels down to the Sea of Galilee and into the region of Decapolis. This region is made up of ten cities—a melting pot of people groups and cultures in this area. And this tad bit of information is needed to understand this healing miracle. This is where the people present Jesus with a deaf and mute man and beg the Messiah to heal him. Jesus does heal him, but in a most unusual way. Together, we will discover the reason for this creative way for healing this man's lame tongue and unhearing ears.

> *Then Jesus left the vicinity of Tyre and went through Sidon, down to the Sea of Galilee and into the region of the Decapolis. There some people brought to him a man who was deaf and could hardly talk, and they begged Jesus to place his hand on him.*
>
> *After he took him aside, away from the crowd, Jesus put his fingers into the man's ears. Then he spit and touched the man's tongue. He looked up to heaven and with a deep sigh said to him, "Ephphatha!" (which means "Be opened!"). At this, the man's ears were opened, his tongue was loosened and he began to speak plainly.*
>
> *Jesus commanded them not to tell anyone. But the more he did so, the more they kept talking about it. People were overwhelmed with*

amazement. "He has done everything well," they said. "He even makes the deaf hear and the mute speak" (Mark 7:31-37 NIV).

FAITH IN ACTION

The first action of faith we see is when the people bring the deaf and mute man to Jesus to make a request for healing. And they are very specific with what they want Him to do for this man. They want Jesus to place His hands on the man; they beg Him to do so.

BE SPECIFIC WITH YOUR REQUEST AND BELIEVE

We read in verse 32, *"they begged Jesus to place his hand on him."* I believe when we present a request to Jesus that we need to be specific. I was taught in my earlier days of my newfound faith that if we want the dog, don't call the cat. In other words, be specific with your request. And these people are being specific; they present this man to Jesus and ask Him to lay His hands on him. And they are not only specific in their request, but they also believe this man will be healed from deafness and a mute tongue.

Matthew 21:22 (AMPC) declares about praying and asking in faith this way: *"And whatever you ask for in prayer, having faith and [really] believing, you will receive."* The same verse in *The Passion Translation* reads as follows, *"Everything you pray for with the fullness of faith you will receive!"* And this Scripture in Tree of Life version says it this way, *"And whatever you ask in prayer, trusting, you shall receive."*

I teach my students to read a specific verse from three different Bible versions in hopes that they will stumble upon unexpected revelation. (See Miracle 2.) In these various versions of Matthew 21:22, it's clear we are to have faith and really believe, we are to pray with the fullness of faith, and we are to trust that we receive what we ask for. I believe this is the testimony of the people that present the deaf and mute man to Jesus in Mark 7:31-37—with the fullness of faith, they really believe and trust this man will be healed.

TAKE HIM ASIDE AND AWAY FROM THE PEOPLE

There are times while ministering to someone when you will discern that the individual needs to be away from others, that privacy is needed. Why do some individuals need privacy? In my experience with healing, they need a place where they feel safe and secure, away from the pressure of ridicule and shame from others.

A specific girl comes to mind from Northern Tanzania. She lives in a harsh community where ridicule is common for someone who is different from the rest. How is she different? She's deaf, has a voice but due to deafness has difficulty speaking, like the man we read about in this portion of Scripture.

After I minister the healing word, I call the sick forward. A mother presents this teenage girl to me, but I can readily see that this young girl is cloaked with shame and feels embarrassed to be surrounded by all the others in attendance, and she is not able to receive in this situation. For her to receive her miracle, I need to create the right atmosphere where she feels safe and secure.

ANOTHER REASON WHY PEOPLE NEED PRIVACY

As Jesus does with Jairus's daughter (see Miracle 15), He chases the people out of this girl's home. Why? Because the doubt and unbelief of the mourners will prevent a miracle from happening.

This deaf teenage girl is not only under the pressure of shame and ridicule of the community, but she has another challenge, a mother who wants to believe but struggles to do so. And the whole while is spewing out doubt and unbelief. If not stopped, negative words will prevent the manifestation of the miracle.

CHANGE THE ATMOSPHERE

I am in a public meeting and am not able to make the people surrounding us leave, so I must take her out of the situation. And so not to lose the expectancy of the people, I must move quickly. So with haste I take her outside the doorway, away from the people, and away from her mother's negative words. This girl feels safe and secure, and the atmosphere is now ripe for healing. I place my hands over her ears and renounce the spirit of deafness; I release the healing power of Jesus to flow into her ears and command them to be open. And immediately she can hear. I present her to her mom and the first word she speaks is *"Mama."*

JESUS USES SPIT TO HEAL

Jesus puts His fingers into the man's deaf ears, and then He does something unique, He spits and touches the man's tongue with His spittle.

If you're anything like me, you might wonder why Jesus uses spit to heal this man's lame tongue. I've been taught when I figure out a problem to start with the obvious and then work my way to the more complicated. So, we will begin with the obvious first, the tongue is an organ of speech. Like the rest of the body, its makeup is mainly water. Saliva is crucial for lubricating the vocal cords, making it easier to speak smoothly. But if you don't use your vocal cords, I think you would have a dry throat. So perhaps the man's vocal cords need a little spittle to jump-start them.

But like I said, start with the obvious and then work your way to the more complicated. And yes, there is something a bit more complex with this healing. And if you were not raised in the Jewish culture, like me you may not know about a specific belief unless someone tells you, or you teach yourself. So, I share with you what I know concerning their belief about spittle.

From *The Passion Translation* of the New Testament, in footnote b for Mark 7:33 it says: "The saliva of firstborn sons in the Jewish culture of Jesus' time was considered to have power to heal infirmities." You see, there is always a reason for what Jesus does. This is the belief of the people, and He is the firstborn Son of God, and He does possess power to heal, and He works with their faith as He does with our faith as well.

THE POWER OF SPEECH

After Jesus places a little spittle on the man's tongue, He then uses the power of speech and looks up to Heaven and with a deep sigh says to the man, *"Ephphatha!" (which means "Be opened!")* and this man's healing manifests.

This extraordinary miracle and the creative methods used during this man's healing are beyond mere words. The power behind these words is faith and the wisdom to use words properly. With a command of faith, *"Ephphatha!"* his ears are recreated, healed and hear. And the first words this man hears are words of faith, spoken by His Messiah. What a beautiful sound he hears!

DON'T TELL ANYONE!

We read in Mark 7:36, *"Jesus commanded them not to tell anyone. But the more he did so, the more they kept talking about it."* I personally find it amusing that He restores someone's ability to speak and must tell the crowds of people not to speak about it. But perhaps, you don't share my sentiments and find it confusing. Why does He command this of them? Some believe it is because He wants them to focus on the greatest miracle—salvation, not on these physical miracles. I get what they are saying, but I am not sure I can agree fully with this belief.

Yes, I believe that believing and receiving Jesus as our Savior is the best miracle that can ever happen to us, but His will is to heal and to make us whole, spiritually, mentally and emotionally and physically too.

Perhaps, as a healing evangelist, I really do see the eternal value of someone who is possessed by devils set free, or someone who is emotionally distraught from trauma at peace by an inward healing of the soul, or the many salvations produced by dramatic physical healings.

Throughout the Gospels, Jesus wins the Lost via healings, miracles, signs, and wonders, and commands us in the Great Commission to do the same. So I do not believe that Jesus is downplaying the importance of these miracles, but that He has a great number of people to reach in a short amount of time, and His popularity as "The Healer" makes it difficult to maneuver among large crowds in the cities. He needs to move outside of heavily populated areas; but even still, the large crowds follow.

THE RICHES OF JESUS ON DISPLAY

- Jesus works with faith.
- He is knowledgeable and understands the cultural beliefs of those with whom He interacts.
- Jesus is okay with doing the unusual to produce a miracle.
- He's wise with His use of words.

CRACK THE MIRACLE CODE

God's creative power and faith-filled words produce creative miracles.

As you read Miracle 24, you will learn how to tap into the empowerment of the Lord's compassion to meet your needs abundantly.

FAITH ASSIGNMENT

Be bold and brave, expect a miracle and offer to minister to someone who has an issue of deafness or speech problem in the name of Jesus.

PRAYER OF FAITH

I sense it is appropriate to include a prayer of faith for those who struggle with some form of deafness. If this is you, or your loved one, lay your hand upon your ears and repeat this aloud over yourself:

> *In Jesus' name, I renounce this curse of deafness. I release and receive the healing power of my Lord Jesus into my ears. I command my ears to be recreated, open, and to clearly hear both high and low sounds. I put my faith in action, I listen, and I hear for the glory of Jesus, amen.*

And for those who struggle with speech problems, here is a prayer of faith for you or for your loved one.

> *In the name of Jesus, I renounce this speech problem. I command this organ of speech to be loosed, the brain, and tongue to all be healed, made whole and to work in harmony for the glory of my Lord and the ability to speak with clarity come forth. I put my faith in action and speak the name of Jesus aloud, amen.*

Questions for Miracle 23: Spittle and a Command of Faith

1. What is the first action of faith we see in this miracle?
2. What are we to be with our request to Jesus?
3. What do some people need when ministering to them?
4. What effect can negative words have if not halted?
5. How does Jesus heal this man from deafness?
6. How does Jesus heal this man from being mute?
7. What does the Jewish culture believe about saliva?

8. What one word does Jesus speak over this deaf man? And what does this word mean?
9. After Jesus heals the mute man, what does He command the crowd to do?
10. Is Jesus is downplaying the importance of these miracles by telling them not to tell anyone?
11. What problem is Jesus facing as "The Healer"?

MIRACLE 24
THE EMPOWERMENT OF COMPASSION

Jesus Feeds 4,000 Plus Women and Children

Jesus continues to disciple His followers about how to fulfill their calling and assignments God's way. And this life lesson is about how to minister to the multitude of 4,000 men, plus women and children, by activating the empowerment of compassion, and supernaturally feed all with just seven loaves of bread and a few fish. This is a powerful message that defies human reasoning.

> *Now Jesus called His disciples to Himself and said, "I have compassion on the multitude, because they have now continued with Me three days and have nothing to eat. And I do not want to send them away hungry, lest they faint on the way." Then His disciples said to Him, "Where could we get enough bread in the wilderness to fill such a great multitude?" Jesus said to them, "How many loaves do you have?" And they said, "Seven, and a few little fish." So He commanded the multitude to sit down on the ground. And He took the seven loaves and the fish and gave thanks, broke them and gave them to His disciples; and the disciples gave to the multitude. So they all ate and were filled, and they took up seven large baskets full of the fragments that were left. Now those who ate were four thousand men,*

besides women and children. And He sent away the multitude, got into the boat, and came to the region of Magdala (Matthew 15:32-39).

JESUS' CALLING

The opening Scripture says that *"Jesus called His disciples to Himself."* This word *call* in Greek is *proskaleō,* and it means "to call or to bid someone into God's service" (Strong's G4341). I find it interesting that with His business Partner, Father God, that they still use similar ways to call and train us for His service.

For example, I am called by Jesus into the fivefold ministry as a prophetess and healing evangelist to teach, preach, and write about His healing Word, to heal the sick, and to be a spiritual mother to many. Therefore, I had been given specific assignments by God to fulfill this calling such as minister at healing events, record teaching television and internet programs, write books about supernatural healing, and raise up a children's home in Guatemala for the fatherless.

And just like the disciples, these assignments given to fulfill the calling have a common purpose—to demonstrate the compassion of Jesus to the multitudes of lost people.

THE COMPASSION OF JESUS

In this same passage of Scripture, Jesus tells the disciples, *"I have compassion on the multitude."* Everything Jesus says or does, whether it appears to be tender or frank, flows from a heart of compassion for the multitude. And in this situation, Jesus is training His disciples how to operate in this supernatural empowerment—compassion.

Compassion is not something you can fake. You either have it or you don't. You may be able to pretend to have it for a while, but you will either burn out, or your phoniness will be discovered. If you lack compassion, you can do something about it, to gain it. How can we gain compassion? By entering personal fellowship with Jesus, like we see with the disciples:

1. *They travel with Jesus.* What does this look like for us? Jesus becomes a lifestyle, not just a religious activity we do on Sunday morning. We become God-conscious, being fully aware that

everywhere we go, He goes with us. He is very clear in His Word, *"Be strong and courageous. Do not be afraid or terrified because of them, for the Lord your God goes with you; he will never leave you nor forsake you"* (Deuteronomy 31:6 NIV).

2. *They fellowship with Him.* Notice as we read through the four Gospels that there are twelve disciples, and they all communicate with Jesus, but there are three out of the twelve—Peter, James, and John—who go beyond mere communication and enter His inner circle of fellowship. They have access to unique opportunities that the others miss out on, such as the transfiguration of Jesus where they witness Jesus in His glory and is seen with Moses (the Law), and Elijah (the Prophets), which is recorded in Matthew 17:1-8, Mark 9:2-13, Luke 9:28-36.

To sum this up, if we will make Jesus a way of life, not a religious act, and go beyond basic communication to press in to really know Him and enter His inner circle of fellowship, this characteristic of His, compassion, will eventually rub off on us. Why? Proverbs 13:20 (TLV) reads like this, *"He who walks with wise men is wise, but a companion of fools suffers harm."* You naturally become like the friends you choose to keep.

JESUS SEES PEOPLE'S NEEDS

Jesus says to the disciples, *"they have now continued with Me three days and have nothing to eat. And I do not want to send them away hungry, lest they faint on the way"* (Matthew 15:32). Jesus knows the people are hungry, their bodies need nourishment, and He does not want to send them away hungry. The people do not ask Jesus to feed them, perhaps some are hopeful for a meal, but no one asks for food. Jesus is the One who speaks up about the situation and tells the disciples that they need to feed the multitude.

JESUS WANTS TO MEET OUR NEEDS

Sometimes we believe falsely that our need is not important enough for God to meet. And that's right where the devil wants us, in doubt about God's love and care for us. But just as Jesus wants to bless the multitude with a meal, He wants to meet our needs too.

A FAITH RESPONSE

The disciples, knowing what He wants before He has a chance to speak it out, reply to Him with a negative response, *"Where could we get enough bread in the wilderness to fill such a great multitude?"* After all they have witnessed, and they ask Jesus, "Where?" He ignores their faithless response with a faith-filled one instead, and says, *"How many loaves do you have?"* They say that there are seven loaves and a few fish. So Jesus takes them and gives thanks.

In the natural His response seems a little bit crazy, perhaps even a little out of touch with reality. But when it comes to matters of faith, we do not use human reasoning or the realm of our five senses. As important as these are, they hinder the activation of God's power in our lives.

The following Scriptures reveal secrets to walking in the supernatural power and provision of God.

Hebrews 11:6 tells us that without faith it is impossible to please Him. Matthew 21:22 says that whatever we ask in prayer, we will receive, if we have faith. And we read in Hebrews 11:1 that faith is the assurance of things hoped for, the conviction or the evidence of things not seen. And in Mark 11:22 Jesus instructs us to have faith in God.

Whatever the situation may be, the solution is faith directed in the right way. Faith in the promises of God supernaturally produce what we lack in the natural, in this case, food for the multitude.

SUPERNATURAL ORDER OF GIVING AND RECEIVING

The disciples release what they have to Jesus, which to feed a hungry crowd is not much. But glory to God, He can take our little and transform it into a lot. And what does Jesus do next? He gives thanks to the Father. Notice He is not begging God to bless and multiply it. He knows He has authority over lack. And He will not allow a lack of provision to hinder His desire to feed this crowd.

Then He gives it to the disciples, and these faithful followers of His give what they receive to the hungry multitude, and supernaturally by the order of giving and receiving, all are fed and there are even leftovers. And not just a random number of leftovers. They give seven loaves of bread and a few fish for this faith project, and they reap seven large baskets of fragments. The number seven means perfect or complete. And when I read this, I shout, *"Hal-*

lelujah!" Jesus fed the multitude of 4,000 men plus women and children not just a few nibbles of bread and fish, but a complete meal. Now that they are fed and full, He can send them away.

THE RICHES OF JESUS ON DISPLAY

- Jesus is full of compassion.
- He sees our needs,
- And wants to meet those needs.
- Jesus does not allow the faithlessness of others to control Him,
- Nor does He allow the power of lack to rule over Him.
- Jesus has faith to meet the needs of all people.

CRACK THE MIRACLE CODE

Tap into the empowerment of the Lord's compassion to meet your needs abundantly.

When you read Miracle 25, you will learn how His compassion breaks down the walls of self-preservation and enables the powers of hope and faith to arise for miracles.

FAITH ASSIGNMENT

Take this faith assignment prayer to the Lord, pray on it, write down what you see, hear, or sense Jesus is speaking to you, and act on it. Pray:

> *I see the importance of understanding my God-given calling and assignments. Show me, Holy Spirit, what my life assignment is, whether it be part of the fivefold ministry, or ministry that is not a pulpit ministry, but ministering to those in my arena of daily influence, I desire to demonstrate Your compassion to the lost people on earth, amen.*

PRAYER OF FAITH

Dear Jesus, I see how You faithfully reveal Your concern for the multitudes of lost people. How deep Your compassion runs to meet not just the spiritual need, although it is most important, but You see and care for our basic needs as well. Teach me to see the needs of those around me and how to operate by the power of faith to meet those needs. I offer You what I have and ask You to take it and use it to help win the multitudes over to Your everlasting love. In Your name I pray, amen.

Questions for Miracle 24: The Empowerment of Compassion

1. What does the word *call* in verse 32 in the Greek mean?
2. What is the Greek word for *call?*
3. About how many people does Jesus feed in this miracle?
4. What are our calling and assignments to demonstrate?
5. When it comes to matters of faith, what are two things we do not use?
6. Faith in the promises of God supernaturally produce what?
7. What can He take and do with our little?
8. Does Jesus beg or ask God to bless and multiply the seven loaves and the few fish?
9. What does Jesus have authority over?
10. What do they reap as they give seven loaves of bread and a few fish?
11. What does number seven mean?
12. What does Jesus feed the people, if not a few nibbles?

MIRACLE 25
RESTORED AND CLEARLY SEES

Jesus Heals a Blind Man at Bethsaida

As Jesus enters the small fishing town of Bethsaida, the birthplace of three of His disciples—Philip, Peter, and Andrew—and the site of numerous recorded miracles, Jesus is presented with a blind man, whom this miracle is about. We will see the progression of this man's miracle from total blindness, to seeing men like trees walking, to complete restoration and being able to see everyone clearly. Let's begin by reading our text in Mark 8:22-26:

> *Then He came to Bethsaida; and they brought a blind man to Him, and begged Him to touch him. So He took the blind man by the hand and led him out of the town. And when He had spit on his eyes and put His hands on him, He asked him if he saw anything. And he looked up and said, "I see men like trees, walking." Then He put His hands on his eyes again and made him look up. And he was restored and saw everyone clearly. Then He sent him away to his house, saying, "Neither go into the town, nor tell anyone in the town."*

FISHER OF MEN

Bethsaida in Hebrew means the "House of Fishermen," and as we read about Jesus' miracles, we see this is where Jesus and His disciples return to often. It is located on the shores of the Sea of Galilee. There is a hidden message in plain sight if we are willing to connect the dots. And it ties in beautifully with the restoration of this blind man's sight.

THE CALL

Let's read about the call from Jesus to Peter, the Rock, and Andrew, the Brave, to become fishers of people in Matthew 4:18-20 from *The Passion Translation* of the Bible:

> *As he was walking by the shore of Lake Galilee, Jesus noticed two fishermen who were brothers. One was nicknamed Keefa (later called Peter), and the other was Andrew, his brother. Watching as they were casting their nets into the water, Jesus called out to them and said, "Come and follow me, and I will transform you into men who catch people for God." Immediately they dropped their nets and left everything behind to follow Jesus.*

Notice the way in which they respond, *"Immediately."* They drop their nets and leave everything behind. There is a witness in their spirit that Jesus is God in the flesh, the Anointed One, and the cherished Messiah standing before them. And they drop everything and immediately follow Him.

And the next day when Jesus calls Philip, another fisherman and native to Bethsaida in John 1:43-51 (TPT), He says to him, *"Come and follow me."* Philip goes straightaway and finds his friend, Nathanel (Bartholomew), to share the good news in verse 45. *"We found him! We've found the One we've been waiting for! It's Jesus, the son of Joseph from Nazareth! He's the One whom Moses and the prophets prophesied would come!"*

God calls ordinary people to do extraordinary feats for Him, as He is doing with these men. They are not the people you would expect God to call. They are not leaders and teachers in the synagogue, nor are they trained to do so; they are fishermen. When Jesus meets them, they are probably sweaty and smelly, with dirt under their fingernails. Their hands and feet, arms and legs most likely are covered with small cuts and abrasions from handling fish, nets, ropes, hooks, and knives. They probably do not meet the standards of the synagogue with fancy robes, sashes, tassels, and turbans. But obviously these things are not important to fulfilling the most important positions in the Church, and this is what Jesus is doing. He is not only calling but entrusting them to the most important work, the Kingdom of God and its inhabitants.

God is not interviewing for perfect-looking people with the latest fashion, nor is He calling for people with a sinless past, for all have sinned and fallen short of the glory of God (Romans 3:23). He is calling out to the ordinary lover and follower of Jesus. The one whose heart is sold out for Jesus and makes serving Him their top priority. Those who will not make lame excuses as to why they can't drop it all and follow Him and catch people for God.

PRIORITIES AND OBEDIENCE

In Matthew 4:18-22 we read about His call to Peter, Andrew, and Philip. These common, everyday fishermen are being called to the mission field with Jesus, not because they have nothing better to do with their time. Fishing is their business, it's their livelihood. Other people are dependent on their earnings. This calling comes at a high price—they left *all* to follow Him.

All means everything familiar to you, everything that gives you comfort. Willingness to leave behind sudden and amazing opportunities. Obedience to not knowing when or if you will see your loved ones back home again. With trust in your pocket and faith in your heart that you see eye to eye with the King of kings and the Lord of lords that together you will catch people for God.

This is what these three fishermen from Bethsaida choose to do, to make Jesus their top priority and obey His call.

BETHSAIDA IS STRONGLY REBUKED

We do not know the exact time frame between Matthew 4:18-22, where the first disciples were called, to Matthew 11:20-24, where the multiplication of the Kingdom of God is being discussed. Let's read from Matthew 11:20-24 where Jesus gives a very strong and stern rebuke to Bethsaida and learn why He rebukes them.

Then He began to rebuke the cities in which most of His mighty works had been done, because they did not repent: "Woe to you, Chorazin! Woe to you, Bethsaida! For if the mighty works which were done in you had been done in Tyre and Sidon, they would have repented long ago in sackcloth and ashes. But I say to you, it will be more tolerable for Tyre and Sidon in the day of judgment than for you. And you, Capernaum, who are exalted to heaven, will be brought down to Hades; for if the mighty works which were done in you had been done in Sodom, it would have remained until this day. But I say to you that it shall be more tolerable for the land of Sodom in the day of judgment than for you."

Bethsaida is being evangelized with powerful teachings, with healings, miracles, signs, and wonders following, and yet they reject the Gospel and choose to remain spiritually blind. This is why the restoration of this blind man's sight is so relevant to this place.

BLIND MAN'S HEALING

In Mark 8:22-23, we read about this blind man's healing: *"Then He came to Bethsaida; and they brought a blind man to Him, and begged Him to touch him. So He took the blind man by the hand and led him out of the town. And when He had spit on his eyes and put His hands on him, He asked him if he saw anything."*

First, it says they begged Him. One would think with such amazing miracles that have already taken place in this land they would not still be begging but thanking Him in advance for healing this man. After all, everyone He was allowed to minister to was healed. But clearly, they are not to this point in their faith yet.

Jesus takes the blind man by the hand and walks him out from among these hard-hearted people. Remember, I taught you in Miracle 15 that we must create and guard the atmosphere of faith for miracles. And with compassion, Jesus creates this atmosphere for this man. He could ask someone else to lead him, but no, Jesus is on a mission, and He willfully leads the man.

I believe while compassion is flooding this man's soul, so too is honor. Why do I believe this? During this time, the blind are treated as outcasts and are often banned to outside the town limits. They are devalued and lack opportunities to work and support themselves, so many are forced into a life of begging for daily existence. So, Jesus escorting him by the hand speaks volumes to this man. For one, he is not an outcast to Jesus, nor is he a burden to Him. These physical acts of honor release inner healing to the man who is accustomed to dishonor. Jesus' actions also break down the walls of self-preservation, which enables hope to build and faith to arise within this broken man.

And I know something else about healers, we have healing in our hands. Along with inner healing, transforming this man's mind and emotions by the virtues of compassion and honor, physical healing power if not already transferring into this man, is at least being felt.

And there's something more, you cannot come into direct contact with Jesus and not be healed, unless you reject His healing power and say, "No" to Him. But as we can see, this man is not saying, "No," he's saying, "Yes, heal me!"

THE POWER OF SPITTLE

I speak of the power of spittle in Miracle 23 when Jesus spits into His hand and touches a man's lame tongue to heal it. I give you a natural reason and a spiritual reason why spittle is used in that creative miracle. And the same reasons apply with this miracle. In this miracle we are dealing with the man's eye. The makeup of human eyes is 98 percent water, so naturally this creative miracle needs water to recreate eyeballs. Then we examine the miracle-working power of faith and that the Jewish people believe that "The saliva of firstborn sons in the Jewish culture of Jesus' time was considered to have power to heal infirmities." Therefore, the people have the faith to receive this way.

SIGHT IS RESTORED CLEARLY THE SECOND TIME

After Jesus spits on the man's eyes and puts His hands on him, He asks the man if he sees anything. He replies, *"I see men like trees, walking."* So Jesus places His hands on the man again and tells him to look up. The man does what Jesus tells him to do, and his sight is restored, he sees everyone clearly.

This healing is not only creative, but it's interesting and forces us to take a second look to understand it.

Does Jesus make a mistake and need to try again? No, I don't believe so. I simply believe that the full manifestation of healing is still in the making. Here we have the original Creator of the eye making an adjustment, this is not failure, it's creating.

NATURAL AND SPIRITUAL RESTORATION

An interesting fact about this healing has to do with the biblical meaning of this word *eye*. According to the footnote for Mark 8:23 (TPT), this is not the common word for "eyes." The Greek word *omma* can refer to both physical and spiritual sight. According to verse 25, the man is restored and sees everyone clearly. This is an odd way to state that his eyes are healed and can see clearly, unless we marry the natural with the spiritual implications in this healing testimony.

Jesus meets a man who is blind in the natural, in a place called Bethsaida, which is rebuked for being spiritually blind. Jesus, being holistic in His approach to healing, not only heals this man from physical blindness, but heals his soul (mind and emotions), as well as heals him spiritually. And yes, he now is restored and can see clearly both physically and spiritually.

THE RICHES OF JESUS ON DISPLAY

- Jesus is willing to work with people individually.
- He understands the importance of creating and guarding an atmosphere of faith.
- Jesus is holistic in His approach to healing.

CRACK THE MIRACLE CODE

Break down the walls of self-preservation with Jesus' compassion and enable faith to arise for your miracle.

As you read Miracle 26, take note and learn to see what Jesus sees that others do not, the Kingdom of God.

FAITH ASSIGNMENT

Examine the condition of your spiritual heart, and ask yourself, *Am I being dishonored and devalued by others? Or am I deliberately dishonoring and devaluing others? If so, am I willing to extend forgiveness to those who hurt me? Or ask those whom I hurt to forgive me?* Pray in faith for God's grace and ability to do what you need to do.

PRAYER OF FAITH

> *Dear Jesus, I ask for Your ability to see with spiritual eyes those who have been dishonored and devalued in this life. Show me how to release this healing power of compassion and honor to build hope so their faith can rise for their miracle. In Your name I pray, amen.*

Questions for Miracle 25: Restored and Clearly Sees

1. In Hebrew, what does *Bethsaida* mean?
2. When Jesus calls Peter and Andrew, how do they drop their nets and leave everything behind?
3. What does Philip do when Jesus calls him?
4. What does Philip say to Nathanel (Bartholomew)?
5. Jesus is doing something more than calling these men to follow Him, what is it?
6. What do these three fishermen from Bethsaida choose to do?
7. What two things do the people of Bethsaida choose to do?
8. What does Jesus do with Bethsaida?
9. What type of atmosphere does Jesus create for this man?
10. What two things are flooding this man's soul?
11. What speaks volumes to this man?
12. What type of healing do these physical acts of honor release?
13. What else do these physical acts of honor do?
14. What do the Jewish people believe about the spittle of the firstborn?
15. Does Jesus make a mistake and need to try to heal this man again?
16. What is still in the making concerning this man's healing?

17. The Greek word *omma* can refer to what?
18. How does verse 25 describe the healing of this man's eyes?
19. What is Jesus in His approach to healing?

MIRACLE 26
RECREATED EYES AND SOMETHING MORE

Jesus Recreates a Blind Man's Eyes with Dirt and Spit

Jesus sees a blind man who needs more than a recreated set of eyeballs—he needs to be healed. Let's read from John 9:1-12 to find out what else is needed in this miracle.

> *Now as Jesus passed by, He saw a man who was blind from birth. And His disciples asked Him, saying, "Rabbi, who sinned, this man or his parents, that he was born blind?"*
>
> *Jesus answered, "Neither this man nor his parents sinned, but that the works of God should be revealed in him. I must work the works of Him who sent Me while it is day; the night is coming when no one can work. As long as I am in the world, I am the light of the world."*
>
> *When He had said these things, He spat on the ground and made clay with the saliva; and He anointed the eyes of the blind man with the clay. And He said to him, "Go, wash in the pool of Siloam" (which is translated, Sent). So he went and washed, and came back seeing.*
>
> *Therefore the neighbors and those who previously had seen that he was blind said, "Is not this he who sat and begged?"*
>
> *Some said, "This is he." Others said, "He is like him."*
>
> *He said, "I am he."*

Therefore they said to him, "How were your eyes opened?"

He answered and said, "A Man called Jesus made clay and anointed my eyes and said to me, 'Go to the pool of Siloam and wash.' So I went and washed, and I received sight."

Then they said to him, "Where is He?"

He said, "I do not know."

JESUS SAW A BLIND MAN

What an ironic subtitle, Jesus Saw a Blind Man, but as we take a closer look it becomes a very powerful statement that breaks a secret code to this person's miracle. Jesus not only notices that the man is blind, but He sees deep into this man's soul and knows what else the man has been plagued with and makes him whole.

LIFE ISN'T ALWAYS FAIR

I think we can agree on this, life isn't always fair. And some seem to suffer far more than others. Let's face it, blindness is extremely cruel.

Have you ever wondered why there are so many blind people in Jesus' day? Practical reasons for this curse would include poor lighting, wind and sandstorms, blinding and intense sunlight, and then add farsightedness, near-sightedness, cataracts, glaucoma, common infections such as pink eye left untreated, trachoma spread by flies, and even leprosy in the eyes.

People just didn't know what we know today about personal hygiene. And they hadn't figured out yet that if they wear curved glass of different thicknesses, many of their vision problems would be taken care of.

The blind were considered second-class citizens; they suffered from discrimination, and great shame was placed upon them by the religious sect as their blindness was considered a punishment for sin. So, no, life isn't always fair, back then or now.

GOD'S GRACE IS SUFFICIENT

In 2 Corinthians 12:9 (AMPC) the apostle Paul writes to the church in Corinth:

> *But He said to me, My grace (My favor and loving-kindness and mercy) is enough for you [sufficient against any danger and enables you to bear the trouble manfully]; for My strength and power are made perfect (fulfilled and completed) and show themselves most effective in [your] weakness. Therefore, I will all the more gladly glory in my weaknesses and infirmities, that the strength and power of Christ (the Messiah) may rest (yes, may pitch a tent over and dwell) upon me!*

In the Greek language the word for *grace* is *charis* (Strong's G5485). And in this portion of Scripture, it says that His grace (His favor, lovingkindness and mercy) is sufficient, more than enough.

If we would be honest with one another, we would admit that sometimes when we face troubles this verse and others like it make us angry at God. But instead of feeling upset at the One who is sinless, I think we ought to do ourselves a favor and face our misunderstanding of His Word.

The message in this verse is not telling us to wallow in our difficulty, but that we have been gifted with something supernatural, *charis,* His grace, and empowered with His favor, lovingkindness, and mercy. We are not left to fend for ourselves, hopeless to remain helpless, but given a strong promise of His strength; when ours feels weak, His strength will carry us through every difficult time in life.

COUNT IT ALL JOY

Okay, we see how His grace is more than enough when we pass through very difficult times in life, now we look at a spiritual tool when we are hit with situations that seem to be out of our control. James 1:2-4 (TPT) says:

> *My fellow believers, when it seems as though you are facing nothing but difficulties, see it as an invaluable opportunity to experience the greatest joy that you can! For you know that when your faith is tested it stirs up in you the power of endurance. And then as your endurance grows even stronger, it will release perfection into every part of your being until there is nothing missing and nothing lacking.*

Whether we like it or not, the trials we face in life enrich us with endurance. And if handled correctly, they strengthen our faith. And being a woman of faith, I choose to look at the bright side of situations and see the goodness of our God at work in my life, and so should you.

There are times when we would like nothing better than to lie low in the doldrums of life. But God's Word teaches us that when everything that could go wrong does, that we are to count it all joy. Holy Spirit is challenging us to put our faith in action, and to use His spiritual power of joy to launch us into His territory of victory.

This might make us feel rip-roaring mad at Jesus, but again we miss what He says to us. He does not say that we are to jump for joy because we are sick, but to count it all joy because we have all the answers we need to rise above sickness and other types of problem—and His name is Jesus. And we rejoice because by His stripes we are healed in spirit, soul, and physical body (Isaiah 53:45).

ALL THINGS WORK TOGETHER FOR OUR GOOD

It's during the trials of life that we will witness with our own eyes the goodness of our God. If we will keep our eyes fixed on Jesus, we will see the amazing ways that *"...in all things God works for the good of those who love him, who have been called according to his purpose"* (Romans 8:28 NIV). Whether the situation is good or bad, big or small, our God is greater; He is more powerful than anything the devil is throwing at us today.

Oh, yes, sometimes life isn't fair, and we feel completely depleted of all strength. During these times we must choose to trust in the power of His grace and count it all joy, because of the difficulties we are passing through, but because we serve the God of the impossible. And if we allow Him to rub a little bit of His spittle on our spiritual eyes, we will experience the glory of God in ways we never dreamed possible.

WHAT A SIGHT TO BEHOLD—JESUS

This man is blind since birth, born blind, never to see with his eyes the sun, moon, and the stars. Never to visualize the beauty in the color of the rainbow. Unable to make imaginary pictures out of the shapes of the clouds, not able to understand the blueness of the sky, or the aqua colors of the sea. Not to be able to lock in his memory the face of mother and father because his eyes do not see. This is when life is unfair. But he is about to behold true justice—Jesus. And what a sight to behold!

COURT IS NOW IN SESSION

The religious community wants to know, *"Rabbi, who sinned, this man or his parents, that he was born blind?"* Blindness is held against this man all his life. But he not only has the Miracle Worker working on his behalf, he also now has the Advocate who is about to set the record straight, *"Neither this man nor his parents sinned, but that the works of God should be revealed in him."* With this public proclamation, Jesus just set this man free from a life sentence of shame. And the glory of the Lord is about to be revealed in this man's life for eternity to witness, not because God is harsh and unloving, but because He is the opposite, kind, loving, and just.

You can believe whatever you want to believe about Jesus, but I choose to believe the report of the Lord found throughout God's Word:

- Jesus is Able (2 Timothy 1:12).
- He is Faithful (1 Corinthians 10:13).
- He is Deliverer (Psalm 18:2).
- He is Healer (Matthew 8:16).
- He is Almighty (Genesis 17:1).
- He is Hope (Romans 15:13).
- He is Gracious (Psalm 145:8).
- He is Victorious (1 Corinthians 15:57).
- He is Comforter and Helper (John 15:26).
- He is Awesome (Nehemiah 1:5).
- He is Conqueror (Romans 8:35-39).
- He is Creator (Genesis 1).
- He is Glory (Psalm 24:7).
- He is Holy (Isaiah 6:3).
- He is Just (Deuteronomy 32:4).
- He is King of kings (Revelation 19:16).
- He is Love (Romans 5:8).
- He is Lord of lords (Revelation 19:16).
- He is Prince of Peace (Isaiah 9:6).
- He is Redeemer (Job 19:25).

- He is Savior (Luke 2:11).
- He is Mighty (Isaiah 9:6).
- He is Worthy (Revelation 5:12).
- He is Messiah (John 1:41).

RECREATING A SET OF SEEING EYES

Our Creator, Jesus, begins to recreate a brand-new set of seeing eyes for this man. Why? Because He came to undo the works of the devil, and blindness is not a gift from God, rather it's a grand theft from the devil.

Let's observe what Jesus does. *"When He had said these things, He spat on the ground and made clay with the saliva; and He anointed the eyes of the blind man with the clay"* (Mark 9:6). The Creator is making new eyeballs out of clay and that life-giving saliva.

Every time I read this miracle, I envision my earlier days as a mom with all my children, and all the fun they had creating with play dough (clay). And the many eyeballs they rolled and placed on their clay animations. And this is how I see with my mind's eye, Jesus making eyeballs out of mudballs. I know it says that He anointed this blindman's eyes with this saliva-enriched clay, but I still envision Him making eyeballs out of mudballs and popping them into his sockets and the man sees.

HE SEES THE LIGHT

I can guarantee you; the first thing this blind man sees is a very bright light with Jesus and His muddy hands in the middle of all this glory. Why do I write this? Because in my experience with the many blind people I have ministered to who have received their sight, over and over the first thing they see is light. Just as Jesus says in John 9:5, *"As long as I am in the world, I am the light of the world."* This blessed man not only sees the physical light, but He sees the Light of the World in the flesh—Jesus.

When the blind receive their sight, utter awe, and total fear of the Lord overtakes them. It is the brightest, purest, holiest light they will ever see while on earth. It's the glory of the Lord manifesting all around them. It is an amazing sight to see. Then comes the joy, jumping, dancing, and praising Jesus. And do you know what else? They do not want to close their eyes. And

I do not blame them. But they must overcome this fear of losing the light and walking in darkness again. And they do.

THE RICHES OF JESUS ON DISPLAY

- Jesus is the Creator.
- He heals what needs to be healed, body, soul, and spirit together.
- Jesus is amazingly logical with His recreation of this man's eyeballs.

CRACK THE MIRACLE CODE

Allow Jesus to create eyes that see what others cannot, the Kingdom of God.

Read Miracle 27 and take comfort in a Savior who never tires to heal and deliver those in need.

FAITH ASSIGNMENT

Do a spiritual heart checkup. Has the devil sentenced you to a life of shame for some reason? If so, what is the reason for the shame? Give this shame to Jesus now and allow Him to recreate your life anew.

PRAYER OF FAITH

Father God, my spiritual eyes have been opened during this lesson, and I see that I no longer need to suffer from dead, or nearly dead body parts. Right now, I align myself with the power of Holy Spirit, that same Spirit that raised You from the dead. Holy Spirit, I receive a new (name body part), and it is full of life, and functions perfectly normal for the glory of Jesus, amen.

Questions for Miracle 26: Recreated Eyes and Something More

1. What is the subtitle that breaks the secret code to this man's miracle?

2. Back in Jesus' day, what type of citizens were the blind considered to be?
3. What is one thing the blind suffered?
4. What did the religious sect place on the blind?
5. What was the reason for the shame?
6. What's one thing life isn't?
7. In 2 Corinthians 12:9, what is His grace?
8. In the Greek language, what is the word for *grace?*
9. Whether we like it or not, what do the trials we face in life enrich us with?
10. If handled correctly, what do these trials do to our faith?
11. What does God do for us in Romans 8:28?
12. With this public proclamation, "*Neither this man nor his parents sinned, but that the works of God should be revealed in him,*" what does Jesus do for the man?
13. What are the materials Jesus uses to recreate the man's eyeballs?
14. What other light does this man see besides physical light?

MIRACLE 27

COME DOWN FROM THAT MOUNTAINTOP EXPERIENCE

Jesus Delivers a Boy from an Unclean Spirit

After a radiant experience where Peter, James, and John witness the transfiguration of Jesus with Moses and Elijah, they must come down from the mountaintop experience and face a great multitude of people with all their problems, including a man with his demon-possessed boy who needs desperate help from Jesus. Read on to find out how Jesus delivers and cleanses this boy from an unclean spirit.

> *Now it happened on the next day, when they had come down from the mountain, that a great multitude met Him. Suddenly a man from the multitude cried out, saying, "Teacher, I implore You, look on my son, for he is my only child. And behold, a spirit seizes him, and he suddenly cries out; it convulses him so that he foams at the mouth; and it departs from him with great difficulty, bruising him. So I implored Your disciples to cast it out, but they could not."*
>
> *Then Jesus answered and said, "O faithless and perverse generation, how long shall I be with you and bear with you? Bring your son here." And as he was still coming, the demon threw him down and convulsed him. Then Jesus rebuked the unclean spirit, healed the child, and gave him back to his father* (Luke 9:37-42).

COME DOWN FROM THE MOUNTAINTOP

It says in the opening verse that Jesus and the disciples come down from the mountain and a great multitude meets Him. This is one of the most difficult experiences in the supernatural life of any believer in Jesus—coming down from a glorious and unexplainable experience with Jesus and then having to confront the multitude of problems this world has to offer.

Naturally you want time to process all that you have witnessed before addressing the surmounting problems that will crowd out that experience. But maybe it's more than the experience He desires you to hold on to. Perhaps you are leaving that mountaintop experience with exactly what He wants you to have, Him.

A SPIRIT SEIZES THIS BOY

In Luke 9:38-39, this man cries out to Jesus, *"Teacher, I implore You, look on my son, for he is my only child. And behold, a spirit seizes him, and he suddenly cries out; it convulses him so that he foams at the mouth; and it departs from him with great difficulty, bruising him."*

This Scripture gives detailed information about what happens when a demon seizes someone. When this occurs, it's a violent takeover. *The Passion Translation* reads this way, *"An evil spirit possesses him and makes him scream out in torment."* Grievously, this demonic spirit torments this boy day in and day out. The New King James version goes on to tell us that this demon convulses him. In the Greek, this word *convulses* is *sparassō* (Strong's G4682), and it means this evil spirit *tears* apart this boy. If you ever encounter a demoniac who convulses, you will witness the shredding of a human being. It is so wrong, and it happens within Christian homes and churches time and time again. We must choose to activate our authority in the Anointed One, Jesus, and cast it out. We must teach and train people how to keep them out.

HE FOAMS AT THE MOUTH

I'm not sure I paid much attention to the fact that this boy foams at the mouth; after all, I have personally seen this time and time again during a deliverance. But Holy Spirit calls me back to it now. Why? Because I write in this work about the Jewish belief of the spittle of the firstborn. (See Miracle 23.)

In Luke 9:38, the boy's father cries out to Jesus, *"Teacher, I implore You, look on my son, for he is my only child."* But in this situation, he was no longer blessed, but accursed, perverted by an unclean spirit, and a visual reminder that his boy, his only son, was demon possessed. But Jesus delivers the boy and there is no longer foaming at the mouth. He heals him from his injuries, even his spittle is cleansed and healed. It's all a testament to the fact that Jesus makes the boy whole again.

ONE LAST TIME

When this demon sees Jesus, this boy's Deliverer draw near, it made the boy convulse (shake violently) one last time. He knows it's a done deal for him. Jesus will command him to leave the boy; but before He does, he is going to wreak hellish terror upon the boy, one last shredding, one last brawl of bruising against him before he must leave. Do you see how evil these demons are? How then can we sit back and do nothing?

A SPIRITUAL HOSPITAL

Our place of worship is like a spiritual hospital where we continually welcome and heal and deliver those in need. This should be a main thrust in our gathering place. A top priority should be to train the body of Christ how to handle a suffering demoniac. How not to walk in fear, but in the authority of Christ. How to activate the supernatural power we have been given to set the captives free in Jesus' name.

HIS DISCIPLES WERE UNABLE TO DELIVER THE BOY

Luke 9:40 tells us what happens next: *"So I implored Your disciples to cast it out, but they could not."* When Jesus hears this, He gives His disciples a strong-worded rebuke and calls them a faithless and perverse generation.

The word in the Greek for *faithless* is *apistos* (Strong's G571), and means "unfaithful, not to be trusted, unbelieving, incredulous, without trust in God." This rebuke is a mouthful of unpleasant revelation about oneself. May this never be spoken over us.

Imagine itinerating with the Messiah. You see Him walk on water, feed thousands of people with a little boy's lunch, He gives sight to the blind. You see the deaf hear and the paralytics walk and more amazing acts than we can imagine. And now when it's our turn to cast out a demon, we can't. And everyone around us knows we can't. I don't know about you, but I would feel embarrassed and ashamed if Jesus has to say this to me.

JESUS FEELS FRUSTRATION

In this encounter with the young boy being tormented by a demon, Jesus walks the earth in human form, and He feels frustration with His disciples. His entire work is about having faith in Him for the miraculous. He knows His time to make ready disciples is about to end. We know this to be true because of what we read in Luke 9:43-45:

> *And they were all amazed at the majesty of God. But while everyone marveled at all the things which Jesus did, He said to His disciples, "Let these words sink down into your ears, for the Son of Man is about to be betrayed into the hands of men." But they did not understand this saying, and it was hidden from them so that they did not perceive it; and they were afraid to ask Him about this saying.*

Jesus is experiencing frustration. They rely upon Him to do it all. But He's preparing them to do it all by faith. And His mission with us is the same.

JESUS REBUKES THE UNCLEAN SPIRIT

Jesus does not pray to the Father, petition, or make a request to the "unclean spirit," He rebukes it. In the Greek, *rebuke* is *epitimaō* (Strong's 2008), and it means that Jesus "straightly charges" this demon out of this boy. This is what someone with authority does, they take charge. They don't play around or try to appease a troublemaker. No, they make the hard call and make them leave. And the sooner the better before more harm can be done.

JESUS HEALS THE CHILD

After the demon is cast out, He then heals the boy of his injuries. The Greek word for *heals* is *iaomai* (Strong's 2390), and it means Jesus *cures* and makes this boy *whole* again. And He then yields this young lad back to his father.

THE RICHES OF JESUS ON DISPLAY

- Jesus always makes time for those who call Him.
- His compassion and mercy are great.
- Jesus gives attention to all the details while ministering to our needs.
- Jesus desires that all His disciples, including us, are equipped to minister to the needs of the people.

CRACK THE MIRACLE CODE

Call out to Jesus, who never tires to heal and deliver those in need.

When you read Miracle 28, you will learn how Jesus requires the activation of our faith for our miracle.

FAITH ASSIGNMENT

Begin to pray and fast for those you know or know about who are either oppressed or possessed by demons. Strengthen your faith about the authority of Christ and learn to operate in the power of the supernatural.

PRAYER OF FAITH

Father God, I desire to be ready to minister to the sick and hurting people I encounter. I do not want to be afraid of people who are sick and disturbed by demons. Teach me who I am in You and the authority that You have given to me over the devil and all his wicked works. In Your name, I pray in faith, amen.

Questions for Miracle 27: Come Down from That Mountaintop Experience

1. Who meets Jesus and the disciples when they come down from the mountain?
2. In this miracle Jesus delivers a boy with what?
3. What is one of the most difficult experiences in the supernatural life of any believer in Jesus?
4. What is the Greek word for *convulses?*
5. What does the Greek word for *convulse* mean?
6. What does this demon spirit do with this boy's spittle?
7. What happened to this boy's spittle was what type of visual reminder?
8. What is the Greek word for *faithless?*
9. This rebuke is a mouthful of what?
10. What is the Greek word for *rebuke?*
11. What does the Greek word for *rebuke* mean?
12. What is the Greek word for *healing?*
13. What does the Greek word for *healing* mean?

MIRACLE 28

MIRACLE MONEY TO PAY THE TEMPLE TAX

Miracle Money Found in a Fish's Mouth

Because this miracle is so rich with revelation, I want to study this miracle from different angles. First, let's discuss the spiritual side of this miracle about Jesus' identity truthfully, and what He lays down to pay this temple tax.

Then we will view it from the angle of God's faithfulness to provide for our needs, and how He supernaturally arranges details to bring about this miracle money.

This miracle coin story is found in Matthew 17:24-27:

> *When they had come to Capernaum, those who received the temple tax came to Peter and said, "Does your Teacher not pay the temple tax?"*
>
> *He said, "Yes."*
>
> *And when he had come into the house, Jesus anticipated him, saying, "What do you think, Simon? From whom do the kings of the earth take customs or taxes, from their sons or from strangers?"*
>
> *Peter said to Him, "From strangers."*
>
> *Jesus said to him, "Then the sons are free. Nevertheless, lest we offend them, go to the sea, cast in a hook, and take the fish that comes up first. And when you have opened its mouth, you will find a piece of money; take that and give it to them for Me and you."*

WHO DO YOU SAY I AM?

To begin our discussion, we scroll back the Scriptures a bit to Matthew 16:13-20:

> *When Jesus came into the region of Caesarea Philippi, He asked His disciples, saying, "Who do men say that I, the Son of Man, am?"*
>
> *So they said, "Some say John the Baptist, some Elijah, and others Jeremiah or one of the prophets."*
>
> *He said to them, "But who do you say that I am?"*
>
> *Simon Peter answered and said, "You are the Christ, the Son of the living God."*
>
> *Jesus answered and said to him, "Blessed are you, Simon Bar-Jonah, for flesh and blood has not revealed this to you, but My Father who is in heaven. And I also say to you that you are Peter, and on this rock I will build My church, and the gates of Hades shall not prevail against it. And I will give you the keys of the kingdom of heaven, and whatever you bind on earth will be bound in heaven, and whatever you loose on earth will be loosed in heaven."*
>
> *Then He commanded His disciples that they should tell no one that He was Jesus the Christ.*

JESUS' IDENTITY RIGHTS ARE BEING TESTED

This miracle runs deep into oceans of revelations of the deity of Jesus, and His obedience to not demand His spiritual rights as the Son of God. Jesus came down to earth for a purpose, to redeem mankind back to the Father. And as much as He might want to, He cannot get ahead of the plan of salvation. I see His rights to His identity being tested in this miracle.

We read what may seem like an innocent question in Matthew 17:24, "*When they had come to Capernaum, those who received the temple tax came to Peter and said,* 'Does your Teacher not pay the temple tax? "For Jesus to pay the temple tax, He would have to agree to the plan of redemption to hide His true identity as the Son of God, the Anointed One, the Messiah to the Son of Man.

So He asks Simon Peter in Matthew 17:25-26,

"What do you think, Simon? From whom do the kings of the earth take customs or taxes, from their sons or from strangers?" Peter said to Him, "From strangers." Jesus said to him, "Then the sons are free."

And for the good of all people, Jesus humbles Himself. He denies the benefits that rightfully belong to Him as the Son of God, identifies as a lowly stranger, and pays the temple tax.

Peter does not understand all that Jesus says, but not too long from now these words His Master speaks during the manifestation of this miracle coin will revisit him. And he will then understand. But for now, Peter does honor Jesus as he speaks from the heart what he believes concerning Jesus, *"You are the Christ, the Son of the living God."* A true disciple is born.

A LOOK INTO MATTHEW'S LIFE

Interestingly, this account is only recorded in the book of Matthew. Matthew is the author of this book. But before his call to follow Yeshua, he is a tax collector. During this time, a tax collector is frowned upon as they are thought to be nothing more than greedy thieves taking from the Jews to enrich the Romans. They are also known for getting rich personally by overtaxing and pocketing the excess for themselves, therefore the people do not trust tax collectors. But despite his portfolio, Jesus calls Matthew to forsake all and to follow Him. And to the glory of our Lord, he does.

GOD CALLS BROKEN PEOPLE INTO HIS SERVICE

I always find God's choice to fulfill positions are not those that the church world would expect. Our Lord continues to use broken people, rich or poor with flawed pasts. And I am a firm believer that when we surrender our weakness to God, He will transform it, and it will become our greatest strength and be used for ministry purpose to win others like us for His glory.

COMPARING THE PHARISEE AND THE TAX COLLECTOR

In Luke 18:9-14 (NASB), Jesus teaches a parable comparing a righteous religious leader with a flawed tax collector. Let's listen in to what He has to say:

> *Now He also told this parable to some people who trusted in themselves that they were righteous, and viewed others with contempt: "Two men went up into the temple to pray, one a Pharisee and the other a tax collector. The Pharisee stood and began praying this in regard to himself: 'God, I thank You that I am not like other people: swindlers, crooked, adulterers, or even like this tax collector. I fast twice a week; I pay tithes of all that I get.' But the tax collector, standing some distance away, was even unwilling to raise his eyes toward heaven, but was beating his chest, saying, 'God, be merciful to me, the sinner!' I tell you, this man went to his house justified rather than the other one; for everyone who exalts himself will be humbled, but the one who humbles himself will be exalted."*

No matter what sins we've committed in our past, if we ask the Lord to forgive us, He does. Our slate is clean, and a brand-new chapter of life opens for us. As God's Word promises us in 2 Corinthians 5:17 (TPT), *"Now, if anyone is enfolded into Christ, he has become an entirely new person. All that is related to the old order has vanished. Behold, everything is fresh and new."*

Let's pray:

> *Dear Jesus, Your act of lovingkindness toward this flawed tax collector warms my heart. I must admit that I have veered away from You because my life is full of flaws, dishonesty, and thievery in one form or another. I humble myself before Youand ask for Your forgiveness. Help me to become the person You created me to be, and may my life turn around and testify of Your goodness to me. I pray this in faith believing, amen.*

DAILY NEEDS, NOT GREED

We all have daily needs that must be met, bills to pay, family to feed, and yet

He tells us not to worry about such things. Matthew records the words of our Lord for us in Matthew 6:25-27 (TPT):

> *This is why I tell you to never be worried about your life, for all that you need will be provided, such as food, water, clothing—everything your body needs. Isn't there more to your life than a meal? Isn't your body more than clothing? Consider the birds—do you think they worry about their existence? They don't plant or reap or store up food, yet your heavenly Father provides them each with food. Aren't you much more valuable to your Father than they? So, which one of you by worrying could add anything to your life?*

Oftentimes, our response to such a promise can be rather negative. We forget that while Jesus is on earth, He leaves His God-powers in Heaven and lives as a human being, with the same needs and trials as anyone else. The difference with Jesus is that He chooses to walk by faith and not by sight, and not by the limitations of human reasoning. He places His trust in a great big God who cares for our every need, big or small.

He declares that everything we need will be provided. Perhaps we overextend ourselves and exit the realm of need and enter greed. If this is where you are, ask the Lord to forgive you and to help you clean up the financial mess you find yourself in today. He's good at cleaning up our mess. We just need to get out of His way and obey what He tells us to do.

DOES JESUS PAY THE TAX?

I don't think too many people like to pay a tax, and often people worry about how they will pay a tax that is due. It's obvious that this concerns Peter. But Jesus knows that Peter begins to worry, and He has a plan of action—a supernatural plan. Jesus sends Peter off on a faith assignment and tells him to do something that does not make sense in the natural. In fact, it sounds downright ridiculous. He sends Simon Peter, a former fisherman, on a fishing trip. Here are the instructions that he is to follow: "*Go to the sea, cast in a hook, and take the fish that comes up first. And when you have opened its mouth, you will find a piece of money; take that and give it to them for Me and you.*" Jesus doubles down paying this tax. He not only pays for Himself, but also for Peter.

You may read this and think to yourself, *Hey, I don't have a magical fish!* And yes, you are right you don't, and neither did Peter, but you do have something greater than a magical fish—faith. And when you activate faith in His faithfulness to provide for your every need, you will witness Him supply in amazing ways.

SUPERNATURAL PROVISION

My husband and I lived on the mission field for 25 years, never knowing where God's provision was going to come from next. But I have learned that I don't have know the details about how He is going to provide, I just know that He does.

God instructed us to purchase property in Guatemala and begin to build homes for hurting children. We knew that we would have to make payments to purchase the property every six months. And God clearly gives us a supernatural plan of provision. He says, "I do not want you to save up for those payments, I will take care of them for you. But I do want you to start to build homes on this property and fill them with children." For us this is a step of faith, we have no way to earn finances. God knows this, and so He sends us out on a faith assignment, and we do what He says to do.

He provides us with a downpayment of $50,000, and then we sign legal documents and agree to pay $10,000 every six months for the next two years, knowing that God clearly spoke to us and said, "I do not want you to save a dime for those payments, I will provide." God waited until the morning of the day that first payment was due before He placed it into our hands. This is how miracle money works.

We had every opportunity to worry, but we chose daily to put our trust in Him, and in Him alone to provide. And He did, and every installment was paid in full, and right on time.

> *So let us seize and hold fast and retain without wavering the hope we cherish and confess and our acknowledgement of it, for He Who promised is reliable (sure) and faithful to His word* (Hebrews 10:23 AMPC).

THE RICHES OF JESUS ON DISPLAY

- Jesus is faithful to the plan of salvation.
- He is willing to deny His rights as the Son of God for the good of the people.
- Jesus is tempted in ways beyond our understanding.

CRACK THE MIRACLE CODE

Jesus requires us to activate our faith for our miracle.

FAITH ASSIGNMENT

Knowing that you might be facing tough times financially, write down on a sheet of paper, one item that must be paid. Commit this financial need to Jesus, ask Him for a plan of action, and do what He says to you to do. And watch the need be met in full.

PRAYER OF FAITH

Oh, Lord Jesus, this miracle involves more than I had anticipated. I must admit at times when asked "Who do I say You are?" that I falter, and that is wrong. It's wrong for me to allow the fear of man and the worry about what others might think of me to stand in the way of my witness to the world. I vow before You now to never deny You, to always take a stand of faith, even when it's not popular. I commit to trust and obey the faith assignments that You require of me. In Your name, I pray, amen.

Questions for Miracle 28: Miracle Money to Pay the Temple Tax

1. How does Simon Peter answer Jesus' question, "Who do you say that I am?"
2. Who reveals Jesus' identity to Peter?

3. What was Matthew before his call to follow Yeshua?
4. When we surrender our weakness to God, how will He transform it?
5. In the parable that Jesus shares who is justified?
6. What does Jesus declare about our needs?
7. What do we have that is greater than a magical fish?
8. According to Hebrews 10:23, what are we to do with the hope we cherish?

MIRACLE 29
QUESTIONS, RUMORS, AND THE BIG LIE

Jesus Heals and Delivers a Blind, Mute Demoniac

In this miracle, we meet up with Jesus as He is itinerating, spreading the Good News about His Kingdom while healing, miracles, signs, and wonders continue to be part of His ministry. On this day, He is ministering deliverance and healing to a demon-possessed man who is also blind and mute. But during this man's glorious miracle, division is being created and falsehoods against Jesus are spreading. Let's read from Luke 11:14-23 to find out the outcome of all this drama:

> *And He was casting out a demon, and it was mute. So it was, when the demon had gone out, that the mute spoke; and the multitudes marveled. But some of them said, "He casts out demons by Beelzebub, the ruler of the demons."*
>
> *Others, testing Him, sought from Him a sign from heaven. But He, knowing their thoughts, said to them: "Every kingdom divided against itself is brought to desolation, and a house divided against a house falls. If Satan also is divided against himself, how will his kingdom stand? Because you say I cast out demons by Beelzebub. And if I cast out demons by Beelzebub, by whom do your sons cast them out? Therefore they will be your judges. But if I cast out demons with the finger of*

God, surely the kingdom of God has come upon you. When a strong man, fully armed, guards his own palace, his goods are in peace. But when a stronger than he comes upon him and overcomes him, he takes from him all his armor in which he trusted, and divides his spoils. He who is not with Me is against Me, and he who does not gather with Me scatters."

Verse 14 says, "*And He was casting out a demon, and it was mute. So it was, when the demon had gone out, that the mute spoke; and the multitudes marveled.*" In Matthew 12:22 we find out a bit more details concerning this man's condition and miracle, "*Then one was brought to Him who was demon-possessed, blind and mute; and He healed him, so that the blind and mute man both spoke and saw.*" So we establish the fact that this man is demon-possessed and mute and blind too. Who is the source of such cruelty? Jesus answers this question in John 10:10, "*The thief does not come except to steal, and to kill, and to destroy"*; and the thief, the devil, has done exactly this to the suffering man. But then we read the purpose of Jesus in the second half of John 10:10: "*I have came that they may have life, and that they may have it more abundantly."*

According to a word search for the second half of this verse from John 10:10, Jesus says that they *"may have,"* this phrase in the Greek is *echō* (Strong's G2192), and it means "to possess," and this word *abundantly* in Greek is *perissos,* (Strong's G4053), and it means "exceeding abundantly, beyond measure." Jesus trades this man's possession of demons for possession of life that is exceedingly abundantly, beyond measure. Now, that's a trade up!

QUESTIONS AND RUMORS BEGIN

Signs and wonders point to the deity of Jesus, and we have people who have hope in their hearts for the Messiah, but can He be the one they long for? Matthew 12:23 reports, *"And all the multitudes were amazed and said, 'Could this be the Son of David?'"* In other words, "Can this Jesus really be the Messiah?" This miracle changes everything for this group of people, and they are amazed, astounded, out of their minds with joy. The speculations are spreading about who He is. But so too, are the falsehoods. The devil and his ghoulish demons have been put to shame and proven to be weaker than Jesus.

And the Messiah just gave them an eviction notice, and they could not remain, they had to leave.

Their chains of bondage fall off the man, and he is now in his right mind, and can now see and speak. The devil is in panic mode, and thinks to himself, *What am I going to do? I know, let's start some rumors of our own and cool down all this chatter about Him being the Messiah.* And a spirit of confusion is loosed among the crowd by the power of lying spirits, backed by that old religious spirit, and fueled by the hate and jealousy of the Pharisees too. And yes, the questions and rumors begin.

THE BIG LIE

When the devil and his ghouls can't accuse you of some unrepented sin, they will make up lies about you. We will momentarily listen in on the big lie they came up with in verse 15 to falsely accuse Jesus: *"He casts out demons by Beelzebub, the ruler of the demons."* Beelzebub is another name referring to satan. But Jesus speaks truth to the lie and says beginning in verse 17-23,

> *But He, knowing their thoughts, said to them: "Every kingdom divided against itself is brought to desolation, and a house divided against a house falls. If Satan also is divided against himself, how will his kingdom stand? Because you say I cast out demons by Beelzebub. And if I cast out demons by Beelzebub, by whom do your sons cast them out? Therefore they will be your judges. But if I cast out demons with the finger of God, surely the kingdom of God has come upon you. When a strong man, fully armed, guards his own palace, his goods are in peace. But when a stronger than he comes upon him and overcomes him, he takes from him all his armor in which he trusted, and divides his spoils. He who is not with Me is against Me, and he who does not gather with Me scatters."*

This is a satanic attack against our Messiah and the people of that time. And what happens in this testimony matters to us today. The devil lies to us every day of our lives. His mission is to possess, and if he can't do that he will oppress. He comes up with wicked plans to bind us to the bondage of sin. I believe he and his creepy fallen angels study us, and they whisper lies to see if we will react to any of them, so they can come up with a battle plan against us.

And if they cannot cause us to fall, they will then stir up trouble with others against us.

We can see this wicked strategy at play in this testimony. Somehow this man became possessed, people are not born possessed. Somewhere, somehow a door is open, and demon possession takes over him. They are constantly trying to get Jesus to fall or fail, but they are never able to cause Him to miss the mark (sin). And because the faith of Jesus overpowers them every time, they stir up trouble with others against Him.

You might think to yourself, *How is Jesus tempted in this situation?* Jesus' time on earth is coming to an end. He has many to reach in just three short years of ministry. He must be about His heavenly Father's business and win the Lost. He travels from city to city, village to village to teach, preach, and reach as many as possible. But Jesus' enemies are a stumbling block to His healing and deliverance ministry. They are creating evil lies about Him to turn people away from His truth. They are full of the devil, and do not desire people to see Kingdom of God, or to witness that there is hope for freedom from demon-possession, sickness, and disease. So what does Jesus battle? Discouragement, weariness, and anger to name just a few temptations.

> *For we do not have a High Priest Who is unable to understand and sympathize and have a shared feeling with our weaknesses and infirmities and liability to the assaults of temptation, but One Who has been tempted in every respect as we are, yet without sinning* (Hebrews 4:15 AMPC).

NO NEUTRAL GROUND

When it comes to spiritual matters, there is no neutral ground. You either believe Jesus, or you don't. The apostle Matthew writes these words of Jesus in Matthew 12:30 (AMPC): *"He who is not with Me [definitely on My side] is against Me, and he who does not [definitely] gather with Me and for My side scatters."*

The apostle John in 1 John 3:10 (AMPC) warns us with this message of truth:

> *By this it is made clear who take their nature from God and are His children and who take their nature from the devil and are his children:*

> *no one who does not practice righteousness [who does not conform to God's will in purpose, thought, and action] is of God; neither is anyone who does not love his brother (his fellow believer in Christ).*

In Revelation 3:16, Jesus says what He will do to us if we become lukewarm toward Him and His ways, *"So, because you are lukewarm and neither cold nor hot, I will spew you out of My mouth!"* This is not a total rejection, but a serious rebuke because He gives an opportunity to repent. So, let's do this together right now:

> *Dearest Jesus, I don't know how I got to this place, but I don't want to remain lukewarm. Forgive me for becoming repulsive to You. I don't want to remain on Your vomit list—I want to be desirable to You again. May the fires of my heart burn with passion for You again, Sweet Jesus. In Your name, I pray, amen.*

YOU MUST CHOOSE

We have decisions to make every day of our life. Some are important, others are so-so, and some just keep the ball of life rolling forward, but there is one decision that all must make. And to not make this decision is to make a decision that will land you in an eternal lake of fire. Revelation 20:15 states, *"And anyone not found written in the Book of Life was cast into the lake of fire."*

With Jesus, there is no neutral ground. You either believe Him, or you don't. To believe Him is to trust what He says is the truth.

Too many people think there is some neutral ground. Well, that type of belief is part of the big lie that all roads lead to the truth. No, they don't. There is only one way to the Father—through the redemptive blood of Jesus. John 14:6 says, *"Jesus said to him, 'I am the way, the truth, and the life. No one comes to the Father except through Me.'"* Luke records this truth concerning salvation in Acts 4:12, *"Nor is there salvation in any other, for there is no other name under heaven given among men by which we must be saved."*

The most important decision to make is to accept Jesus Christ as our Savior. If you do, eternal life with Him in Heaven is your eternal destination. If not, hell is where you will go. Romans 10:9 tells us how to make this choice, *"If you confess with your mouth the Lord Jesus and believe in your heart that God has raised Him from the dead, you will be saved."* It really is this simple, but the key is that you first believe that Jesus is your Savior. And this is the decision you must choose. Let's pray:

> *Dear Jesus, I ask You to forgive me of my sins, my every bad thought, word, and deed. I do believe in my heart that You are who You say You are. And with the words of my mouth, I confess that You are my Savior. Holy Spirit, I ask for Your help to grow in this newfound faith, and to become all that You desire me to be. In Your name, I pray, amen.*

THE RICHES OF JESUS ON DISPLAY

- Jesus is unstoppable.
- He knows His deity.
- Jesus stays true to His mission.
- He does not allow the enemy to get away with lying to people.

CRACK THE MIRACLE CODE

The devil enters panic mode when you receive your healing and will lie about what happened to you.

While you read Miracle 30, you will discover how a religious spirit will try to keep you in bondage; but to Jesus, you are more important than religious rules and regulations.

FAITH ASSIGNMENT

Honestly examine your life. *Ask yourself, Are there any areas where I know I'm not living right? Are there open doors that need to close to shut out the work of the enemy in my life? If so, what are they?* And, *Am I willing to do what I need to do to close the open doors in my life?*

PRAYER OF FAITH

> *Dear Holy Spirit, Your voice of conviction has been speaking to my spirit during this lesson. I humbly ask for Your forgiveness, dear Jesus. Create in me a clean heart with the power of Your forgiveness. Holy*

Spirit, lead me into the newness of Your Spirit, where all is fresh and made new. In Your name I pray this in faith, amen.

Questions for Miracle 29: Questions, Rumors, and the Big Lie

1. What was this man's problem?
2. Who was the source of such cruelty to this man?
3. In the Greek, what is the phrase *may have?*
4. And what does this phrase *may have* in the Greek mean?
5. What is the word *abundantly* in Greek?
6. What does *abundantly* in Greek mean?
7. What does Jesus trade this man's possession of demons for?
8. What will the devil and his ghouls do if they can't accuse you of some unrepented sin?
9. What was the big lie against Jesus in this miracle?
10. What type of ground does not exist when it comes to spiritual matters?
11. According to Revelation 3:16, what will Jesus do with us if we are lukewarm?
12. What is this if not total rejection?
13. What is the most important decision we must all make?

MIRACLE 30
LOOSED FROM YOUR BONDAGE

Jesus Heals a Crippled Woman from 18 Years of Bondage

As we listen to Jesus teach the Scriptures on this fine Sabbath, something forbidden but amazing happens to a woman who is stricken by a spirit of infirmity and is literally bent over for the past 18 years and cannot stand up straight and tall.

Let's take a seat and witness Luke 13:10-17 play out before our eyes:

Now He was teaching in one of the synagogues on the Sabbath. And behold, there was a woman who had a spirit of infirmity eighteen years, and was bent over and could in no way raise herself up. But when Jesus saw her, He called her to Him and said to her, "Woman, you are loosed from your infirmity." And He laid His hands on her, and immediately she was made straight, and glorified God.

But the ruler of the synagogue answered with indignation, because ***Jesus had healed on the Sabbath****; and he said to the crowd, "There are six days on which men ought to work; therefore come and be healed on them, and not on the Sabbath day."*

The Lord then answered him and said, "Hypocrite! Does not each one of you on the Sabbath loose his ox or donkey from the stall, and lead it away to water it? So ought not this woman, being a daughter of Abraham, whom Satan has bound—think of it—for eighteen years, be loosed from this bond on the Sabbath?" And when He said these things, all His adversaries were put to shame; and all the multitude rejoiced for all the glorious things that were done by Him.

JESUS SEES HER

Because of her infirmity this woman is an outcast, the people believe that this physical suffering is her punishment for sin. She carries the brand of a "sinner" in society. And being a woman during this time in history does not help her cause either. It is prohibited for a man to speak to a woman in public. Jesus breaks the rules of Jewish tradition to call her out publicly. And time and time again, He forgoes the traditions and religious laws to undo the wicked works of the devil, to deliver those who are possessed or oppressed by devils and He heals the infirmed.

But something wonderful happens to this invisible woman, Jesus sees her. Out of the crowd of people in the synagogue, she draws His attention. When someone walks in the healing anointing, they can't help but notice the suffering of those around them. Jesus is the Great Physician, the Great Healer, and He sees what others do not see, all the invisible, hurting people.

When others do notice the people and their infirmity, most only see the physical symptoms, but Jesus perceives the real culprit, a spirit of infirmity. *Infirmity* in the Greek language is *astheneia* (Strong's G769), and it means "disease, infirmity, sickness, weakness." And in this woman's case, this demon of infirmity has a strong hold, a grip that debilitates her spine, and causes it to twist and deform to the point of a permanent bend.

HEALING METHODS

The healing methods that Jesus exercises with this miracle are the power of words and the laying on of hands. Both are very prominent avenues of healing the sick in the Bible. *"When Jesus saw her, He called her to Him and said to her, 'Woman, you are loosed from your infirmity.'"* These declarations of faith break the chains of bondage that keep this woman bent over. After He rescues her spirit from the enemy, then He is free to administer healing by the laying on of His hands. As He lays His hands on her, she is immediately made straight, and glorifies God (Luke 3:13).

A RELIGIOUS SPIRIT KEEPS PEOPLE IN BONDAGE TO PAIN

A religious spirit keeps people in bondage to pain. I can't tell you how many times I encounter people living like this. They are suffering needlessly, as those in the local pulpits teach that Jesus no longer heals today.

This miracle about a woman who is set free from a debilitating weakness of the spine brings to my mind a woman who suffered from a tethered spine for 25 years. She is not a member of a church that questions her being healed on the Sabbath, but rather she seeks no healing at all. They teach her slanderous lies that Jesus no longer heals, and that He wills for her to live with unrelenting pain. But she dares to defy that lying religious spirit and makes her way to the front of the church. I take one look at her and ask if she is ready to receive her healing. She answers, "Yes," then falls into my arms and her spine heals immediately.

LOOSED FROM YOUR INFIRMITY

What a glorious medical report this woman receives from Jesus, her Great Physician, *"Woman, you are loosed from your infirmity!"* (Luke 13:12). What glorious news, the past 18 years of severe pain and suffering are instantly gone. A spine grossly twisted suddenly made straight. Extreme weakness transforms by His strength. And this spirit of infirmity that bound her to the curse is gone by a word of authority, and she is a free woman with a brand-new start in life.

And her testimony can be your testimony. You do not need to allow this stronghold to cling to you any longer. You can be free from it today and walk in your healing now.

JESUS UNDER ATTACK

As normal, the religious spirit breaks out and attacks; while the multitude rejoices, the religious leader responds with indignation. In the Greek, *indignation* is *aganakteō,* and it means here that this religious leader is "very displeased" (Strong's G23) with Jesus. He does not see this miracle as something good, but believes it to be sacrilegious, dishonoring to the holiness of the Sabbath.

His entire calling as a religious leader in the local synagogue is founded upon the law. There's no grace and mercy for the people, just an outward appearance of fulfilling the requirements. He is spiritually blind to the miraculous intervention of God in this woman's life. And so, he attacks Jesus for healing on the Sabbath. And then rebukes the people for breaking the religious Sabbath rules. Sadly, in many places of worship it is no different today than it was back then.

JESUS IS ALL-KNOWING

Jesus calls this man out and says in essence, *"Hypocrite! You care more about your ox or donkey then you do about this suffering woman"* (Luke 13:15). The man knows that Jesus reads what he thinks is hidden in his heart, but Jesus is spiritually perceptive, He's omniscient, all-knowing.

The Bible teaches us:

> *For nothing is secret that will not be revealed, nor anything hidden that will not be known and come to light* (Luke 8:17).
>
> *He knows the hearts of all* (Acts 1:24).
>
> *You know what I am going to say even before I say it, Lord* (Psalm 139:4 NLT).
>
> *There is not one person who can hide their thoughts from God, for nothing that we do remains a secret, and nothing created is concealed, but everything is exposed and defenseless before his eyes, to whom we must render an account* (Hebrews 4:13 TPT).

It's best to lay all the evil intentions of our hearts before Him and repent, so we can be forgiven and free from them. Otherwise, we will be held accountable for them.

HE PUTS HIS ENEMIES TO SHAME

Luke 13:17 tells us that all His adversaries, His enemies are put to shame. In the Greek this word *shame* is *kataischynō*, and it means that Jesus "disgraced this religious leader for his hypocrisy" (Strong's G2617).

REJOICE!

Jesus receives a tongue lashing filled with blasphemous lies for doing good on the Sabbath. And like Jesus, we too will face verbal persecution and possibly even worse for following the law of grace.

Peter the apostle writes in his first epistle, 1 Peter 4:12-14:

> *Beloved, do not think it strange concerning the fiery trial which is to try you, as though some strange thing happened to you; but rejoice to the extent that you partake of Christ's sufferings, that when His glory is revealed, you may also be glad with exceeding joy. If you are reproached for the name of Christ, blessed are you, for the Spirit of glory and of God rests upon you. On their part He is blasphemed, but on your part He is glorified.*

Not if, but when this hypocritical spirit of this world revolts against us for doing what's right— like taking a stand for the preborn, praying silently near an abortion clinic, exercising our parental rights on behalf of your children at the local school board meeting—don't be surprised when this hypocritical spirit rises from within the local religious establishment. After all, it would not be so offensive if it came from anywhere but there. But because you know that they should behave like Christ—but instead crucify Him again with twisted beliefs and wicked acts— their betrayal hurts.

THE RICHES OF JESUS ON DISPLAY

- Jesus never backs down from doing what's right.
- He is willing to suffer the slander for our sake.

CRACK THE MIRACLE CODE

People are more important to Jesus than religious rules and regulations.

When you read Miracle 31, you will learn how Jesus does not bow to hypocrisy but operates in the new law of grace.

FAITH ASSIGNMENT

Examine your heart, *Is there any area in my life that I struggle with either a religious spirit, or a spirit of hypocrisy? If so, Holy Spirit, help me to get my priorities in order.*

PRAYER OF FAITH

Dear Jesus, may it be said of me that I place greater value on the people than how I will appear to others. That they are more important than the ministry or the calling—and they matter more than rules and requirements. May I have my priorities in order. In Your name I pray, amen.

Questions for Miracle 30: Loosed from Your Bondage

1. Why is this woman considered an outcast?
2. What do the people believe concerning her physical suffering?
3. What brand does she carry in society?
4. It is prohibited for a man to what?
5. What does Jesus see that others do not?
6. What type of spirit does this woman have?
7. What is the Greek word for *infirmity?*
8. What does infirmity in the Greek language mean?
9. What are the healing methods used in this miracle?
10. What does a religious spirit keep people in bondage to?
11. What was this woman loosed from?
12. What is the Greek word for *indignation?*
13. What does *indignation* mean?
14. What is the Greek word for *shame?*
15. And what does the Greek word for *shame* mean?

PART FOUR
MIRACLES 31-37

Dear Holy Spirit, allow us to follow You into the supernatural realm of healing, miracles, signs, and wonders, and learn the powerful lessons that Jesus intends for us to understand and walk out while on earth. In Jesus' name, we pray, amen.

We now follow Jesus and His mighty miracles in Part Four, Miracles 31-37. We begin this journey with Miracle 31 and witness His mercy heal a man with dropsy on the Sabbath and the ruckus He must overcome for caring for and healing this hurting man.

MIRACLE 31
HYPOCRISY VERSUS GRACE

Jesus Heals a Man with Dropsy on the Sabbath

As we follow Jesus on His mission to spread the message of the Kingdom, we find ourselves in the house of one of the rulers of the Pharisees to eat bread on the Sabbath. Let's read about a miracle that happens with a man who has dropsy found in Luke 14:1-6:

> *Now it happened, as He went into the house of one of the rulers of the Pharisees to eat bread on the Sabbath, that they watched Him closely. And behold, there was a certain man before Him who had dropsy. And Jesus, answering, spoke to the lawyers and Pharisees, saying, "Is it lawful to heal on the Sabbath?"*
>
> *But they kept silent. And He took him and healed him, and let him go. Then He answered them, saying, "Which of you, having a donkey or an ox that has fallen into a pit, will not immediately pull him out on the Sabbath day?" And they could not answer Him regarding these things.*

WHAT IS DROPSY?

I find it very helpful to do a brief word search to find out what the Bible is talking about when I'm not familiar with a particular word. In this case *dropsy.* What is it? Dropsy is a medical condition characterized by fluid retention in the body's tissues, commonly known today as edema. It can affect any part of the body but is most noticeable in the ankles, feet, and legs. It is a common problem today as well.

ABIDING BY THE RULES

As a guest in someone's home, it is socially acceptable to abide by the basic rules of that household. But you know as well as I know, sometimes their rules are unacceptable, and we must take a stand for what is right in the sight of God. So, Jesus takes such a stance in the household of a prominent Jewish religious leader.

WHO ARE THE PHARISEES?

The Pharisees are both powerful and influential men within the Jewish community. They are mostly middle-class businessmen and leaders of the synagogues. They accept the Holy Scriptures as divinely inspired by God but also place equal importance on the Jewish traditions of the time. Because of this, there is great conflict between them and Jesus. Jesus openly calls them *"hypocrites"* and *"whitewashed tombs"* and rebukes them for being physically clean on the outside, but spiritually filthy on the inside.

The Pharisees plan many traps to catch Jesus doing something wrong by their laws and traditions, but Jesus, being who He is, the Son of David, and the Son of God, perceives their evil intentions and by the gift of the prophetic working in Him, cuts to the chase and asks pertinent questions that cut to the heart and leaves them speechless, fearful that if they do reply they will expose themselves for the hypocrites they really are.

TO EAT BREAD ON THE SABBATH

In the first verse of this chapter we see the opening scene, "*Now it happened, as He went into the house of one of the rulers of the Pharisees to eat bread on the Sabbath, that they watched Him closely.*" Eating bread on the Sabbath was acceptable, but according to the Sabbath laws, it had to be prepared before this day of rest. I mention this here as a reminder that the Pharisees are all about fulfilling their laws and traditions, and so far, so good, everything is in order.

Jesus is at the table of a very important ruler of the Pharisees, and they watch Him closely. Yet, with all their evil intentions to try to entrap Him doing or saying something evil, they never can. And He faithfully continues to teach God Word with an authority they do not know of. And with every available opportunity, Jesus publicly presents a word of correction to their false teachings and beliefs. Again, He is on a mission to evangelize the people, including the Pharisees.

ANOTHER TEST

While breaking bread with this prominent leader and others, Jesus is presented with another test concerning the Sabbath. Will He adhere to their harsh rules and traditions, or will He obey a new law of grace? The subject of the test presents himself before Jesus in Luke 14:2, *"And behold, there was a certain man before Him who had dropsy."* Will Jesus break their interpretation of the law of the Sabbath and heal this suffering man? Or will He bend to their harsh understanding of the law and allow this man to suffer another day?

WHAT DOES JESUS DO?

I suppose the atmosphere is tense in this room, with legalistic eyes glaring at Jesus, closely watching and waiting for an opportunity to catch Him in the act of breaking their graceless law. They hope He does what they say He should not do so they can trap and accuse Him of being a lawbreaker. Jesus heals the man and lets him go right in front of this room filled with Pharisees and lawyers who themselves are filled with religious spirits, legalism, and hypocrisy.

WHO ARE THE LAWYERS?

The lawyers are the scribes in the Bible, a group of learned men whose primary role is to study, interpret, and teach the Scriptures. They take their task of preserving the Word very seriously. They copy every word by hand. They count and recount every letter and every space for accuracy. They are committed to perfection in their work. But they commit error when they add the traditions of men into their interpretations of the Scriptures. Henceforth, Jesus has legal ground on which to cross-examine their written laws and the motives of their beliefs. And He does.

JESUS ASKS THE LAWYERS THE HARD QUESTION

As they all witness this man's healing from dropsy, Jesus then asks the lawyers the hard question, *"Is it lawful to heal on the Sabbath?"* Before this divine encounter they think they know the answer, but before they have a chance to answer this question, Jesus asks another question, a very convicting one too. *"Which of you, having a donkey or an ox that has fallen into a pit, will not immediately pull him out on the Sabbath day?"* With authority Jesus pierces their hearts with conviction. And they dare not reply with their uncaring interpretation about the law of the Sabbath.

Jesus calls them out on the carpet, and they all know He speaks the truth. But do they have ears that are spiritually open, and will they mend their hypocritical ways? Or will they block their ears with pride and stubbornness? Like us, each one will have their chance to answer for themselves.

ANOTHER IMPORTANT QUESTION REMAINS

Another important question remains to be answered—does Jesus break the law of the Sabbath when He heals this man on the Sabbath? The answer is "No." According to God's law concerning the Sabbath, no law is broken. But He does break the scribes and Pharisee's interpretation concerning the law of the Sabbath.

Jesus addresses a crowd of people who gather to hear Him, and He says to them, "*Do not think that I have come to do away with or undo the Law or the Prophets; I have come not to do away with or undo but to complete and fulfill them*" (Matthew 5:17 AMPC).

Jesus responds to the Pharisees who saw His disciples pluck off some heads of grain to eat on the Sabbath, "*The Sabbath was made for man, and not man for the Sabbath. Therefore the Son of Man is also Lord of the Sabbath*" (Mark 2:27-28).

THE RICHES OF JESUS ON DISPLAY

- Jesus does not come to break the law, but to fulfill the law.
- He perceives the evil intentions of the scribes and the Pharisees.
- Not only does Jesus call out the Pharisees and the scribes for their hypocrisy but He takes the time to teach them why they are wrong.
- Jesus does not bend to their hypocrisy.
- He operates in the law of grace.
- It is not the will of Jesus for this man to suffer another day.

CRACK THE MIRACLE CODE

Jesus does not bow to hypocrisy but operates in the new law of grace.

As you read Miracle 32, you will discover the power of His mercy and how it cleans, heals, and makes us whole.

FAITH ASSIGNMENT

Be honest with yourself and examine your beliefs. Are you operating under a harsh interpretation of God's Word? Do you understand God's grace? What steps, if any, are you willing to take to break free from false teachings?

PRAYER OF FAITH

Dear Jesus, my heart's desire is to follow after You and Your ways. I give You permission to show me if there be any wicked way in me, so that I may ask for Your forgiveness and change my behavior or wrong thoughts. Holy Spirit, I ask for Your comfort as I walk through this process of change in my life. In Your precious name I pray, amen.

Questions for Miracle 31: Hypocrisy Versus Grace

1. What must we do, as a guest in someone's home, when their rules are unacceptable to God?
2. According to our lesson, why is there great conflict between Jesus and the Pharisees?

3. What does Jesus openly call the Pharisees?
4. Why does He rebuke the Pharisees?
5. What are the Pharisees all about?
6. Can the Pharisees with their evil intentions ever entrap Jesus doing or saying something wrong?
7. With every available opportunity, what does Jesus do publicly with these Pharisees?
8. Who else besides the people is Jesus on a mission to evangelize?
9. In one word, what is dropsy?
10. What was the hard question Jesus asks the lawyers?
11. What was the second convicting question He asks them?
12. With what does Jesus pierce their hearts with conviction?
13. Who are the lawyers?
14. What was their error when interpreting the Scriptures?
15. Does Jesus break the law of the Sabbath when He heals the man of dropsy on the Sabbath?
16. What does He break?

MIRACLE 32
ONE OUT OF TEN RETURNS TO GIVE THANKS

Jesus Cleanses Ten Lepers on the Way to Jerusalem

Let's continue our journey with Jesus and enter into a village where He meets up with ten leprous men who call out to Him for mercy. We will read about this miracle in Luke 17:11-19.

> *Now it happened as He went to Jerusalem that He passed through the midst of Samaria and Galilee. Then as He entered a certain village, there met Him ten men who were lepers, who stood afar off. And they lifted up their voices and said, "Jesus, Master, have mercy on us!"*
>
> *So when He saw them, He said to them, "Go, show yourselves to the priests." And so it was that as they went, they were cleansed.*
>
> *And one of them, when he saw that he was healed, returned, and with a loud voice glorified God, and fell down on his face at His feet, giving Him thanks. And he was a Samaritan.*
>
> *So Jesus answered and said, "Were there not ten cleansed? But where are the nine? Were there not any found who returned to give glory to God except this foreigner?" And He said to him, "Arise, go your way. Your faith has made you well."*

THE PLIGHT OF THE LEPER

Here we have a group of ten lepers. And as they say, "there's power in numbers," but in this case because of their numbers it's more difficult for them to draw near to Jesus. Not because Jesus will not accept them, but because the crowds fear their disease. But even though they stand afar off from where Jesus is, He sees them. He knows their plight.

FAR FROM JESUS

Like these ten men stand afar off, you might be in the same position, far from Jesus. You may fear that Jesus will reject you because of past failures and sin issues. Or you doubt He cares for you. You listen to lying spirits that say there's no hope for you. You continue to convince yourself that you are unlovable, undesirable for God. These are bold-faced lies that keep you far from Jesus.

Society rejects these ten men because of their leprosy, but Jesus does not. He openly welcomes lepers, as He does all of us. There is no disease too great that He cannot or will not heal. Your spiritual disease, sin, is not too much for Him to forgive. Your broken heart is not too tough for Him to touch and mend. Instead of keeping your distance far from Jesus, take a step of faith forward and draw near to Him.

> *Move your heart closer and closer to God, and he will come even closer to you. But make sure you cleanse your life, you sinners, and keep your heart pure and stop doubting* (James 4:8-9 TPT).

CALL OUT TO HIM

From a distance, for fear that Jesus too will reject them like the rest, these men call out to Him to have mercy and show compassion for the afflicted, contagious, rejected, and wretched condition they are in.

Back in the early 1980s, I was a young wife and mama of three (and eventually a total of eight) and I also was a baby believer growing up in the faith. I taught them a verse that I have carried with me throughout all these years, even now as a grandma of fourteen. And I share this with you today, *"The Lord will hear when I call to Him"* (Psalm 4:3).

Just as these ten leprous men with all their pain and suffering call out to Him, even from a distance for fear that they are not acceptable to Him, He hears them. And He is faithful to hear us too.

Our words to Jesus do not fall on deaf ears. He actually listens with His heart. He understands our struggles, our trials, those inward hurts that others may not know.

So, I encourage you, especially if you are in a tough spot, to call out to Him now, and He will hear you.

JESUS, MASTER

When these ten men lift their voices, they call their healer by His name, "Jesus, Master." This is powerful because they are vocally acknowledging who He is. And doing so, publicly.

When they call out to Jesus as Master, they acknowledge His authority. His authority over them, over the leprosy that encapsulates their bodies. They acknowledge His supernatural deity over all things.

As one who operates in the healing ministry, people call me their teacher, because this is what I do. I teach people how to heal, and to be healed. But they do not call me their "Master," nor would I allow anyone to do so. This title does not belong to me, but to the One I serve and represent, Jesus.

Why do I bring this up? Because there is power in our words; and in this situation with these ten lepers, there is power in the names of God. When they call Him "Master," they are calling down upon His authority and governing leadership over them and the situation. By the power of their words they are releasing supernatural power for their miracle.

HAVE MERCY ON US!

They call out to Jesus to have mercy on them. Mercy is His nature, and intertwines with His compassion, which is love in action. We read about His acts of love, compassion, and mercy throughout the Gospels.

Jesus willingly reaches out to these ten men with kindness and goodness to heal them of their misery and affliction. This is the definition of mercy (Strong's G1656).

And whatever ails us, whether spiritually, emotionally or physically, Jesus desires and can heal us by His kindness and goodness toward us too. There is no need for us to remain in misery and affliction because He does have mercy on us.

HE SEES AND HEARS US

A dangerous area that hurts people deeply is invisibility. They believe the lie that no one sees them. But the truth is, there is Someone who always sees, and not just with physical eyes, but with spiritual eyes.

In the Old Testament, we read about a slave by the name of Hagar who comes between a man and his barren wife. The situation lands her in a heap of trouble; in fact, she finds herself abandoned in a desert. But amid her earthly mess, she meets God by a spring of water that means, "Well of the One Who Lives and Sees Me." *God* sees her affliction, reaches out to her in her time of need, protects her, provides for her needs, and even blesses her and her future descendants. He informs her that she is pregnant with a son, and instructs her to name her son *Ishmael*, which means *God hears*. (See Genesis 16:6-15 to read Hagar's story.)

Just as God sees and hears Hagar in her time of distress, so too Jesus sees into the heart of the matter of these ten leprous men. He also sees and hears us when we think we are invisible, and no one cares. The Lord is ever-present, He's all-seeing, all-hearing, all-knowing, and all-caring. He's waiting for us to call out to Him. Do so now.

THEY RECEIVE A FAITH ASSIGNMENT

From a distance, these ten men—completely covered with a highly contagious and disfiguring disease—call out to Jesus. He hears and sees them and responds with a faith assignment. How peculiar. I'm sure they desire Him to heal them right on the spot, but instead He tells them to *"Go, show yourselves to the priests."*

Sometimes Jesus lays hands on the sick and they recover; other times He heals with a verbal word of faith; and other times He assigns faith assignments, as He does with these ten lepers.

The healing does not take place until they do as He says, *"Go."*

ONE OUT OF TEN RETURNS

Heaven records the spiritual stats, only one out of ten returns to give thanks for his miracle. Whoa! This shows us that God sees every moment of a miracle, from the start to the finish. And the miracle begins in the heart with hope, and during the miracle faith activates, and the miraculous event finishes deep in the soul of the recipient, a thankful or thankless heart.

WITH A LOUD VOICE GLORIFIED GOD

This group of men have been very vocal during this miracle. They are not timid in their request for Jesus to show mercy on them and heal them from this dreadful leprosy. But one in particular is more vocal than the rest. It's the one man out of the group of ten men who returns to give thanks. Again, being very outspoken and with a loud voice, this time he glorifies God.

His response shows me that not only is his body cleansed and healed from all leprosy, so too is his soul (his mind and emotions). No longer fearful of being rejected or run out of town, the shame has lifted. He does not need to throw rocks at someone passing near him and shout disgraceful things about himself, “Unclean!” Instead, he uses his loud voice to openly glorify God.

HE FELL ON HIS FACE AT JESUS' FEET

This man truly gets it. He understands the outpouring of mercy that Jesus bestows upon him. Not only does he loudly give shouts of praise, but he physically throws himself at the feet of Jesus in worship and adoration of his Master. This is evidence of a truly changed man, not just physically healed, but inwardly too. This man is made whole in every way a person can be, physically, mentally, emotionally, and spiritually too.

GIVING THANKS

Giving thanks to God for the things He has done for us is extremely important. It keeps us humble and solidifies His sovereignty in our lives. It shows appreciation for the little things as well as the big things He does for us. It shows spiritual growth and maturity. And it keeps us free from the sin of entitlement.

A SAMARITAN

While we do not know about the ethnicity of the other men in this group, this man is a Samaritan. As stated earlier in this work, there is a lot of animosity between the Jews and the Samaritans. The main conflict between the two people groups has to do with where they worship God. The Jews believe the true place of worship is in the temple, while the Samaritans believe worship is to take place on top of Mount Gerizim. What God truly wants is for us to worship Him in Spirit and in truth. This is a matter of the heart, not a physical place. And as we can see, this Samaritan man receives the revelation of who heals him, the true Messiah, Jesus Christ, the Anointed and Promised One, and he falls at His feet to worship Him in Spirit and in truth.

> *But the hour is coming, and now is, when the true worshipers will worship the Father in spirit and truth; for the Father is seeking such to worship Him. God is Spirit, and those who worship Him must worship in spirit and truth* (John 4:23-24).

YOUR FAITH HAS MADE YOU WELL

Again, we hear these beautiful words from the lips of Jesus, *"Your faith has made you well."* Faith is limitless; whatever we apply it to, it will produce. And this man activates his faith in the healing power of Jesus, and his faith produces healing from that all-consuming power of this torturous deadly disease, leprosy. Not one spot of leprosy remains. He is completely cleansed by the power of his faith in Jesus.

THE RICHES OF JESUS ON DISPLAY

- Jesus' mercy heals the afflicted.
- Jesus is all-seeing.
- Jesus is all-hearing.
- Jesus is ever-present to help us in our time of need.

CRACK THE MIRACLE CODE

Faith in His mercy cleanses, heals and makes us whole.

When reading Miracle 33, you will learn how to resurrect your miracle, even though it sleeps.

FAITH ASSIGNMENT

Do a self-check and examine your spiritual heart, does it need a cleansing from Jesus? Are you holding on to doubt and unbelief that God is able and willing to heal you in every area of your life? Are you believing a lie that He does not care about you, or that He loves everyone, except you? These are forms of spiritual leprosy that only Jesus can heal you from. And He is more than willing to do so. Starting right now, call out to Him and accept His love and forgiveness.

PRAYER OF FAITH

Dear Jesus, I have believed lies that I am too far gone for You to reach, and so I have stood afar off from You. But I lay down at Your feet my broken heart, my sin-filled life, and the strength of this disease that has caused so much suffering in my life. I call upon Your mercy to cleanse me, to heal me, and to make me whole again. In Your beautiful name I pray, amen and amen.

Questions for Miracle 32: One Out of Ten Returns to Give Thanks

1. Usually “there's power in numbers,” but in this case because of their numbers it's what?
2. Why is it difficult for them to draw near Jesus?
3. Even though these ten men stand afar off from Jesus, what does He see?
4. What do these ten men call out to Jesus for?
5. In Psalm 4:3, what does the Lord do when we call Him?
6. What do they acknowledge when they call Jesus "Master"?
7. What is Strong's definition of mercy?
8. What does the spring of water mean where Hagar meets God?

9. What does *Ishmael* mean?
10. What does Jesus give the ten lepers?
11. How many out of the ten return to give Jesus thanks?
12. Instead of declaring with a loud voice "Unclean" about himself, what does he now do with a loud voice?
13. Giving thanks protects us from what sin?
14. What was the main conflict between the Jews and the Samaritans about?
15. The Jews believe the true place of worship is where?
16. Where do the Samaritans believe they are to worship God?
17. How does God want us to worship Him?
18. Worship is not about a physical place, but what?

MIRACLE 33
THAT YOU MAY BELIEVE

Jesus Raises Lazarus from the Dead

Jesus and His disciples are at Bethabara, about 30 miles, or a day's journey from Bethany, when He hears that Lazarus is sick. Instead of rushing to his deathbed, Jesus waits two more days. It's not until He receives the news that His dear friend is dead that He begins the journey to his tomb. Now, when He arrives, Lazarus has been laid to rest for four days. Here at the grave of His close friend, He weeps, prays a prayer of faith, and performs a mighty miracle so that we may believe.

Miracle 33 is found in John 11:1-45, and due to its length please first read this portion of Scripture in your own Bible, then return here as we discuss it together. We will begin our discussion with John 11:1-3:

> *Now a certain man was sick, Lazarus of Bethany, the town of Mary and her sister Martha. It was that Mary who anointed the Lord with fragrant oil and wiped His feet with her hair, whose brother Lazarus was sick. Therefore the sisters sent to Him, saying, "Lord, behold, he whom You love is sick."*

The name *Lazarus* means "whom God helps," and Jesus certainly does help him. But His timing is different from Mary and Martha's. Jesus is not moved by their urgency, but as we will find out, His delay has a purpose—to glorify the Son of God.

In *The Passion Translation*, verse 4 reads: *"When he heard this, he said, 'This sickness will not end in death for Lazarus, but will bring glory and praise to God. This will reveal the greatness of the Son of God by what takes* place.'" Jesus is laying the foundation of this miracle by the power of faith-filled words. *"Now Jesus loved Martha and her sister and Lazarus. So, when He heard that he was sick, He stayed two more days in the place where He was"* (John 11:5-6). How curious is Jesus' response to their news.

With a surface glance, one would think Jesus doesn't care, but as we take a deep look we understand just how much He really does care for all. So much so that He denies Himself for the sake of the others.

JESUS RESPONDS WITH A PARABLE

Jesus is aware that they are afraid when He says, "*Let us go to Judea again.*" The disciples said to Him, "*Rabbi, lately the Jews sought to stone You, and are You going there again?*" He responds to their fear with a parable, "*Are there not twelve hours in the day? If anyone walks in the day, he does not stumble, because he sees the light of this world. But if one walks in the night, he stumbles, because the light is not in him*" (John 11:7-10).

With the use of this parable, Jesus reminds His disciples that the time is short, and we must be about our heavenly Father's business and win souls. We are to be bold and not fear our enemies, or what they may do to us.

LAZARUS SLEEPS

In John 11:11, Jesus gives a word of knowledge, a prophetic word concerning His dear friend Lazarus that is happening now that in the natural He would have no knowledge about. He says to them, *"Our friend Lazarus sleeps, but I go that I may wake him up."* But they misunderstand His faith talk and think because He says *"Lazarus sleeps,"* that He means he is sick and resting and will get well. But Jesus knows they do not understand Him yet, even though they have heard their Master use this term before when He raised Jairus' daughter from the dead. *"Now all wept and mourned for her; but He said, 'Do not weep; she is not dead, but sleeping.'"*

LAZARUS IS DEAD

Jesus clarifies Himself in John 11:14, *"Then Jesus said to them plainly, 'Lazarus is dead.'"* I can understand the disciples' confusion with His faith verbiage when He uses the term *sleep* for *death* in Miracle 15 when He raises Jairus' daughter from the dead. But they have been traveling with Jesus almost three years now, witnessing many miracles, more miracles than this world can even hold. I would think at least one of the disciples would ask if He meant Lazarus is dead. But they do not.

SPIRITUALLY ATTENTIVE

The disciples' lack of understanding in this matter of His faith speech shows me that we need to be spiritually attentive. We should pay close attention when He speaks to us. And realize that He doesn't just make small talk with us—His message runs deep.

THAT YOU MAY BELIEVE

Then Jesus speaks a convicting statement that cuts to the heart of the matter concerning belief and unbelief. He says in John 11:15, *"And I am glad for your sakes that I was not there, that you may believe. Nevertheless let us go to him."* Jesus is super perceptive. He knows our level of faith, and when we struggle to believe. So for their sake, Jesus waits for His friend to pass before going to minister to him.

Why? Jesus loves His disciples, and His greatest work on Calvary draws near. And He knows it will be very difficult for them when they see Him die on the Cross. Time is running out to prepare their faith to take over the work of the ministry.

BE CAREFUL WHAT YOU SAY!

Negative people, like Thomas, are careless with their words. He and others like him with their faithless speech, talk themselves into doubting Jesus constantly. His loose lips earn him a dishonorable title, "Doubting Thomas." Let us read his sarcastic reply to Jesus in John 11:16, *"Then Thomas, who is called the Twin, said to his fellow disciples, 'Let us also go, that we may die with Him.'"* This snide response is probably due to the conversation in verses 7 and 8, *"Then after this He said to the disciples, 'Let us go to Judea again.' The disciples said to Him, 'Rabbi, lately the Jews sought to stone You, and are You going there again?'"*

I don't know if Thomas said this aloud or muttered it under his breath, either way, Jesus heard his disrespectful tongue. Be careful what you say!

THE COMFORT OF FRIENDS

> *So when Jesus came, He found that he had already been in the tomb four days. Now Bethany was near Jerusalem, about two miles away. And many of the Jews had joined the women around Martha and Mary, to comfort them concerning their brother* (John 11:17-19).

The comfort of friends is much needed and appreciated at a time like this, but not so for Jesus. He knows that this is not a Going Home celebration, but a Resurrection Party.

Unity is a powerful force, but the unity of grief in this situation works against faith to believe in a miracle of resurrection. He will need to meet with both Martha and Mary alone and do so quickly.

HIS ENCOUNTER WITH MARTHA

> *Then Martha, as soon as she heard that Jesus was coming, went and met Him, but Mary was sitting in the house. Now Martha said to Jesus, "Lord, if You had been here, my brother would not have died. But even now I know that whatever You ask of God, God will give You"* (John 11:20-22).

These three verses give us profound insight into Martha's life, who is known for her servant's heart, but now we see a deep revelation into the depth of her faith in her Lord, Jesus. She verbally acknowledges her faith that her brother, Lazarus, would still be alive if Jesus had been there to heal him from sickness. And takes it a step further indirectly referring to His intimate relationship with Abba, *"Whatever You ask of God, God will give You."* She knows that not only does Jesus have the power to heal the sick, but also to raise the dead.

For the most part, Martha sees Him as the Son of God who has no limits to what He can do. Why do I say, "for the most part?" Because usually this is how she sees Him. In matters of faith, He has no limits, but on this day, she grieves the death of her brother, and her emotions cloud her faith.

DO YOU BELIEVE THIS?

Jesus speaks prophetically to Martha. He says to her, *"'Your brother will rise again.' Martha said to Him, 'I know that he will rise again in the resurrection at the last day.' Jesus said to her, 'I am the resurrection and the life. He who believes in Me, though he may die, he shall live. And whoever lives and believes in Me shall never die. Do you believe this?' She said to Him, 'Yes, Lord, I believe that You are the Christ, the Son of God, who is to come into the world'"* (John 11:23-27).

She might wonder why He asks her to confirm her belief in His deity. And it's fantastic that even in her time of pain and grief she believes that Jesus is the Son of God, but that's not what He asks. He asks if she has the faith to believe in a miraculous resurrection from the dead for Lazarus now. But her thoughts are taken over by death, not in miracles.

WEEPING AND GROANING

Let's leave the scene of Martha and check in with Mary to see what's happening with her.

> *Therefore, when Jesus saw her weeping, and the Jews who came with her weeping, He groaned in the spirit and was troubled* (John 11:33).

It says here that Jesus groans in the spirit. This does not mean intercession in the Holy Spirit, but groaning because of the pain He experiences. It's the type of pain we physically feel as we try to suppress our own emotions, but it becomes unbearable, and we begin to moan on the inside.

It also states that Jesus is troubled. In Greek this word for *trouble* is *tarassō* (Strong's 5015), and means He was "emotionally agitated." *The Passion Translation* describes it that Jesus *"shuddered with emotion."*

And He said, "Where have you laid him?" They said to Him, "Lord, come and see." Jesus wept. Then the Jews said, "See how He loved him!" And some of them said, "Could not this Man, who opened the eyes of the blind, also have kept this man from dying?" (John 11:34-37)

At this point in the story, people are weeping, but we will find out for different reasons. Mary and the Jews who come with her are weeping, in Greek this weeping is *klaiō* (Strong's G2799), and it means they are "mourning for their dead." But the tears Jesus sheds is different, in the Greek this *weeping* is *dakryō* (Strong's G1145). Jesus already knows that He is about to raise Lazarus from the dead, so He is not mourning the death of Lazarus, but senses great emotion, compassion, and mercy for the deep pain He perceives in Mary and the others.

IF YOU WOULD BELIEVE

Then Jesus, again groaning in Himself, came to the tomb. It was a cave, and a stone lay against it. Jesus said, "Take away the stone" (John 11:38-39).

Even during His personal frustration from their lack of faith and understanding about the supernatural power He possesses as the Son of God, He commands them to, *"Take away the stone."* And dear Martha is mortified, and begins to express her concern in verse 39, *"Lord, by this time there is a stench, for he has been dead four days."* But even in her grief and misunderstanding, in verse 40 He reprimands her, *"Did I not say to you that if you would believe you would see the glory of God?"*

LAZARUS, COME FORTH!

Then they took away the stone from the place where the dead man was lying. And Jesus lifted up His eyes and said, "Father, I thank You that You have heard Me. And I know that You always hear Me, but because of the people who are standing by I said this, that they may believe that You sent Me." Now when He had said these things, He cried with a loud voice, "Lazarus, come forth!" And he who had died came out

> *bound hand and foot with graveclothes, and his face was wrapped with a cloth. Jesus said to them, "Loose him, and let him go"* (John 11:41-44).

Jesus prays in faith, thanks His Father that He hears Him, and clarifies this confession is not for Him, but for the sake of the witnesses, that they might believe that He is sent to them by Father God. He commands dead Lazarus to come out of that grave! And all witness him, bound in his grave clothes, waddle out of that tomb. Jesus commands them to unbind him and let him go. And as they do, dead flesh is fresh, full of life, as his blood circulates, his color returns, no longer cold but warm to the touch. The impurities of death leave by the power of faith. He lives, he breathes, and has his being for the glory of our Lord, amen!

THE RESULTS

Many of the Jews that witness the resurrection of Lazurus believe Jesus is the Son of God: *"Then many of the Jews who had come to Mary, and had seen the things Jesus did, believed in Him"* (John 11:45). But a few hard-hearted witnesses depart to report what Jesus did to the Pharisees. And the fear-filled Pharisees and the chief priests call a special meeting of the High Council and agree to kill Jesus. (Read John 11:44-54.) They also plot to silence the testimony of Lazarus by assignation. (Read John 12:9-11.)

THE ENEMY FIGHTS THE MIRACULOUS

The enemy, the devil, fights the miraculous, before, during, and after. Why? Because he fears the results of souls won for Jesus—more people believing for miracles, producing more souls for Christ. So, he fights hard and nasty to abort a miracle before it has opportunity to birth; and after he fights to kill the miracle, to stop the work of the Kingdom from reproducing.

THE RICHES OF JESUS ON DISPLAY

- As the Son of Man, Jesus' faith is unwavering.
- Jesus understands the battle that must be won.
- And Jesus never gives up on His friends.

CRACK THE MIRACLE CODE

Resurrect your miracle!

As you read Miracle 34, answer the question, what do you want Jesus to do for you? And learn to grab hold of Jesus' attention with your faith.

FAITH ASSIGNMENT

What miracle in your life has died? How can you resurrect it? Pray in faith and ask Holy Spirit to reveal to you the steps to take to bring it back to life.

PRAYER OF FAITH

Oh, Father God, this miraculous resurrection of Lazarus from the dead speaks volumes to my faith. I hear Your Spirit call out to mine not to give up, but to fight the good fight of faith and to resurrect that miracle I heard You speak to me before. Dear Jesus, I take the limits off You. Have Your way and be the Miracle Worker in my life today. In Your precious name I pray, amen.

Questions for Miracle 33: That You May Believe

1. What does the name *Lazarus* mean?
2. What is the purpose behind Jesus' delay?
3. With the use of a parable, what does Jesus remind the disciples about?
4. Where have the disciples heard Jesus refer to someone's death as being asleep?
5. Why does Jesus say to His disciples in verse 15, *"And I am glad for your sakes that I was not there"?*
6. What dishonorable title does Thomas have?
7. Jesus knows that this is not a Going Home celebration, but what type of party?
8. But even in Martha's grief and misunderstanding in verse 40 what is the reprimand He gives her?
9. What are the well-known words Jesus calls out to Lazarus while he is dead in the tomb?

10. What three acts of faith does Jesus do as He stands in front of Lazarus' tomb?
11. What was the main result of this resurrection miracle?
12. What do the Pharisees and the chief priest agree to do with Jesus?
13. What else do they plot to do?
14. Why does the devil fight the miraculous before, during, and after a miracle?

MIRACLE 34
WHAT DO YOU WANT JESUS TO DO FOR YOU?

Jesus Restores Sight to Blind Bartimaeus

Jesus is about to leave Jericho, "A City of Palm Trees," that caters to rich and powerful people. This city is also known for a victorious battle where the walls tumble down, a story filled with redemption and grace for Rahab, a Canaanite harlot, and a life-changing encounter for a wealthy tax collector, Zacchaeus, who climbs a sycamore tree for a better view of Jesus and is never the same again. It is also here where Jesus meets blind Bartimaeus who receives a glance into what the supernatural power of his faith in Jesus can do.

This supernatural event is found in Mark 10:46-52.

> *Now they came to Jericho. As He went out of Jericho with His disciples and a great multitude, blind Bartimaeus, the son of Timaeus, sat by the road begging. And when he heard that it was Jesus of Nazareth, he began to cry out and say, "Jesus, Son of David, have mercy on me!" Then many warned him to be quiet; but he cried out all the more, "Son of David, have mercy on me!" So Jesus stood still and commanded him to be called. Then they called the blind man, saying to him, "Be of good cheer. Rise, He is calling you." And throwing aside his garment, he rose and came to Jesus. So Jesus answered and said to him, "What do you want Me to do for you?" The blind man said to Him, "Rabboni,*

that I may receive my sight." Then Jesus said to him, "Go your way; your faith has made you well." And immediately he received his sight and followed Jesus on the road.

By reading the first two verses, we see that even before Bartimaeus meets Jesus, he believes Him to be the Messiah. We know this to be true because of the way he calls out to Jesus, Son of David. This Son of David title is in reference to the Messianic promise found in Isaiah 9:6-7. And the Messiah is also a descendant of the lineage of King David.

OBSTACLES THAT STAND IN THE WAY OF OUR HEALING

Then many warned him to be quiet; but he cried out all the more, "Son of David, have mercy on me!" (Mark 10:48).

Often, people in need of a miracle face discouragement from others. But we must be persistent, like Bartimaeus is, and push through the obstacles that try to block us from our Miracle Worker, Jesus.

Some of this discouragement may be from the rigid religious community or unbelieving family members and friends who are unlearned in spiritual matters concerning healing. Either way, you must break through the negative thoughts and opinions of others and pursue your faith for your healing.

HAVE MERCY

Twice, Bartimaeus publicly cries out to the Messiah to have mercy on him. He calls out for His compassion. Some may find his mannerism to be unabashed, and I agree it is. But to understand his life situation better, it helps to remember that the blind are outcasts in society in this time. They consider Bartimaeus to be a burden to them, he might get in their way. So, they do not allow him or others like him to enter the city, or be among the crowds. He has no real opportunities to fend for himself. He must rely upon the kindness of others for daily substance. Society forces him to become a beggar.

Jesus has a big heart for the outcast—and He is about to dish out a heaping helping of mercy for him today.

JESUS STOOD STILL

> *So Jesus stood still and commanded him to be called. Then they called the blind man, saying to him, "Be of good cheer. Rise, He is calling you." And throwing aside his garment, he rose and came to Jesus* (Mark 10:49-50).

Jesus is accustomed to pleas for help for healing. But there is something about Bartimaeus that grabs the attention of Jesus and causes Him to stop. Is it his persistence? Is he the squeaky wheel that demands oil? I don't believe so. Why not? Because faith operates by love, you could say that love fuels faith. And a response to a squeaky wheel is out of frustration, and so it's not this.

What could it be that causes Jesus to stand still? Faith. Faith grabs hold of Jesus' attention every time. It's like a magnet that draws His attention.

"And whatever you ask for in prayer, having faith and [really] believing, you will receive" (Matthew 21:22 AMPC). Bartimaeus has the faith he needs to believe and receive his vision from the Son of David.

WHAT DO YOU WANT?

> *So Jesus answered and said to him, "What do you want Me to do for you?" The blind man said to Him, "Rabboni, that I may receive my sight"* (Mark 10:51).

It's amazing, but sometimes people are confused about what they really want. Some people want their physical healing but want to hold on to their disability checks from the government at the same time. While others want healing but don't want to let go of all the added attention they receive from family members who tend to their illness. Others are afraid to say what they personally want out of fear that other family members are worn out and do not want to fight the good fight of faith any longer.

And then there are those who know what they want—healing. And they are not afraid to face the changes that will occur in their life and actually embrace not only a body that is strong and healthy, but they long for a life that is radically different from what they have been in bondage to for so long. And Bartimaeus is in this category, he longs for eyes that see the people and the beauty all around him. He desires to be free and independent, no longer in need of others to guide him and fend for him. He unashamedly embraces the mercy of Christ to come into his life. He knows what he wants.

YOUR FAITH HAS MADE YOU *SŌZŌ*

> *Then Jesus said to him, "Go your way; your faith has made you well." And immediately he received his sight and followed Jesus on the road* (Mark 10:52).

Depending on which version of the Bible you read from, it says, *"Your faith has made you well."* The New King James Version uses the word, *"well,"* which in the Greek is *sōzō* (Strong's G4982),on and it means that Bartimaeus' faith in Jesus, his Messiah, saves, heals, and makes him whole. Not only can he see with new miracle eyes, but his faith in Jesus saves his spirit and makes his mind and emotions whole again from years of suffering. Bartimaeus' faith in Christ makes him *sōzō*.

This is such a beautiful testimony about a man who suffers from the ugliness of life. He knows darkness, cruelty, rejection, want, boredom, and loneliness. And now, He meets Jesus of Nazareth, the Son of David, Messiah, the Son of God, face to face, and he will never be the same. Bartimaeus' faith in the Lord Jesus gives him eyes that see, and the vision to appreciate life that very few understand. No longer is he in a situation that forces him to follow others, but now he chooses to follow Jesus for an adventure of a lifetime. Giving glory to God all the way. And leads others who see him to give praise to His God too.

THE RICHES OF JESUS ON DISPLAY

- Jesus is drawn to our faith.
- He sees beyond our negative situations.
- Jesus fulfills the desires of our heart.
- He opens more than physical eyes—He opens spiritual eyes too.

CRACK THE MIRACLE CODE

Grab hold of Jesus' attention with faith.

As you read Miracle 35, take courage that miracles are always in season.

FAITH ASSIGNMENT

Ask yourself, *What do I want or need Jesus to do for me?* Write it down. And find three promises from the Bible to back your faith for this request.

PRAYER OF FAITH

Dear Jesus, my faith is once again challenged by the miracle You gave to Bartimaeus. May I have the eyes of faith that he demonstrates in this miracle and to be so outspoken that I no longer care about what others think about me. And may I lead and guide others to follow and glorify You. All this I pray in Your most holy name, amen.

Questions for Miracle 34: What Do You Want Jesus to Do for You?

1. Who does Bartimaeus believe Jesus to be, even before he meets Him?
2. How do we know this to be true?
3. The title Son of David is in reference to what promise found in Isaiah 9:6-7?
4. What do people in need of a miracle often face from others?
5. Where does some of this discouragement come from?
6. What must you do to pursue your healing?
7. How many times does Bartimaeus cry out to the Messiah for mercy?
8. What are the blind considered to be by the society of that day?
9. What does Jesus have toward the outcast?
10. What is Jesus about to dish out to Bartimaeus?
11. What is it about Bartimaeus that grabs the attention of Jesus and causes Jesus to stop?
12. What does Matthew 21:22 say?
13. What does Jesus ask Bartimaeus?

14. What is Bartimaeus' response to Jesus?
15. How does Bartimaeus embrace the mercy of Christ in his life?
16. What does Jesus say in response to Bartimaeus' request?
17. What does the Greek word *sōzō* mean?
18. What does he do after immediately receiving his sight?

MIRACLE 35
CURSE A SPIRIT OF LACK IN YOUR LIFE

Jesus Curses a Barren Tree and It Withers and Dies

Jesus and His disciples approach Jerusalem, at Bethphage (in Greek means "the house of unripe figs" (Strong's G967), Mark 11:1 NASB). As we read on, Jesus gives two of His disciples a faith assignment with a word of knowledge that involves a donkey and people waving palm branches with shouts of Hosanna. It's been a glorious day, but now it's late and they leave for Bethany. In Matthew 21:18-22 we read the story of the barren fig tree and come to understand what it means.

> *Now in the morning, as He returned to the city, He was hungry. And seeing a fig tree by the road, He came to it and found nothing on it but leaves, and said to it, "Let no fruit grow on you ever again." Immediately the fig tree withered away.*
>
> *And when the disciples saw it, they marveled, saying, "How did the fig tree wither away so soon?"*
>
> *So Jesus answered and said to them, "Assuredly, I say to you, if you have faith and do not doubt, you will not only do what was done to the fig tree, but also if you say to this mountain, 'Be removed and be cast into the sea,' it will be done. And whatever things you ask in prayer, believing, you will receive."*

An additional fact that adds an interesting take to this story is found in Mark 11:13-14, "*And seeing from afar a fig tree having leaves, He went to see if perhaps He would find something on it. When He came to it, He found nothing but leaves, for it was not the season for figs. In response Jesus said to it, 'Let no one eat fruit from you ever again.' And His disciples heard it.*" This is a puzzling, but fascinating detail about the faith of Jesus.

WHAT'S THIS ABOUT?

First, I want to say that there are multiple layers in this miracle about the fig tree, but to keep in tune with the theme of this book, I focus on the faith of Jesus, not on end-time beliefs.

We observe that Jesus curses the fig tree for not bearing fruit, even though it's not the season to bear fruit. What is this all about?

There is a foundational teaching in the miracle of the fig tree about the power of faith, faith-filled words, and about the potency in the prayer of faith. And this is where we will focus our attention.

JESUS HAD NEED OF A DONKEY

Let's read Mark 11:2-3, "*and He said to them, 'Go into the village opposite you; and as soon as you have entered it you will find a colt tied, on which no one has sat. Loose it and bring it. And if anyone says to you, "Why are you doing this?" say, "The Lord has need of it," and immediately he will send it here.'*"

This is the only time that we read in the Gospels that Jesus has *need* of anything. The call for this beast of burden is to carry the weight of Salvation —Jesus upon its back. The colt ushers Him into the gates of Jerusalem where the people celebrate His arrival and wave palm branches with shouts of praise, "*Hosanna! BLESSED IS HE WHO COMES IN THE NAME OF THE LORD.*"

Everything that Jesus has need of comes to fruition by the power of faith. In this case, it's faith in an old-time prophecy in Zechariah 9:9 (NIV), "*Rejoice greatly, Daughter Zion! Shout, Daughter Jerusalem! See, your king comes to you, righteous and victorious, lowly and riding on a donkey, on a colt, the foal of a donkey.*" Even the disciples who are sent have faith in the prophetic word of knowledge. And it all comes to pass.

NO FIGS

The time of Jesus living among us as one of us nears the end. Calvary is just around the corner for Him. He fulfills the prophecy where the people usher Him in with honor and praise as the Son of David, the true Messiah. The next morning after He awakes in His earth suit, like the rest of us, He's hungry. So He goes to the now famous fig tree and only finds leaves, no fruit. He speaks to it and says, *"Let no fruit grow on you ever again."*

It is of utmost importance that we as lovers and followers of Jesus bear fruit, and not just a little bit of fruit, but fruit in abundance. John the apostle encourages us with these words about fruit bearing, *"When you bear (produce) much fruit, My Father is honored and glorified, and you show and prove yourselves to be true followers of Mine"* (John 15:8 AMPC).

LET'S LOOK FOR MORE DETAILS

To help us understand this miracle with the fig tree, we need to look for more details to know what happens around this miraculous event. Jesus gives the disciples prophetic insight while using the example of the barren fig tree about what will happen to the nation of Israel (in biblical days) because she rejects Jesus, her king. (See Mark 11:12-14.)

In Mark 21:15-19, we observe how Jesus enters the temple and begins to clean house as He turns over the tables of the merchants who were doing business in the Lord's House of Prayer. And as the scribes and the chief priests hear about this, they begin to hatch a plot destroy Him. The next morning the disciples pass by the fig tree and see that it is dried up from the roots. Peter remembers what Jesus said the day before and now says, *"Rabbi, look! The fig tree which You cursed has withered away."* And I should add an extra detail here that Jesus *speaks* to the fig tree, while Peter reports that Jesus *curses* the fig tree.

I think it is important for us to know the difference between the word, *said* as in *"Jesus said"* in verse 14, and where Peter reports that "*Jesus cursed*" the fig tree in verse 21. In verse 14, the word *said* is *eipon,* and it means "to say, speak, tell or command" (Strong's G2036). Whereas in verse 21 the word *cursed* in the Greek language is *legō* (Strong's G3004), and it's linked to divine "judgment, sin and consequences" (Strong's G3004). This may appear to be a minute detail, but it has great significance about the power of our words.

First, Jesus speaks a stern word of faith to the barren fig tree, and it hears and obeys its Creator—Jesus. And then the next day, Peter and the other disciples see the consequences of the words they hear Jesus speak to the tree the day before.

There is a potent Scripture about the power of our words in Proverbs 18:21 (AMP), *"Death and life are in the power of the tongue, and those who love it and indulge it will eat its fruit and bear the consequences of their words."*

OUT OF SEASON

Have you ever craved a specific type of fruit, only to find out that it is out of season. Well, this is partly what Jesus runs into at the fig tree. He wants figs to eat, but there are no figs, because they are out of season. It's not the time of the year to harvest figs. But this doesn't seem to matter to the Creator of the universe. His expectations for sweet, ripe figs, although out of season, are astounding. And it should speak to us volumes of wisdom about His faith. The following are a few things that should speak to our souls concerning faith.

1. Faith is limitless. Because we believe in the power of our Miracle Worker activated in us, our fig tree of faith should have a bumper crop of miracles.
2. It's the open season on faith. It does not matter that the miracle fig that you so desire, even though out of season, is not there. Your faith should produce what you desire or have need of because you believe in the promises of God.
3. Faith is not based on the natural realm. Faith never has been, nor will it ever be based on the natural realm of earth. Faith supersedes the natural realm, including human reasoning, and the realm of the five senses.

ANOTHER LOOK AT THE MEANING OF FAITH

Some may think that it takes great faith to expect to pick and eat a fig off the tree when it's not the season for fig-picking. Let's take another look at the meaning of faith.

In Mark 11:22-24, Jesus answers and says to them: *"Have faith in God. For assuredly, I say to you, whoever says to this mountain, 'Be removed and be cast into the sea,' and does not doubt in his heart, but believes that those things he says will be done, he will have whatever he says. Therefore I say to you, whatever things you ask when you pray, believe that you receive them, and you will have them."*

Jesus says to have faith in God. This word *faith* in the Greek is *pistis,* and it means that we are "to trust, be assured in God's faithfulness" (Strong's G4102). Perhaps it helps to look at faith in this way. It's not so much our level of faith, which can at times be daunting or condemning, but easier to understand is our level of trust in God, and in His faithfulness. We should ask ourselves if we trust God.

1. Do you trust that Jesus is the Son of God?
2. Do you trust that He died on the Cross and rose from the dead? Do you trust that the Holy Bible is the infallible Word of God?
3. Do you trust that Jesus created the heavens and the earth?
4. Do you trust that He created people?

These five questions ask if you trust in things that you must believe by faith. And yet, you know that you do. So when Jesus asks us to "Have faith in God" for other unexplainable, way-out miraculous figs, such as deliverance from demon-possession, healing from sickness or disease, creative miracles for a new heart, set of lungs, functional kidneys, eyes and ears or whatever ails you, don't be afraid. Have faith in God. Trust Him.

THE CREATIVE-DESTRUCTIVE POWER OF WORDS

Another characteristic of Jesus is that He doesn't put up with lack in His life, and neither should we. Whether in season or out of season, He expects there to be an ample supply of sweet and delicious figs on this tree. And because this tree doesn't produce the fruit it ought to for Him, He uses the creative-destructive power of words and speaks death to it.

I am a strong proponent of speaking life, but I also teach that we need to learn how to wield the power of the tongue, our words, effectively. When it comes to a spirit of death, such as cancer, we need to first speak words of faith and speak death to that cancer at its very seed and command it to dry up at the roots. Supernaturally zap the deadly power out of your cells, tissues, organs, and systems in the name of Jesus. Then we speak life, healing, good health, and strength to our body.

CURSE THE SPIRIT OF LACK

Curse the spirit of lack not only in your finances, but also in the areas of your health, your faith, your peace, and every area where you see lack. The following are some confessions of faith against lack in different areas of your life to vocalize with faith.

CONFESSION OF FAITH AGAINST FINANCIAL LACK

In the name of Jehovah Jireh (Genesis 22:7-8), a spirit of lack will not control my finances. For in my God, I trust. My God shall supply all my needs according to His riches in glory. (Philippians 4:19). No matter what earthly currency is going under, God is my Source, and I have no lack of supply. In the name of the Lord who supplies, I pray with thanksgiving, amen.

CONFESSION OF FAITH AGAINST LACK OF HEALTH

In the name of the Lord, my God, I renounce a spirit of death, sickness, disease, and weakness in my body. I declare by faith that God is my Healer (Exodus 15:26), Jesus is my Strength (Ephesians 6:10), and by His healing stripes I am healed and made whole in spirit, soul, and in my physical body too (Isaiah 53:4-5).

CONFESSION OF FAITH AGAINST LACK OF FAITH

In Jesus' name, I renounce the power of weak faith in my life. I ask for forgiveness for all doubt and unbelief in my heart. I repent and do a 180-degree turn, and I choose this day to build up my most holy faith (Jude 1:20) by hearing (Romans 10:17), studying (2 Timothy 2:15), and living (Hebrews 4:12) out the word of faith in my life, starting today I confess words of faith, *"I have strong faith."* In your name, I pray believing, amen.

CONFESSION OF FAITH AGAINST LACK OF PEACE

In the name of the Lord, my High Tower (Psalm 144:2), I renounce this danger that surrounds me. Despite the unrest in this world, I put my trust in Jehovah Shalom (John 14:27, 16:33). I rely upon His peace that surpasses all understanding (Philippians 4:7). I do not surrender to a war-mongering spirit, rather I take up my shield of faith (Ephesians 6:16) and effectively use the sword of the Spirit (Ephesians 6:17) and fight the good fight of faith (1 Timothy 6:12), holding on to His peace (John 14:27). In Jesus' name, I rest in His peace, amen.

> *Everything you pray for with the fullness of faith you will receive!* (Matthew 21:22 TPT).

THE RICHES OF JESUS ON DISPLAY

- Jesus' trust in God is unwavering.
- Undeniably strong is Jesus' faith.
- Jesus produces miracles in all seasons of life by the power of faith.

CRACK THE MIRACLE CODE

Miracles are always in season.

When you read Miracle 36, you will learn how to hearken and listen to what God speaks to you.

FAITH ASSIGNMENT

Is there any area in your life where you see lack? If so, write it down. Look for a few promises of faith to combat this lack, write them down and begin to confess them over this area of lack in your life. And believe that God will supply that need in your life.

PRAYER OF FAITH

Dear Jesus, I surrender all doubt and unbelief at Your feet today. Help me to overcome this battle of lack in my life. Lead me into Your promise of plenty and show me where to share abundance in my life. In Your name I pray, amen.

Questions for Miracle 35: Curse a Spirit of Lack in Your Life

1. What is a foundational teaching in the miracle of the fig tree?
2. What is the one thing in the Gospels that Jesus was in need of?
3. What does Jesus find when He goes to the fig tree?
4. What was unusual about Jesus looking for fruit from this fig tree?
5. What does Jesus say to this fig tree?
6. What does Peter say to Jesus the next day concerning this fig tree?
7. What is the word *said* in the Greek language?
8. What does the word *said* mean in verse 14?
9. What is the word *cursed* in the Greek language?
10. What is the word *cursed* in the Greek language linked to?
11. According to Proverbs 18:21, what is in the power of the tongue?
12. What is faith?
13. What should your faith produce?
14. What does faith supersede?
15. What is another way to look at our level of faith?
16. What does Jesus use to speak death to the fig tree?
17. According to Matthew 21:22 (TPT), what type of faith should we pray with to receive?

MIRACLE 36
EARS TO HEAR

Jesus Reattaches an Enemy's Ear While Being Wrongfully Arrested

Jesus has been warning His disciples of this dark hour that must come to pass. And His enemy and ours, satan himself, enters into Judas Iscariot to betray Jesus. We find ourselves in the Garden on the night Jesus is betrayed. And as the arrest takes place and emotions get out of hand, impulsive Peter valiantly takes his sword and cuts the right ear off the high priest's servant. Listen to what God's Word speaks to us in this portion of Scripture from Luke 22:50-51:

> *And one of them struck the servant of the high priest and cut off his right ear. But Jesus answered and said, "Permit even this." And He touched his ear and healed him.*

We will start our study of Miracle 36 by looking into the names of two major characters in this miracle—Judas Iscariot and Simon Peter.

JUDAS ISCARIOT

Let's look at the meaning of Judas Iscariot's name. *Iscariot* is not his last name, but from a Hebrew word meaning *lock*, therefore, he is *Judas the locksmith.*[1] Names during Bible times have great meaning, and this surely lines up prophetically that he is the one the devil works through to arrest and lock up Jesus. Judas also has the keys to the treasure box. He is a traitor, a liar, and a thief, and he sells out Jesus for 30 pieces of silver.

Unfortunately, we have seen that a financial responsibility position is full of great temptation within the ministry. Often while training pastors and leaders how to operate in the realm of the supernatural when addressing this issue, the room is so full of silent conviction that a pin drop can be heard on the carpet. The treasure box is a revealer of character. If they can be trusted with its contents, they can be trusted with just about anything.

PETER

Jesus forewarns Peter about his denial of his Lord. He lets him know that the father of all lies, the devil, has sought permission to sift him as wheat in Luke 22:31-32:

> *And the Lord said, "Simon, Simon! Indeed, Satan has asked for you, that he may sift you as wheat. But I have prayed for you, that your faith should not fail; and when you have returned to Me, strengthen your brethren."*

What does it mean to *"sift him as wheat"*? The Greek word for this is *siniazō*, and it means "to sift him by inward agitation to try one's faith to the verge of overthrow" (Strong's G4617).

It's such disturbing news Jesus reveals to Peter. And it does come to pass just as He prophesies. But so too, the second half of this prophecy, *"But I have prayed especially for you [Peter], that your [own] faith may not fail; and when you yourself have turned again, strengthen and establish your brethren"* (Luke 22:32 AMPC). And the restorative power of forgiveness takes an imperfect and impulsive man, Simon (shifting sands), and turns him into Peter (the Rock). And he proves to be a true lover and follower of Jesus.

Simon is Peter's official given name. We've been taught that it means *"shifting sand."* Let's dig in to find revelation in this name. Sand is ground-up rock, and it's finer than gravel, and it forms beaches and deserts, and it's also used in construction. Jesus gives Simon a new name, Cephas, which translates to Peter (John 1:42) and means rock. Let's look at a rock. It's a solid formation made up of small granular pieces of sand. Peter goes through the spiritual process of shifting (transforming) from being a small, loose granule of sand found on the beach as a fisherman, to a solid rock foundation that Jesus will use to construct the early Church. Let's dig further in the sand for biblical affirmation about this name change.

Jesus uses the prophetic power of words and declares His call upon this man's life and the role he will have in the future of the Church.

> *And I tell you, you are Peter [Greek, Petros—a large piece of rock], and on this rock [Greek, petra—a huge rock like Gibraltar] I will build My church, and the gates of Hades (the powers of the infernal region) shall not overpower it [or be strong to its detriment or hold out against it]* (Matthew 16:18 AMPC).

I want to excavate a little deeper into Peter's new name, because the more we dig, the more we find. Listen to this, when Peter authors his second epistle to the Church in 2 Peter 1:1, there's a slight change of his name. *Simon* is now *symeōn* (G4826) and it means "harkening." This is a very important detail in the 36th miracle of Jesus recorded.

HOW DID THE ENEMY KNOW?

Matthew 16:18 also answers another question concerning the devil's request to sift Peter. How did the enemy know to sift Peter like wheat? Because he and his army of demons listen in on Jesus' conversations, and from there they plan their attacks against Peter, and us as well.

HARKEN

Harken means "to listen, to give special attention to something." Let's hear what the Spirit wants to say to us here. Jesus knows they will come to arrest Him this night. He tries to prepare the disciples for the danger that lies ahead and tells them to gather up the supplies they will need. In Luke 22:38 (TPT) they respond to Him, *"Lord, we already have two swords!"* Jesus responds to them, *"You still don't understand."* They leave the upper room, and He takes them to His secret place of prayer, to the Mount of Olives. He instructs them, *"Keep praying for strength to be spared from the severe test of your faith that is about to come"* (Luke 22:40 TPT). But they fail to pray and sleep instead.

Meanwhile Jesus intercedes and bleeds drops of blood from the intense agony He battles.

A lot of insight is given in this portion of Scripture. He tells His disciples they do not understand. This is why we need to harken and give special attention to what the Spirit of the Lord says to us, so we *do* understand. We receive this understanding as we stay alert and pray and intercede. Wake up! And hear what the Spirit of God speaks to you.

PETER CUTS OFF THE SERVANT'S EAR

Peter, out of fear and righteous indignation, takes a swing with his sword and slices off the right ear of the high priest's servant. Jesus puts a stop to this violence for several reasons, He knows it is the start of His journey to the Cross. The second reason is this is illegal, and Peter could go to jail; and thirdly, He cares for this lost man, the servant.

But then there is a profound spiritual lesson for us. This word *ear* in Greek is *ous,* and it is a metaphor that means "the faculty of perceiving with the mind, the faculty of understanding and knowing" (Strong's G3775). And it isn't just any ear, it's his right ear. In Greek, the *right* is *dexios,* and again is a metaphor meaning "a place of honor or authority" (Strong's G1188).

Spiritually speaking, when Peter cuts off this man's right ear, he deafens his ability to hear the Gospel of Jesus Christ. We've all heard the saying, "Preach the Gospel and only use words when necessary." If Jesus doesn't do something now, this man will be lost forever.

What does Jesus, the Son of God, do? With all compassion He reaches out and supernaturally reattaches the servant's right ear. I tell you the truth, this man just hears the greatest sermon anyone ever preaches to him. And no matter what the high priest or anyone else says or does against Jesus, they will never convince him that Jesus is not the Messiah. Jesus just won another convert for eternity.

ARE YOU BEING SIFTED?

Every true minister, and believer as well, is tried and tested, sifted as wheat. It's a painful process we must go through. It's not optional. Pray for God's grace, mercy and strength. Remember, He intercedes for you.

THE RICHES OF JESUS ON DISPLAY

- No matter the battle Jesus is fighting off, He stops and fights for us.
- He prophetically speaks hope into our future.
- Jesus calls things that are not as though they already are (see Romans 4:17).
- He intercedes for His beloved.
- Jesus believes in us.

CRACK THE MIRACLE CODE

Harken and listen to what Jesus is speaking to you.

As you read Miracle 37, take courage when you are spiritually spent, Jesus wants to minister to your grief and revive your faith.

FAITH ASSIGNMENT

This is a serious assignment of faith. Stop! Listen! And pray! What has God been speaking to you about? Will you listen and obey His commands to you today?

PRAYER OF FAITH

Well, Jesus, I must honestly confess that I have not been a good listener to You lately. I know You speak to me, but I am not harkening to Your voice. And for this, I am truly sorry. There are no excuses for this. I ask for Your forgiveness, and vow to listen better to You. In Your name, I pray, amen.

Questions for Miracle 36: Ears to Hear

1. What is the meaning of *Iscariot?*
2. According to the meaning of Judas' name, he was what?
3. How does the devil work through Judas?
4. What does Judas have the keys to?
5. What is Judas?

6. What does it mean to *"sift him as wheat"*?
7. What is the Greek word for *sift him?*
8. What have we been taught that Simon means?
9. What is the new name of Simon?
10. What is the translation of Simon's new name?
11. Rock is the translation for what name?
12. What is the slight change to Simon in 2 Peter 1:1?
13. What does *symeōn* mean?
14. How did the enemy know how to sift Peter?
15. What does *harken* mean?
16. Which ear does Peter cut off the high priest's servant?
17. What are three reasons Jesus stops the violence at this scene?
18. What is the Greek word for *ear*?
19. Metaphorically, what does *ear* mean?
20. What is the Greek word for *right*?
21. In Greek what does *right* mean here?
22. Spiritually speaking, what does Peter do when he cuts off this man's ear?
23. What does Jesus, the Son of God, do for this man?
24. Will anyone ever be able to convince this man that Jesus is not the Messiah?

MIRACLE 37
FAITH REVIVES

The Second Miraculous Catch of Fish

Where are we in the story of Jesus and His disciples and closest followers? They are full of grief as they witness His tortuous death on the Cross. They fear the retaliation of their enemies and are hiding.

During their time of grief, they must come to grips that Judas Iscariot betrays Jesus, and later hangs himself. They struggle with guilt because they abandon their Lord in His greatest hour of need. They hear and rehear Jesus' words and teachings play over and over in their minds, as they try to sort this all out.

Three days later, Mary Magdalene faces the confusion of Jesus' missing body and finds out that He gloriously rose from the dead, as He first appears from behind her at the site of His empty tomb (John 20:16).

And Matthew 28:9 records Jesus' appearance to the other women at the tomb. In the Gospel of Luke 24:31, Jesus appears to two of the disciples on the road to Emmaus. And the apostle John records that on the evening of His resurrection, Jesus appears and stands among them while they are behind locked doors in fear for their lives, and He gives them a salutation of peace (John 20:19).

Eight days later, Jesus appears again to them in the same place with another greeting of peace for their fearful and weary souls, but this time doubting Thomas is with them and Jesus rebukes him for his unbelief (John 20:26).

And now, Jesus appears to them once again on the shores of the Sea of Galilee. And this is where we begin our 37th recorded miracle of Jesus.

HIS FOLLOWERS ARE EMOTIONALLY SPENT

> *After this, Jesus let Himself be seen and revealed [Himself] again to the disciples, at the Sea of Tiberias. And He did it in this way: There were together Simon Peter, and Thomas, called the Twin, and Nathanael from Cana of Galilee, also the sons of Zebedee, and two others of His disciples. Simon Peter said to them, I am going fishing! They said to him, And we are coming with you! So they went out and got into the boat, and throughout that night they caught nothing* (John 21:1-3 AMPC).

At this point, the disciples are emotionally spent, and discouragement sets in. Why? They are accustomed to living and traveling with Jesus, ministering to big crowds, witnessing mighty miracles, and the excitement of the supernatural became a normal part of life for them.

Jesus appears suddenly from time to time, and this brings great comfort and joy to them, but then He departs once again. They don't quite yet understand it all. And frankly, they miss Him. And when people feel lonely, and misplaced, there is a normal tendency to want to go back to the way life used to be. For instance, Peter says, *"I am going fishing!"* and the others respond, "And we are coming with you!" Interesting observance here, even when Peter is at a low point in life he still leads the others to follow.

Jesus knows their struggles; He too has been through a lot. But now everything is different for Him, He is in His glorified body, no longer living in human flesh as the Son of Man but now He is alive as the Son of God. But He remembers the emotions that humans feel and the struggles we must work through. Hebrews 4:15 (AMPC) beautifully describes why He can sympathize with the disciples and us:

> *For we do not have a High Priest Who is unable to understand and sympathize and have a shared feeling with our weaknesses and infirmi-*

> *ties and liability to the assaults of temptation, but One Who has been tempted in every respect as we are, yet without sinning.*

CHILDREN

It's now His third appearance to the disciples (see John 21:14), and it's obvious to me that these mighty men of God are in a low place right now. And when Jesus appears to them on the shores of the Sea of Galilee, He calls out to them with the title, "Children." When He first calls them to follow Him, He promises to make them fishers of men. He trains them to be leaders, to carry on the work of the ministry, and to establish the Church for Him. Yet now, He calls out to them as children.

> *But when the morning had now come, Jesus stood on the shore; yet the disciples did not know that it was Jesus. Then Jesus said to them, "Children, have you any food?" They answered Him, "No"* (John 21:4-5).

Jesus loves these mighty men, He lays down His life for them, they are His friends, and His brothers in the family of God. There is no belittlement in the way in which He calls out to them, "Children," in the spiritual and emotional place they are in right now. In fact, it's the opposite. This is a term of endearment and brotherly affection toward them. He's healing their inward man. He's touching their souls, their minds and emotions that are beaten down, and are badly in need of repair. This is His way to reach out to show them that He cares about them.

HE BLESSES AND REVIVES

He loves them so much that He blesses them again with something that brought joy and excitement once before, and He knows that this miraculous catch will revive their faith.

> *And He said to them, "Cast the net on the* ***right*** *side of the boat, and you will find some"* (John 21:6).

So they cast, and soon they were not able to draw in the net because of the multitude of fish.

Not only does this word *right* in the Greek speak of the right versus the left side of the boat, it also speaks metaphorically to us about a place of honor or authority. Jesus not only blesses His workers of the Word, but He requires the same from His people.

The following are three reminders for the body of Christ to treat their leaders with honor, respect, tend to their needs, and bless them.

1. 1 Thessalonians 5:12-13: *And we urge you, brethren, to recognize those who labor among you, and are over you in the Lord admonish you, and to esteem them very highly in love for their work's sake. Be at peace among yourselves.*
2. 1 Timothy 5:17 (AMPC): *Let the elders who perform the duties of their office well be considered doubly worthy of honor [and of adequate financial support], especially those who labor faithfully in preaching and teaching.*
3. Luke 10:7 (TPT): *Don't shift from one house to another, but stay in one home during your time in that city. Eat and drink whatever they serve you. Receive their hospitality, for you are my harvester, and you deserve to be cared for.*

JOHN RECOGNIZES JESUS

If we quickly skim over the Word, we miss important details and lessons like *"the disciple whom Jesus loved said to Peter."* Who is the unnamed disciple who is first to recognize Jesus here? It's John. How do we know John is the disciple whom Jesus loves? Numerous times throughout Scripture this is how John is referenced. One of most touching references in the Bible about John being referred to as *"the one whom He loved,"* I believe, is while Jesus is dying on the Cross. He commissions John to tend to His mom after He passes: *"When Jesus therefore saw His mother, and the disciple whom He loved standing by, He said to His mother, 'Woman, behold your son!'"* (John 19:26).

PETER REMOVES HIS OUTER GARMENT

Therefore that disciple whom Jesus loved said to Peter, "It is the Lord!" Now when Simon Peter heard that it was the Lord, he put on his outer garment (for he had removed it), and plunged into the sea (John 21:7).

As briefly mentioned in Miracle 14, garments throughout the Bible have spiritual significance, and in this case, Peter removes his garment. What is the condition of his spiritual heart currently? Grief, discouragement, confusion, guilt, and anger to name some of the emotions overwhelming him. Basically, he throws in the towel, and this is the spiritual significance when he removes his garment while he works. But when he hears that Jesus is at the shoreline, he immediately puts on his garment and jumps in the water. Joy returns and so does his garment. He abandons the boat and heads straight for Jesus.

We can surely apply Isaiah 61:3 (AMPC) to this situation:

To grant [consolation and joy] to those who mourn in Zion—to give them an ornament (a garland or diadem) of beauty instead of ashes, the oil of joy instead of mourning, the garment [expressive] of praise instead of a heavy, burdened, and failing spirit—that they may be called oaks of righteousness [lofty, strong, and magnificent, distinguished for uprightness, justice, and right standing with God], the planting of the Lord, that He may be glorified.

And Psalm 30:5 tells us that joy returns in the morning—and hey, it's another beautiful morning for the disciples.

A SPIRITUAL FISH FRY

I shared with you a whopper of a fish story in Miracle 6 when I said it's time for us to take the limits off our God. Now with this second miraculous harvest of fish, it's time to have a spiritual fish fry with our favorite host, Jesus.

But the other disciples came in the little boat (for they were not far from land, but about two hundred cubits), dragging the net with fish. Then, as soon as they had come to land, they saw a fire of coals there, and fish laid on it, and bread. Jesus said to them, "Bring some of the fish which you have just caught." Simon Peter went up and dragged the net to land, full of large fish, one hundred and fifty-three; and although there were so many, the net was not broken (John 21:8-11).

Jesus wants not only to show His team of personal disciples that He loves and cares for them, but that He is still with them, and always will be. And even though things are different from before, He never leaves them, He's always with them and for them.

Jesus uses this time of spiritual fish-fry fellowship to instill hope and to remind them of their calling as fishers of people.

THE RICHES OF JESUS ON DISPLAY

- Jesus never gives up on His disciples, including us.
- He rebuilds us when we feel discouraged.
- Jesus invites us to move forward in our callings and assignments from Him.
- He blesses us with good things.
- Jesus supernaturally provides for us in outstanding ways.

CRACK THE MIRACLE CODE

Allow Jesus to minister to your grief and revive your faith.

FAITH ASSIGNMENT

Examine your heart, write down the areas of grief, and great loss in your life, and then take these pains and sorrows to Jesus in prayer. Allow Him to minister to your grief and revive your faith.

PRAYER OF FAITH

Lord Jesus, Your Spirit is speaking to my spirit about the great loss and grief that needs Your healing touch. From day to day, I struggle in different ways. I know that You are faithful and true to perform Your promise in my life. I ask You to take this brokenness of mine and make me whole again. In Your name I humbly pray, amen.

Questions for Miracle 37: Faith Revives

1. What sets in as Jesus' disciples are spiritually spent?
2. What became a normal part of life for the disciples?
3. When people feel lonely and misplaced, there is a normal tendency for some to want to do what?
4. What does Peter say when he feels so discouraged?
5. What do the other disciples with him say in reply to Peter?
6. What is our High Priest in Hebrews 4:15 able to understand and sympathize about us?
7. In John 21:14, what does Jesus call the disciples?
8. Is this term a belittlement?
9. When He calls them by this name, how is it used?
10. What does Jesus do with their faith?
11. What does the Greek word for *right* metaphorically speak to us?
12. Who is the unnamed disciple who is first to recognize Jesus here?
13. What is the spiritual significance when Peter removes his garment?
14. What does Peter do when he hears Jesus is at the shore?
15. What does Jesus use to instill hope and remind them of their calling as fishers of people?

There are also many other signs and miracles which Jesus performed in the presence of the disciples which are not written in this book. But these are written (recorded) in order that you may believe that Jesus is the Christ (the Anointed One), the Son of God, and that through believing and cleaving to and trusting and relying upon Him you may have life through (in) His name [through Who He is] (John 20:30-31 AMPC).

ANSWER KEY

MIRACLE 1: WHATEVER HE SAYS TO YOU, DO IT!

1. You need the Creator, the Creative Word made visible, and the empowerment of His Spirit to work a miracle.
2. He fulfills the role of the eternal Bridegroom.
3. Because Mary knew Him, she understood Him, and was quick to respond to His command.
4. The number six in the Bible symbolizes people and all our frailty.
5. Living a lifestyle of service to her Lord.
6. She ponders upon them.
7. *Phaneroō,* which means to become known, to be plainly recognized, thoroughly understood for who and what one is.
8. *Doxa,* in reference to Jesus the Messiah, it means, splendor, brightness, magnificence, excellence, preeminence, dignity, grace, majesty.

MIRACLE 2: BELIEVE BY FAITH, NOT BY SIGHT

1. You people, the crowd of people who follow Him only to see signs and wonders.

2. To save the Samaritans.
3. An event that defies the laws of nature, often attributed to divine action.
4. Indicators or symbols that signify something greater than themselves, often pointing to God's authority and purpose. The biblical meaning of *signs* encompasses both miraculous occurrences and everyday events that carry spiritual significance.
5. Extraordinary events or acts that invoke awe and amazement. The Hebrew word for wonders is *mofet,* while in Greek, it is *teras.* Both terms encapsulate the essence of miraculous phenomena that transcend ordinary experiences. These wonders are portrayed as manifestations of God's power and sovereignty, serving as signs to affirm faith and reveal divine truth.
6. A people who believe what He has to say.
7. He is testing his faith.
8. Our faith.
9. Victory-believing faith.
10. Jesus is aware that time is of the essence but also knows that there is no distance in the spirit realm, so He issues a word of faith, *"Your son lives,"* and tells the man to go home.
11. A dangerous zone of weak faith.

MIRACLE 3: DELIVERED FROM AN UNCLEAN SPIRIT

1. The religious community became enraged and drove Him to the edge of town, to throw him off the cliff.
2. Capernaum.
3. In the "Village of Comfort."
4. A circuit.
5. A place where the miracles and teachings of Jesus Christ are manifested.
6. *Shabbat* and it means to rest.
7. In a moral sense it is unclean in thought and life. It's impure (ceremonially, morally (lewd) or specially, (demonic)—foul, unclean.
8. To set the captives free.
9. Pray and fast.

MIRACLE 4: SEE THROUGH THE FATHER'S EYES

1. He saw.
2. *Eidō.*
3. It means to perceive, notice, discern, and discover.
4. Reach out and touch the infirmed and they would heal.
5. *Phobos.*
6. Exceeding fear, dread or terror.
7. *Agapē* love.
8. It possesses no earthly perversion—it is benevolent brotherly love and affection from God.
9. It lacks nothing necessary for completeness.
10. *Ballō.*
11. *Kolasis.*

MIRACLE 5: HEALED SPIRITUALLY AND PHYSICALLY

1. With a word.
2. He restored their health.
3. It means that a demon (demons) has taken ownership of this person.
4. A stronghold, an evil influence to lead people into sinful behavior.
5. Evil.
6. Jesus.
7. This sexual tie must be broken in Jesus' name.

MIRACLE 6: TAKE THE LIMITS OFF GOD!

1. They pressed in, crowded around Jesus.
2. Courage.
3. The nets and the chains of discouragement.
4. The laws of nature.
5. Something greater than themselves.
6. The awe of amazement.
7. The great number of people who will be harvested and brought into the Kingdom of God when we do what He has asked of us.

MIRACLE 7: HE IS WILLING TO HEAL

1. Confidence.
2. Physically unclean, highly contagious, and spiritually unclean.
3. It means healer, to cure, heal, repair, and make whole.
4. Because they lack the confidence of His love for them.
5. He reached out and touched him.
6. Back in biblical times the priest diagnosed someone with leprosy, not a doctor.
7. Are You willing to heal me?
8. Prostrate facedown.

MIRACLE 8: GREAT FAITH

1. The centurion.
2. Great faith.
3. He marvels.
4. *Thaumazō.*
5. To wonder.
6. That in the realm of faith, there is no distance.
7. The centurion's faith.

MIRACLE 9: FORGIVEN AND HEALED

1. The power of the Lord.
2. At least one obstacle.
3. He perceives, spiritually discerns the thoughts and the intentions of the hearts of those around Him.
4. The faith of this man's friends, and He also discerns the evil intentions in the hearts of the scribes and Pharisees.
5. Back in these times, any type of sickness, disease, or physical malady was directly equated with sin.
6. He is proving His deity to the scribes and Pharisees that He has both the authority and power to forgive sins and to heal by healing this man of paralysis, by addressing sin issues.
7. The power of life and death.

MIRACLE 10: DEFY THE RELIGIOUS SPIRIT AND HEAL

1. Because they are filled with a religious spirit.
2. This spirit is legalistic, all about appearance, and has nothing to do with compassion and what will truly help and bless people.
3. Seven times.
4. Blind guides, snakes, brood of vipers, and whitewashed tombs.
5. Eight times.
6. Jesus came to earth to destroy the works of the devil, and He is planting a new seed of freedom from the law of sin and death and introducing grace.
7. With Jesus' verbal command and this man's obedience, his hand is instantly restored.

MIRACLE 11: LIFE OVERPOWERS DEATH

1. Beauty.
2. Pleasant place.
3. Jesus, the Resurrection and Life.
4. A widow is a married woman whose husband has died, and she remains unmarried, and due to her loss, she is in a vulnerable position, lacking emotional support, and financial provision.
5. He's loving and perfectly good.
6. *Splagchnizomai*.
7. Dancing.

MIRACLE 12: WHERE IS YOUR FAITH?

1. They are doing something good and the enemy, the devil hates and fears them for it. So, they can't complete their mission with Jesus on this earth.
2. Fight the good fight of faith. The power of praise and worship, and the fear of God.
3. To be strong and courageous, and not to be afraid or discouraged.
4. He expects them to activate their faith instead of asking Him to do this for them.

5. Are we going to put our trust in that negative report, or will we trust in the promises of God?

MIRACLE 13: DELIVERED AND CLOTHED IN HIS RIGHT MIND

1. An unclean spirit.
2. Wearing no clothes.
3. Because in the Jewish culture pigs are unclean.
4. Torture their victims.
5. The once naked man living in the tombs is now found sitting at the feet of the Savior and clothed in his right mind.
6. Reward at the end.

MIRACLE 14: A SPECIAL TOUCH

1. Unclean and untouchable.
2. Incurable.
3. Desperate things.
4. Unnoticed.
5. To touch the hem of His garment and be healed.
6. He sees me, and He notices me.
7. Because of a special touch.
8. He possesses all knowledge, He's all-knowing.
9. He is restoring her back into the community, declaring her clean, touchable, and acceptable.
10. Her faith.
11. Very powerful, has no limits, and produces great works—miracles.

MIRACLE 15: GUARD THE ATMOSPHERE

1. With expectancy.
2. It does not return void.
3. To beseech, call to one's side.
4. Too short, his daughter was too young to die.
5. She is robbed of life as the past 12 years of suffering is long and hard, and unfair to her.

6. Jesus, the wild crowd, and Heaven.
7. By faith.
8. With boldness.
9. Doubt and unbelief.
10. The power of life and death.
11. It means "to amaze, to astonish, to be beside oneself, to be out of one's mind, or to be flabbergasted."
12. The miracle-working power of Jesus over their daughter.

MIRACLE 16: HAVE MERCY ON US

1. Son of David.
2. Jesus is the true Messiah.
3. Man, and human weakness.
4. Divine inspiration of Holy Spirit.
5. "Jehovah is salvation."
6. Anointed or Chosen One.
7. *Eleeō,* and it means "to help the afflicted."
8. Their own faith heals them.

MIRACLE 17: IRRESISTIBLE FORCE

1. *Daimonizomai.*
2. To be under the power of a demon.
3. *Kōphos.*
4. A lame tongue.
5. Deafness.
6. *Ekballō.*
7. To lead one forth or away somewhere with a force which he cannot resist.
8. A lifestyle of prayer and fasting.
9. Holy Spirit's.
10. Cast them out.

MIRACLE 18: DO YOU WANT TO BE MADE WELL?

1. Bethesda means "house of mercy" or "flowing water."
2. It is known for its angelic visits and waters with curative powers.
3. Our Provider.
4. Encouragement.
5. Pity.
6. *Agōnizomai.*
7. It means to contend with adversaries.
8. The devil.
9. No.
10. Faith is simple and uncomplicated. It trusts, and stems from the heart. It's founded in the riches of God's grace and mercy.

MIRACLE 19: SPIRITUAL MULTIPLICATION

1. He's testing Philip's faith.
2. No.
3. No.
4. The little boy.
5. Childlike faith.
6. A lack of provision.
7. It all begins with a willing heart that's not afraid to give it all away, if need be.
8. A pure heart.
9. *"I am the Bread of Life."*
10. By sharing in word, and demonstrating by miracles, signs, and wonders.
11. Our sacrificial Lamb who takes away the sin of the world.

MIRACLE 20: RESCUED FROM THE STORMS OF LIFE

1. Wait with faith.
2. To have Jesus with you.
3. Tribulations, personal difficulties.
4. Because you know who I am.

5. Two times.
6. Catch (away, up), pluck, pull, take (by force), to be translated.
7. Called and committed to the cause of Christ.

MIRACLE 21: HEALING IN HIS WINGS

1. By touching the hem of His garment.
2. Tunic.
3. Cloak.
4. Corner of garment.
5. *Tzitzit*.
6. He's the true Messiah.

MIRACLE 22: UNRELENTING FAITH

1. A non-Jew who lives in Canaan.
2. She recognizes Jesus as the fulfillment of Old Testament prophecies and declares His identity as the Messiah.
3. She believes in her heart that Jesus is the *"Son of David,"* and she publicly acknowledges His deity.
4. Humbles herself before Him and calls Jesus, *"Lord"* and worships Him.
5. Jesus is spiritually healing this woman, remaining silent, and granting her mercy, giving her time to call on His name for salvation.
6. No.
7. The Lost.
8. He uses real-life situations to teach the policy of His grace and mercy, and to institute everlasting change.
9. Part of His mission is to extend the bridge of salvation to the Gentile population.
10. To allow their differences to stand in the way.
11. The Gentiles.
12. The Jews.
13. No.
14. To become His disciples—lovers and followers of Him.

15. Her daughter was instantly set free from demonic torment.

MIRACLE 23: SPITTLE AND A COMMAND OF FAITH

1. The people bring the deaf and mute man to Jesus to request healing.
2. Specific.
3. A place where they feel safe and secure, away from the pressure of ridicule and shame from others.
4. Prevent the manifestation of this miracle.
5. He puts His fingers into the man's ears.
6. He spits and touches the man's tongue with His spittle.
7. "The saliva of firstborn sons in the Jewish culture of Jesus' time was considered to have power to heal infirmities."
8. *"Ephphatha!" (which means "Be opened!").*
9. Not to tell anyone.
10. No.
11. It is difficult to maneuver among large crowds in the cities, so He needs to move outside of heavily populated areas, but even still the large crowds follow.

MIRACLE 24: THE EMPOWERMENT OF COMPASSION

1. To call or to bid someone into God's service.
2. *Proskaleō.*
3. 4,000 men plus women and children.
4. The compassion of Jesus to the multitudes of lost people.
5. Human reasoning or the realm of our five senses.
6. What we lack in the natural.
7. Transform it into a lot.
8. No.
9. Lack.
10. They reap seven large baskets of leftovers.
11. Perfect or complete.
12. A complete meal.

MIRACLE 25: RESTORED AND CLEARLY SEES

1. "House of Fishermen."
2. Immediately.
3. He goes straightaway and finds his friend, Nathanel (Bartholomew), to share the good news.
4. *"We found Him! We've found the One we've been waiting for! It's Jesus, the son of Joseph from Nazareth! He's the One whom Moses and the prophets prophesied would come!"*
5. Entrusting them to the most important work, the Kingdom of God and its inhabitants.
6. To make Jesus their top priority and obey His call.
7. They choose to reject the Gospel and remain spiritually blind.
8. He rebukes them.
9. Faith for miracles.
10. Compassion and honor.
11. He is not an outcast to Jesus, nor is he a burden to Him.
12. Inner healing.
13. They break down the walls of self-preservation, which enables hope to build and faith to arise within this broken man.
14. "The saliva of firstborn sons in the Jewish culture of Jesus' time was considered to have power to heal infirmities."
15. No.
16. The full manifestation of healing.
17. Both physical and spiritual sight.
18. Restored and sees everyone clearly.
19. Holistic.

MIRACLE 26: RECREATED EYES AND SOMETHING MORE

1. Jesus saw a blind man.
2. Second class.
3. Discrimination.
4. Shame.
5. Their blindness was considered a punishment for sin.
6. Always fair.

7. Enough for you.
8. *Charis.*
9. Endurance.
10. Strengthen.
11. *Works for the good of those who love Him, who have been called according to His purpose.*
12. Sets the man free from a life sentence of shame.
13. Clay and saliva.
14. The Light of the World in the flesh—Jesus.

MIRACLE 27: COME DOWN FROM THAT MOUNTAINTOP EXPERIENCE

1. A great multitude.
2. An unclean spirit.
3. Coming down from a glorious and unexplainable experience with Jesus and having to confront the multitude of problems this world has to offer.
4. *Sparassō.*
5. This evil spirit *tears* apart this boy.
6. Perverted it and caused it to foam at the mouth.
7. Demon possession.
8. *Apistos.*
9. Unpleasant revelation about oneself.
10. *Epitimaō.*
11. Jesus *straightly charges* this demon out of this boy.
12. *Iaomai.*
13. Jesus *cures* and makes this boy *whole* again.

MIRACLE 28: MIRACLE MONEY TO PAY THE TEMPLE TAX

1. *"You are the Christ, the Son of the living God."*
2. Our Father who is in heaven.
3. A tax collector.
4. It will become our greatest strength and be used for ministry purposes to win others like us for His glory.

5. The tax collector.
6. They will be provided.
7. Faith.
8. Seize *and* hold fast *and* retain without wavering.

MIRACLE 29: QUESTIONS, RUMORS AND THE BIG LIE

1. Demon-possession, and he was blind and mute.
2. The devil, the thief.
3. *Echō.*
4. Possess.
5. *Perissos.*
6. Exceeding abundantly, beyond measure.
7. Possession of life that is exceeding abundantly, beyond measure.
8. They will make up lies about you.
9. *"He casts out demons by Beelzebub, the ruler of the demons."*
10. Neutral ground.
11. "*I will spew you out of My mouth!*"
12. A serious rebuke.
13. Accept Jesus Christ as our Savior.

MIRACLE 30: LOOSED FROM YOUR BONDAGE

1. Because of her infirmity.
2. It is her punishment for sin.
3. Sinner.
4. Speak to a woman in public.
5. All the invisible, hurting people.
6. A spirit of infirmity.
7. *Astheneia.*
8. Disease, infirmity, sickness, weakness.
9. Power of words, and laying on of hands.
10. Pain.
11. Her infirmity.
12. *Aganakteō.*
13. Very displeased.

14. *Kataischynō.*
15. Disgraced.

MIRACLE 31: HYPOCRISY VERSUS GRACE

1. We must take a stand for what is right in the sight of God.
2. They accept the Holy Scriptures as divinely inspired by God, but also place equal importance on the Jewish traditions of the time.
3. *"Hypocrites"* and *"whitewashed tombs."*
4. For being physically clean on the outside, but spiritually filthy on the inside.
5. Fulfilling their laws and traditions.
6. No.
7. Presents a word of correction to their false teachings and beliefs.
8. The Pharisees.
9. Edema.
10. *"Is it lawful to heal on the Sabbath?"*
11. *"Which of you, having a donkey or an ox that has fallen into a pit, will not immediately pull him out on the Sabbath day?"*
12. With authority.
13. The scribes in the Bible.
14. They add the traditions of men into their interpretations of the Scriptures.
15. No.
16. The scribes and Pharisee's interpretation concerning the law of the Sabbath.

MIRACLE 32: ONE OUT OF TEN RETURNS TO GIVE THANKS

1. It's more difficult for them to draw near to Jesus.
2. The crowds fear their disease.
3. Their plight.
4. His mercy.
5. He hears us.
6. His authority.

7. Jesus' willingness to reach out to these ten men with kindness and goodness to heal them of their misery and affliction.
8. "*Well of the One Who Lives and Sees Me.*"
9. God hears.
10. A faith assignment.
11. One.
12. Glorifies God.
13. Sin of entitlement.
14. Where to worship.
15. The temple.
16. Mount Gerizim.
17. In Spirit and in truth.
18. A matter of the heart.

MIRACLE 33: THAT YOU MAY BELIEVE

1. "Whom God helps."
2. To glorify the Son of God.
3. The time is short, and we must be about our heavenly Father's business and win souls. We are to be bold and not fear our enemies, or what they may do to us.
4. When He raised Jairus' daughter from the dead.
5. *That they may believe.*
6. Doubting Thomas.
7. A Resurrection Party.
8. *"Did I not say to you that if you would believe you would see the glory of God?"*
9. *"Lazarus, come forth!"*
10. Jesus prays in faith, thanks His Father that He hears Him, and commands dead Lazarus to come out of that grave!
11. Many of the Jews that witness the resurrection of Lazurus believe Jesus is the Son of God.
12. Kill Him.
13. To silence Lazarus' testimony by assignation.
14. Because he fears the results of souls won for Jesus, and more people who will believe for their miracle that produces more souls for Christ.

MIRACLE 34: WHAT DO YOU WANT JESUS TO DO FOR YOU?

1. Messiah.
2. Because he calls out to Jesus, as the Son of David.
3. The Messianic promise.
4. Discouragement.
5. The rigid religious community or unbelieving family members and friends who are unlearned in spiritual matters concerning healing.
6. You must break through the negative thoughts and opinions of others.
7. Twice.
8. Outcasts.
9. A big heart.
10. A heaping helping of mercy.
11. His faith.
12. *"And whatever you ask for in prayer, having faith and [really] believing, you will receive."*
13. "*What do you want Me to do for you?*"
14. That I may receive my sight.
15. Unashamedly.
16. "*Go your way; your faith has made you well.*"
17. Saves, heals, and makes whole.
18. Follows Jesus.

MIRACLE 35: CURSE A SPIRIT OF LACK IN YOUR LIFE

1. The power of faith, faith-filled words, and about the potency in the prayer of faith.
2. A donkey.
3. No fruit.
4. It was not the season for figs.
5. *"Let no fruit grow on you ever again."*
6. *"Rabbi, look! The fig tree which You cursed has withered away."*
7. *Eipon.*
8. To say, speak, tell or command.
9. *Legō.*

10. Divine judgment, sin and consequences.
11. Death and life.
12. Limitless.
13. What you desire or have need of because you believe in the promises of God.
14. The natural realm, including human reasoning, and the realm of the five senses.
15. Our level of trust in God and in His faithfulness.
16. The creative-destructive power of words.
17. Fullness of faith.

MIRACLE 36: EARS TO HEAR

1. Lock.
2. A locksmith.
3. To arrest and lock up Jesus.
4. The treasure box.
5. A traitor, a liar, and a thief.
6. To sift him by inward agitation to try one's faith to the verge of overthrow.
7. *Siniazō*.
8. Shifting sand.
9. Cephas.
10. Peter.
11. Peter.
12. *Symeōn*
13. Harkening.
14. Because he and his army of demons listen in on Jesus' conversations.
15. To listen, to give special attention to something.
16. Right.
17. He knows it is the start of His journey to the Cross. The second reason is this is illegal, and Peter could go to jail; and third, He cares for this lost man.
18. *Ous*.
19. The faculty of perceiving with the mind, the faculty of understanding and knowing.

20. *Dexios.*
21. A place of honor or authority.
22. He deafens his ability to hear the Gospel of Jesus Christ.
23. With all compassion reaches out and supernaturally reattaches this servant's right ear.
24. No.

MIRACLE 37: FAITH REVIVES

1. Discouragement.
2. The supernatural.
3. Go back to the way life used to be.
4. *"I am going fishing!"*
5. "*And we are coming with you!*"
6. Our weaknesses and infirmities and liability to the assaults of temptation.
7. Children.
8. No.
9. As a term of endearment and brotherly affection toward them.
10. Revives.
11. A place of honor or authority.
12. John.
13. He throws in the towel.
14. Puts on his garment and jumps in the water.
15. He uses this spiritual fish-fry fellowship time to instill hope and remind them of their calling as fishers of people.

NOTES

MIRACLE 1

1. "Logos," The Passion Translation, John 1:1, footnote b.
2. "Ponder," https://www.biblestudytools.com/dictionary/ponder, accessed February 7, 2025.
3. Strong's Concordance G5319.

MIRACLE 2

1. "Road through Samaria," Study Guide for John 4 by David Guzik; accessed April 24, 2025.
2. "Miracle," Miracle: Biblical Meaning and Origin of This Name in the Bible, https://bibledictionarytoday.com/biblical-names/miracle; activated February 24, 2025.
3. "Signs," What Does "Signs" Mean in the Bible?, https://bibledictionarytoday.com/words/signs; accessed February 14, 2025.
4. "Wonders," What Does "Wonders" Mean in the Bible?, https://bibledictionarytoday.com/words/wonders; accessed February 24, 2025.
5. "What is the distance from Galilee to Capernaum?" *Answers,* https://www.answers.com/math-and-arithmetic/What_is_the_distance_from_Galilee_to_Capernaum; accessed April 24, 2025.

MIRACLE 3

1. Lisa Loraine Baker, "Why Was Capernaum Such an Important City in the Bible?" *Bible-StudyTools.com,* https://www.biblestudytools.com/bible-study/topical-studies/why-was-capernaum-such-an-important-city-in-the-bible.html; accessed April 25, 2025.
2. "Galilee, a circuit," *galilaia,* Strong's Greek Lexicon (KJV) #G1056, https://www.blueletterbible.org/lexicon/g1056/kjv/tr/0-1; accessed April 25, 2025.
3. Galilee, Galilea: Biblical Meaning and Origin of This Name in the Bible, https://bibledictionarytoday.com/biblical-names/galilea; accessed April 25, 2025.
4. "What does 'Sabbath' mean in the Bible?" *BibleDictionaryToday.com,* https://bibledictionarytoday.com/words/sabbath; accessed April 25, 2025.

MIRACLE 4

1. "To see," *eidō,* Strong's Greek Lexicon, G1492.
2. "Fear," *phobos,* Strong's Greek Lexicon, G5401.
3. "Love," *agape,* Strong's Greek Lexicon, G26.
4. "Perfect," *teleios,* Strong's Greek Lexicon, G5046.
5. "Casts," *ballō,* Strong's Greek Lexicon, G906.
6. "Torment," *kolasis,* Strong's Greek Lexicon, G2851.

NOTES

MIRACLE 6

1. "Gennesaret, What is GENNESARET?" *Gennesareth,* WebBible Encyclopedia, ChristianAnswers.Net, https://christiananswers.net/dictionary/gennesaret.html; accessed May 3, 2025.
2. "Simon Peter, Meaning Of The Name Simon Peter In The Bible," *Our Bible Heritage,* https://ourbibleheritage.com/meaning-of-the-name-simon-peter-in-the-bible; accessed July 6, 2025.
3. Tiffany Christensen, "James, Biblical Meaning Of The Name James—Biblical Pathway, September 5, 2024, https://biblicalpathway.com/biblical-meaning-of-the-name-james; accessed July 6, 2025.
4. "What the Bible Says About the Biblical Meaning of the Name John," *God's Blessing,* https://godsbless.ing/definitions/names-and-characters/biblical-significance-of-the-name-john; accessed July 6, 2025.
5. "Zebedee," Topical Bible: Zebedee, https://biblehub.com/topical/t/the_sons_of_zebedee.htm; accessed July 6, 2025.

MIRACLE 7

1. "Hansen's Disease (Leprosy)," *CDC,* https://www.cdc.gov/leprosy/about/index.html; accessed July 7, 2025.

MIRACLE 11

1. "Nain," beauty, a village in Galilee located at the north base of Little Hermon, Strong's G3484, Blueletterbible.org.
2. נָאָה nâ'âh, naw-aw'; Strong's H4998; a home; figuratively, a pasture:—habitation, house, pasture, pleasant place; Blueletterbible.org.
3. "Widow, What Does 'Widow' Mean in the Bible?" https://bibledictionarytoday.com/words/widow; accessed July 7, 2025.

MIRACLE 16

1. "Meaning of Number Six," https://www.biblestudy.org/bibleref/meaning-of-numbers-in-bible/6.html; accessed July 8, 2025.
2. "Jesus means salvation," Strong's G2424.
3. "Messiah, What does Messiah mean?" GotQuestions.org, https://www.gotquestions.org/what-does-Messiah-mean.html, accessed July 8, 2025.

MIRACLE 21

1. "The Hem of Jesus' Garment," *BibleHub.com,* https://biblehub.com/topical/t/the_hem_of_jesus'_garment.htm; accessed July 8, 2025.
2. "Jewish Dress and Custom - A Study of Haluk, Tallit, Kanaf, Tzitzit, and Tfillin" - Acts 242 Study, accessed May 24, 2025.

MIRACLE 36

1. "Judas Iscariot," *The Passion Translation Bible,* Luke 6:14-16, footnote b, page 169.

ABOUT BECKY DVORAK

Becky is a dynamic preacher of the Gospel, healing evangelist, prophetess to the nations for 30+ years, Destiny Image author, and host of the powerful teaching program, *Empowered for Healing and Miracles*, featured globally on the *It's Supernatural!* Network on ISN. Becky conducts healing services, seminars, and conferences globally. And she offers online healing courses.

Becky spent 25 years in the trenches of service for Jesus Christ in an orphanage in Guatemala, Central America. God performed many miracles through Becky during that time, including the raising of the dead. Now the Lord is releasing Becky to equip the Body of Christ in the earth realm on a much greater scale.

Becky and her husband, David, celebrate 44 years of marriage, have 8 children, 3 adult biological and 5 adopted, 1 son-in-law, 5 daughters-in-law and 15 grandchildren, and live in Arizona, USA.

Connect with Becky

Website
www.authorbeckydvorak.com

Email:
becky@healingandmiraclesintl.org

Facebook
www.facebook.com/authorbeckydvorak

YOUR *Prophetic* COMMUNITY

Sign up for a **FREE** subscription to the Destiny Image digital magazine and get awesome content delivered directly to your inbox!

destinyimage.com/signup

Sign up for Cutting-Edge Messages that Supernaturally Empower You

- Gain valuable insights and guidance based on biblical principles
- Deepen your faith and understanding of God's plan for your life
- Receive regular updates and prophetic messages
- Connect with a community of believers who share your values and beliefs

Experience Fresh Video Content that Reveals Your Prophetic Inheritance

- Receive prophetic messages and insights
- Connect with a powerful tool for spiritual growth and development
- Stay connected and inspired on your faith journey

Listen to Powerful Podcasts that Propel You into God's Presence Every Day

- Deepen your understanding of God's prophetic assignment
- Experience God's revival power throughout your day
- Learn how to grow spiritually in your walk with God

From

Becky Dvorak

Defeat Sickness and Disease Once and for All

Are you or a loved one discouraged by sickness in your life? Does it seem like even your most fervent prayers go unheard? But what if it didn't have to be this way?

Prophetic healing evangelist Becky Dvorak has spent years ministering around the world to those caught in the trenches of physical illness. And time and again she has witnessed the power of God heal some of the most hopeless conditions.

In this practical, hope-filled book, Becky shares the prophetic insight and the authoritative, effective prayers she uses on the frontlines of healing ministry, equipping you to defeat disease and step boldly into wholeness.

You have the Spirit of Jesus living inside you. It's time to cast down discouragement and fearlessly declare the supernatural, targeted prayers that release miracle power—and overcome disease once and for all.

Purchase your copy wherever books are sold